Step Up
to Networking

JoAnne Woodcock

PUBLISHED BY
Microsoft Press
A Division of Microsoft Corporation
One Microsoft Way
Redmond,Washington 98052-6399

Library of Congress Cataloging-in-Publication Data
Woodcock, JoAnne.
    Step Up to Networking / JoAnne Woodcock.
       p. cm.
    ISBN 0-7356-0572-6
    1. Computer networks. I. Title.
    TK5105.5.W65   1999
    004.6--dc21   98-55330
                                            CIP

Printed and bound in the United States of America.

1 2 3 4 5 6 7 8 9   MLML   4 3 2 1 0 9

Distributed in Canada by ITP Nelson, a division of Thomson Canada Limited.

A CIP catalogue record for this book is available from the British Library.

Microsoft Press books are available through booksellers and distributors worldwide. For further information about international editions, contact your local Microsoft Corporation office or contact Microsoft Press International directly at fax (425) 936-7329. Visit our Web site at mspress.microsoft.com.

Acquisitions Editor: Juliana Aldous
Project Editor: Lynn Finnel

CONTENTS *at a Glance*

Acknowledgments

Every book has a beginning, a middle, and an end—not only in terms of pages, but, more important, in terms of *process* and the people who contribute significantly to its development. This book has benefited from the efforts of many people who have done their best to make it readable, understandable, and not too embarrassing for its writer. And this is the page, traditionally saved on their behalf, where public thanks can be offered to all. So, then…

To Jim Brown, publisher; Anne Hamilton, acquisitions manager; and Juliana Aldous, program manager, content acquisition: thanks for making this book happen. To Lynn Finnel, book project manager, and Joel Panchot, art direction at Microsoft, and—at Helios Productions—to Sybil Ihrig, project manager and compositor; Greg Guntle, technical editor; Gail Taylor, copy editor; Ken Yaecker, illustrator; Rebecca Taft, principal proofreader; and Rebecca Plunkett, indexer: thanks for taking this book from raw manuscript to printed page—a not inconsiderable feat, and one much appreciated for the professional (and painless) way in which it happened.

To Karen Steckler and Darla Nyren of Microsoft Skills 2000, thanks for being part of this, for providing the material on the CD, and for helping with the introduction to the book.

To the staff, the horses, and the special riders at the Little Bit Therapeutic Riding Center, thanks for permission to show the Web page created for you by Current Image Web designers.

And finally, to Kate and Mark, Kay and Skeet, Karen, Arabella, Hamlet, and the four-footed clans—thanks for being there. You, above all, make everything worthwhile.

Introduction

This is a book about networking. It's not a "point here, click there" kind of book. Nor is it the kind of book that tells you how to build a network, use a network, manage a network, or fix a network.

"But," you say, "if it's not going to do any of the above, what is it going to do for me, for 300 pages or so?" Well, it's going to help you figure out what a network *is* (and figuring that out will not depend on what you think the definition of "is" is).

What You Will Find Here

This book will show you how the idea of a network underlies the reality of a network. It will show you how hardware, software, and telecommunications blend with a host of standards and ways of working that, together, define a network. Along the way, you will meet blueprints known as architectures, rules of etiquette known as protocols, guidelines known as reference models, and even dreams of the future that are instrumental in the design of high-speed transports capable of moving all kinds of data faster and in greater quantities than ever before.

Starting with the evolution of networking and a look at the different ways in which people rely on computer-to-computer communication, the book will introduce you to the basics underlying small PC-to-PC connections (peer-to-peer networks), medium-sized local area networks (LANs), large wide area networks (WANs), and gigantic networks (the Internet and the World Wide Web).

In addition, you will begin (and not incidentally) to pick up the vocabulary of networking—the abbreviations, acronyms, and (yes) even the whole, pronounceable words that describe the networking environment. This is the vocabulary that defines the world of a networking professional, and it is a particularly rich one. In fact, it is so rich that it can end up swirling through the mind of a newcomer like confetti at a big parade.

But—and this is an important but—this vocabulary is not beyond anyone's reach. Like any "language," it just needs to be learned, one step at a time. You weren't born knowing how to speak your native tongue, but that didn't stop you from learning how. Networking lingo is no different. In this case, you are just a little older, the words are a little more technical, and you will be relying on a different teacher. Take your time, don't expect to become fluent overnight, and if need be, remind yourself now and then that things worth knowing often ask for a little patience (and a little effort) on your part.

That, in a nutshell, is what you'll find here—an introduction to a fascinating world. It's a world that was born around about the 1960s, grew through the 70s, expanded in the 80s, flourished in the 90s...and will be indispensable in the next millennium.

About You

As you may have gathered by now, learning about networks is not quite the same as learning about, say, how to use your computer. It's a little more involved than that. But does that mean you need to be some kind of genius or technical wizard? No, at least not at this level.

Being a genius never hurts, but if networking required that only geniuses need apply, it would never have amounted to much. As for technical wizardry, well, it's a buildable skill, one that you will concentrate on later if you want or need to become actively involved in building, administering, or troubleshooting networks. For the purposes of this book, you need meet only one requirement: you should know something about computers. That means you should not be an absolute beginner. You don't have to be a programmer, but you should be comfortable around computers—for example, playing games and using standard productivity software, such as a word processor. You will not be quizzed on your knowledge, but the book will assume that you understand words like *operating system* and *circuit board*.

Whether you are considering a career in networking or are simply a curious person wanting to know more about the world in which you live, that is the one and only requirement as far as this book is concerned.

Except, of course, it will also help if you are actually interested in learning about networks. That one is more or less assumed, though, given the subject matter....

What's Next?

When you finish this book, suppose you find yourself hungry for more? For more knowledge, for the ability to gain hands-on experience with a network, and possibly for a future of some type as a network professional? Where should you go? That question can be answered, at least in part, by the following sections.

Skills 2000

Microsoft Skills 2000 is a Microsoft initiative designed with one overriding goal: to help eliminate the shortage of Information Technology (IT) professionals needed by small and large companies in the United States and elsewhere. This shortage exists today and is projected to grow in the future. And unlike a shortage of, say, coffee stirrers or doodle pads, it is a critical shortage, because businesses that lack adequate technical support to fuel growth must pull back on their plans, and that can ultimately impact both their competitiveness and their profitability.

IT professionals are therefore valuable and needed members of the workforce. What types of professionals are needed? Well, all kinds, from programmers to database experts to Web developers to...network specialists. Network specialists are, in fact, among the IT professionals most in demand.

So the picture looks rosy, and Microsoft Skills 2000 is there with help if you want it. Through this program, you have access to information, assessment, job matching, loan programs, and other resources that can help you on your way.

But, you might be wondering, can *I* do it? Well, why not? Here are some facts:

- You *don't* need a background in technology, nor do you necessarily need a degree in computer science.

- You *don't* have to be a certain age or have a certain level of education, although being 18 or older with a high-school diploma will help, as will an interest in (and aptitude for) technical or mechanical subjects. IT training can thus benefit you whether you are entering the workforce or seeking a career change, if it is a type of work you will enjoy doing.

- And finally, you *don't* have to be the stereotypical computer nerd. Although eyeglasses are common in this industry, pocket protectors and ponytails are optional, as are middle-of-the-night cravings for fast food and caffeinated soft drinks. It's what you can do that counts, not who you are.

In other words, you can be *you* and be valued for it.

What to Do Next

If all this sounds promising, here are some specific steps you can take (preferably, but not necessarily) after finishing the book:

- Visit the Microsoft Skills 2000 Web site at *http://www.microsoft.com/skills2000/*.

- Take the Microsoft Skills 2000 IT Tour (on the CD in the back of the book), a fun and friendly way to learn about information technology, including networks.

- Try the free online Aptitude Tool found at the Microsoft Skills 2000 Web site to find out where you might fit in the Information Technology industry.

- If you need financial assistance, check into IT Career Loans, also provided through the Microsoft Skills 2000 Web site *http://www.microsoft.com/skills2000*.

- Explore the various Microsoft Training and Certification resources, which include classroom, online, and self-paced training.

- Attend an IT Career Night (listed on the Microsoft Skills 2000 Web site).

And go for it.

Networks:
Past, Present, and Future

In today's world, networks are almost as essential as computers. Without networks, computers sit in lonely isolation, chewing quietly on their data, able to share what they do only by displaying the results on the screen, saving them to disk, or sending them to a printer. Picture, for example, computer A and computer B. Each is working, say, on designing pigs that fly. Without a network, A and B are completely unaware of each other, unable to share what they do unless the people using them are already in contact and are willing to swap information using disks, the telephone, or even *snail mail*.

Given a network, however, the two computers can immediately begin to access the same database of information, add their results to it, and make those results available to one another. They, as well as computers C, D, and E for that matter, can join forces and work on complementary projects instead of working alone and possibly reinventing the wheel by duplicating each other's efforts on the same task. Thanks to networking, the people who use these computers can share ideas, work, and information no matter how far apart they happen to be in either time or distance.

Of course, networks aren't only for people and computers working on arcane or silly projects. Networks are for everyone, and they are used for purposes ranging from purchasing, sales, billing, and online commerce to payroll, e-mail, scheduling, group meetings, and file and resource sharing. Consider some of the ways that people around the world rely on networks:

■ A salesperson carrying a laptop along on a sales trip uses a modem and *dial-up networking* to tap into the main business computer in the home office and send e-mail or access a product database.

■ A consultant working from home cables a few desktop computers together in a *peer-to-peer network* so the machines can share communal files and a printer.

■ A small business uses a high-end computer as the hub of a *client/ server network* from which less powerful (and less expensive) desktop workstations can request shared files, application updates, e-mail services, printers, and storage space.

■ A multinational enterprise with offices scattered throughout many countries connects an eclectic mix of Macintoshes, MS-DOS and Windows computers, heavy-duty workstations, terminals, and mainframes as part of a *distributed system* that serves as the organization's information and application backbone.

■ And the family with a little sub-$1,000 computer connects to servers on the Internet—the mother of all networks—for gaming, chatting, shopping, and just plain looking around to see who and what exist in the virtual world of the Web.

Networks are everywhere, and they are essential. Whether they are large or small, whether they connect two or twenty or twenty thousand or more computers, networks make communication happen. In this, they are awesome.

The Idea of a Network

At heart, networks are simply a combination of computers, plus special-purpose networking hardware and software that enable the kind of sharing shown in the following simple illustration:

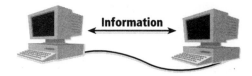

But of course networks are also just a tad more complex than this. After all, information flows through a network in streams of bits and bytes—electrical signals—that no one can see. Yet, though they are invisible, those signals, which are transferred as small packages of information, move at incredible speeds and sometimes cross continents or even pass from one network to another in order to reach their destination. And no matter how long or short the journey, those packages must travel with a high degree of accuracy, arriving error-free and only at the intended destination—because the whole purpose of a network would be subverted if files and messages were routinely garbled in transmission or mistakenly delivered to the wrong party.

That's a tall order, but networks manage quite well on a daily, often round-the-clock basis. This is an amazing feat when you consider that, in order to perform so well, they must depend on the interaction of numerous technologies running the gamut from hardware to communications and even to (these days) Internet-enabling software.

But how did the world reach this point, this place and time where such technology actually stars in television commercials and newspaper ads? Where, thanks to networks, "everyone" who is "anyone" has an e-mail address; where businesses from mom-and-pop shops to multinational corporations trust their finances and most sensitive data to computers; and where organizations as diverse as oven manufacturers, the Federal government, auto dealers, and dog breeders feel a need to spread the word about their work on the global Internet?

To see how networks came to be such a force in computing, start with a quick look at the past, at how they developed over time. This look is not only interesting in itself, but in many ways it provides a glance at the future through the mirror of the past, because some of the currently developing technologies, including network computers, the *Java* programming language, and *Windows terminals*, are turning basic networking concepts back on themselves. They are returning to ways of working reminiscent of the early days of centralized storage, management, and even information processing.

The Road Behind

The combination of two technologies, communications and computers, underlies all networks. Communication obviously got started when the first cave person grunted meaningfully at another. And depending on how you choose to define the word *computer*, you can wander back 2,000 years or more to the invention of the first known calculating device, the abacus. However, grunts and abaci never blended to create what we know today as a network, so you don't have to go that far back. In fact, you need only go back about 35 years, to the computing era known broadly as the Stone Age or, to those courting more precision, the Iron Age (after the ferrite metal used to create the core, or memory, in the mainframes that defined computing at the time).

The 1960s

Back in the 1960s, mainframes dominated the computing landscape. They were marvels of technology—lightning fast, complex, and very expensive. They were also very large. Even though today's high-end workstations provide more computing power, those early mainframes far outstripped today's mighty mites in size. They were, in fact, room-sized behemoths that consisted of multiple cabinets and assorted peripheral hardware.

Nowadays often referred to as "dinosaurs" or "big iron," these mainframes took their name from the fact that their processing and, often, their memory were housed in a single cabinet known as the "main frame." As befitted their price and their position as fast, high-powered calculating machines, these mainframes lived in dust-free, air-conditioned luxury and were attended only by the technological elite.

Initially, mainframes were so-called batch-processing machines. That is, they were not interactive in the same way a PC is, because they handled jobs in batches scheduled to be run at particular times. Because these jobs did not require—indeed, did not allow—human/machine interaction, the computers were initially fed their data on envelope-sized punched cards.

Historical aside: These cards were printed with a "do not spindle, fold, or mutilate" message meant to ensure that the cards could be fed through and accurately read by a machine known as a card reader. Unfortunately, the wording also had a tendency to irritate people, some of whom delightedly spindled, folded, mutilated, or did all three when they could get away with it.

At any rate, batch processing greatly improved the speed at which data could be manipulated when compared to doing the same job by hand. But because the machines were so expensive, job scheduling was economically unthrifty when the computer ended up sitting idle between jobs. The arrival of magnetic tapes and, later, disk storage improved the situation by speeding up input/output times, but even then the processing part of the computer remained idle while data was being moved into and out of memory.

To utilize the computer's time as completely as possible, people began turning to the idea of *multiprogramming*, which offered a means of putting multiple jobs in memory and parceling out the computer's processing time among the different jobs. Multiprogramming, because it allowed the computer to handle more than one job at the same time, meant that the operating system of the computer had to be revamped to ensure the safety of the jobs in process. Each job, for example, had to be allotted its own memory and had to be protected from the other jobs being run at the same time. And the operating system itself had to "know" how and when to switch the processor from one task to another.

Dumb Terminals and Timesharing

Although the computer itself remained batch-like in that programmers and other users still had to wait for their jobs to be run…and rerun…and re-rerun if a small mistake—even a typing error—made the job "bomb," multiprogramming opened the door to more, and more efficient, processing. As in the *multitasking* operating systems of today, the processor could turn its attention to one job while another was held up waiting for input or output. Within a few years, the concept of running multiple jobs at the same time led to yet another advance, this one advantageous to the human half of the computing equation. It was called *timesharing*.

Like multiprogramming, timesharing required operating systems that were tailored to the job at hand. The first timesharing operating system, known as MULTICS (for multiplexed information and computing service), was developed in the late 1960s by a group including General Electric, Bell Laboratories, and the Massachusetts Institute of Technology. Ken Thompson, one of the developers who worked on the MULTICS project, later went on to join forces with Dennis Ritchie to develop UNIX—famous today not only because it is a venerable (by some, venerated) operating system, but also because the C programming language was created as part of its development.

Timesharing, like multiprogramming, was based on the idea of switching the computer's processing from one task to another. Unlike multiprogramming, however, timesharing also incorporated user interactivity in the form of *terminals* wired to the main, or *host*, computer. It was at this point that computing evolved from a localized, essentially standalone model like this:

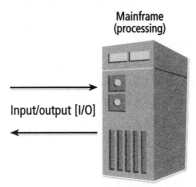

to a more accessible, spread-out, "networking" model in which many workstations could simultaneously access and use the processing power of the computer, like this:

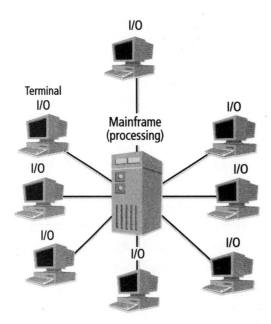

Unlike the workstations typical of current networks, however, the terminals used with timesharing computers were *dumb*—that is, they had little or no processing power of their own. Nor did they have any local storage. They essentially consisted of keyboards for input and screens for output, and they were wired directly to the host computer.

Although these dumb terminals sound much like the *network computers* being developed and marketed today, there are two important differences. First, network computers are "smart" rather than dumb. That is, network computers, or *NCs*, are fully capable of processing information on their own. Second, although network computers, like dumb terminals, rely on larger machines for programs, data, and storage, they are not directly wired to a single host. Rather, they are able to connect to any server in the network, not just to a single computer as in the host/terminal timesharing situation.

Long-Distance Timesharing

Timesharing allowed terminals scattered throughout a business to interact with a large computer. But not all businesses that needed such processing power could afford a computer, nor could they necessarily count on being in the same building as the big machine. By the 1970s, however, computing became more accessible, thanks to the invention of the *modem* and its support of machine-to-machine communication via the telephone. The modem's job was—and still is—to convert information to and from the *digital* form needed by computers (and terminals) to the *analog* form in which it must travel over telephone lines.

With the arrival of long-distance timesharing, terminals could connect to the host via dedicated phone lines leased from the phone company. Another option, especially in situations in which businesses leased or rented computer time from a business that offered timesharing services, was to connect terminals to the host over ordinary voice lines. Given a modem and, often, an *acoustic coupler* into which the user plugged the handset of a telephone, a terminal could now be located far from the host, even in a different city, and still depend on and take advantage of work performed by the big machine.

ARPANET

But even though distance had now been added to the computing picture, processing remained the sole responsibility of the host computer. The terminals were still dumb and were often still reliant on batch-style job scheduling. Terminals and telephone communications advanced the cause of networking, to be sure, but this form of networking had not progressed beyond a kind of master/slave relationship in which terminals could freely access the host while the host itself sat alone, without anyone but the terminals to talk to. Yet it was the host, rather than the terminal, that was the brain of the operation and therefore had the most to share.

This fact was not lost on the researchers and academicians of the time. By the 1970s, the idea of host-to-host communication was being advanced through the development of a revolutionary new means of connecting computers, the network known as ARPANET. Named after its sponsor, the Advanced Research Projects Agency of the United States Department of Defense, ARPANET became the glue that linked host computers at universities and research labs around the country and provided a data highway for military communications. Through ARPANET, host computers were finally able to communicate and to share files through a peer-based network something like this:

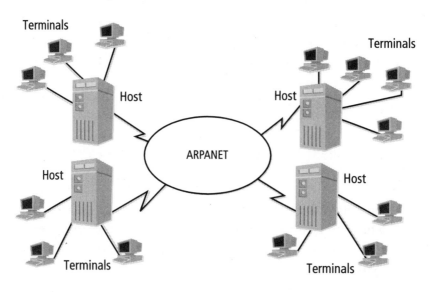

In order to communicate, each host was assigned a unique *address* and exchanged messages with the others with the help of a *packet-switching* computer, which essentially "bundled" the messages, addressed them for delivery, and sent them on their way.

ARPANET is significant not only because it was an early host-to-host network, but because (drum roll) it was the ancestor of the incredible worldwide Internet.

The PC Revolution

While ARPANET was growing on one side of the computing universe, another development was beginning to take shape in the technological arena: a small, smart machine called the personal computer that, by the 1990s, would revolutionize information processing throughout the world. The first of these *microcomputers* was a hobbyist's machine that appeared in 1975. Known as the MITS Altair, it was a smallish, rectangular box with 256 bytes (roughly, characters) of memory and with lights and switches on the front. The lights served for output, and the switches, which needed to be flipped on or off manually to represent instructions entered as strings of binary numbers, were the one and only source of input. There was no screen and no keyboard. Neither was there any standardized software, until Bill Gates and Paul Allen, founders of Microsoft, created a BASIC programming language for the Altair.

Dating from the introduction of this computer, the latter half of the 1970s and the early 1980s became a time of rapid change in the budding microcomputer industry. Within two years, the Altair—truly a machine limited to the interests and abilities of electronics hobbyists—was essentially defunct and had been supplanted by a number of more advanced computers. Notable among them was a friendly, soon to be famous, new machine built and sold by a brand-new company known as Apple Computer. This machine, introduced at the West Coast Computer Faire in 1977, was the Apple II. Fully equipped with a screen and a keyboard and, later, a disk drive, the Apple II was instrumental in moving the idea of home computing out of hobbyists' basements and into the world at large.

Soon after, in 1981, the IBM PC burst onto the computing scene. Bolstered by the high regard in which IBM was held in the business community, and helped along by work-related applications such as the VisiCalc spreadsheet and the dBase relational database, the IBM PC became the first of a line of computers (including so-called IBM compatibles) that popularized—or, perhaps more accurately, legitimized—the microcomputer invasion of the business world. The Information Revolution, as it came to be called, had officially begun.

Standalone PCs

Initially, however, personal computing was intensely personal. It was you and the computer. Your data. Your applications. Your directory structure. Your CONFIG.SYS, and your AUTOEXEC.BAT customized setup file. To many people, especially the adventurous, this sense of ownership combined with the ability to actually interact with a machine in real time was invigorating. It was, to use a 90s type of word, empowering. Typewriters and calculators had never offered the fun or the challenge that these computers did. Even nonprogrammers could feel strong, technical, and in charge after mastering the intricacies of the Dir command or, better yet, after creating a batch file that not only worked but made the computer do something it hadn't been preprogrammed to do.

But as computing became ever more important, especially in business, people also realized that solitary communing with the computer sometimes collided with the demands of the real world. Creating a report, a budget, or a database might be challenging or fun, but the real purpose of the document was to aggregate and, usually, share the information. Sharing happened in one of three ways: (1) printing the document, (2) relying on "sneakernet" to walk floppies to another machine, or (3) allowing multiple users to access the same files on the same computer.

While these methods did—and still do—work, they were not the most efficient ways, in terms of either cost or time saved, to make information widely available. A much better solution, and one that businesses have embraced from the 1980s to the present, is a *local area network*, or *LAN*.

Local area networks

Developed in the 1970s but becoming a real force in computing during the 1980s and 1990s, LANs link computers that are geographically close to one another—in the same office, on the same floor of a building, or in a relatively small office campus. The computers are known as *nodes* on the network, and they are connected by cabling and by networking hardware known as *network interface cards*, or *NICs*. The purpose of a LAN is to allow the computers on the network to communicate and to share not only information (files) but also resources such as printers.

Early LANs consisted of perhaps a few dozen computers and were limited to about 600 feet of cabling. As the technology developed, however, so did network size and scope. Today, LANs can cover hundreds of yards rather than hundreds of feet, and they can support hundreds, rather than dozens, of nodes. In addition, they can include a mix of computers from PCs to minicomputers or mainframes, and they have grown up to provide a welter of options in speed, layout, and ways of moving information around. At heart, though, LANs still remain networks for relatively small areas.

Wide area networks and Internetworks

But of course, organizations that need networks aren't always small or limited to a smallish area. Some are huge, others rely on offices in far-flung places, and still others are both huge and widespread. Typically, the larger or more dispersed the organization, the greater its need for the computing power and rapid communication that networking brings. For example, a governmental, educational, or business organization with branches scattered across and between countries clearly benefits if the computers in one branch are able to share information with the computers in other branches.

With the development of increasingly sophisticated computer, communications, and networking technologies, it has become possible to connect computers located far from one another in a *wide area network*, or *WAN*. Through a WAN, messages can travel across the country or around the world with the aid of high-speed communications—an enormous benefit, especially in the 1990s, when individuals and businesses have become so reliant on personal and networked computers.

A WAN can be made up of a mainframe computer to which distant terminals connect through a telephone line, or (more typically) it can consist of a network of interconnected LANs. Although the line to draw is not very clear—and not always agreed on by experts—you'll sometimes see the term *internetwork* applied to WANs made up of such interconnected networks. That's especially the case with WANs that link LANs built upon distinctly different *architectures*, that is, those that rely on different technologies and follow essentially different rules of networking behavior. (These subjects are covered in more detail later in the book).

WANs, although they rely on far more advanced technology, resemble the original ARPANET in linking widely separated computers. Communication can still be based on modem and telephone, but newer technologies, including satellite, microwave transmission, and cable (television) are also coming into play. As with the original ARPANET, the computers in a WAN also rely on mediating hardware and software that help them (1) prepare and address messages for transmission and (2) route transmissions both efficiently and accurately. A number of such technologies are now used for this purpose, including the *routers*, *bridges*, and *gateways* described later in the book. (Gateways, by the way, are particularly interesting because they connect networks built on different architectures, essentially repackaging transmissions in such a way that each network thinks it is communicating with another network exactly like itself.)

Going Global

As mentioned above, the word internetwork is sometimes used to describe a WAN consisting of separate LANs. It is also the word, as you've probably guessed, that is the basis for the name of the greatest internetwork in the world, the Internet.

The Internet

If any aspect of computing has taken the world by storm over the past two to three years, it must be the Internet. Increasingly important not only as a global resource for e-mail, research, chatting, special-interest groups, and bulletin boards, the Internet also has become a new medium for buying, selling, advertising, educating, and even broadcasting. In addition, the Internet—or rather the part of it known as the World Wide Web—is significantly altering the way people view, create, and use information.

As mentioned earlier, the Internet started out as a Department of Defense project that became the research lab/university/military network called ARPANET. ARPANET was responsible for the development of numerous technologies, such as packet switching, that networks rely on today. Chief among ARPANET's contributions, however, especially in terms of the Internet, was the development of a set of *protocols* (roughly, sets of rules followed by communicating computers) known as *TCP/IP*—itself short for the combined names of the two initial protocols developed, Transmission Control Protocol and Internet Protocol. The TCP/IP protocols govern the packaging (TCP) and routing (IP) of information across a network. How important is TCP/IP? It defines communication on the Internet. In that sense, TCP/IP *is* the Internet.

Originally a network of four nodes, ARPANET ran at a whopping 56 kilobits per second (Kbps)—the same speed at which current modems operate. Although the network sounds small and antiquated today, it fired the imagination back then, and universities everywhere clamored to connect to it. Unfortunately, however, only those with Department of Defense grants were given the privilege.

In response, in 1986 the National Science Foundation began work on a separate network, called NSFNET, which would be open to all comers. Unlike ARPANET, NSFNET was built on a central *backbone* of interconnected supercomputers, to which regional networks connected to provide access for users at universities and other sites. NSFNET grew at a rapid pace, and sometime during the later 1980s, as more and more hosts joined the NSFNET backbone, and as other networks blended into the mix, this ever-expanding collection of networks came to be known as the Internet.

Growth continued almost exponentially. By the early 1990s, the Internet boasted multiple high-speed backbones and more than one million host computers. By the mid-1990s, the number had jumped to almost 10 million. In 1995, access to the Internet shifted from NSFNET to public, for-profit,

Internet Service Providers (ISPs); NSFNET, apparently gratefully, began the process of reverting to its original identity as a research network. By the end of 1997, the number of Internet hosts had climbed near the 30 million mark. These hosts belonged to scores of geographic and organizational *domains* around the world, domains familiar to Internet users from the abbreviations, such as .com and .org, and the country codes, such as.fr (France), and .dk (Denmark), that serve to identify and categorize the hosts' owners. And there it stands. By the time you read this, there will no doubt be well over 30 million computers on the Internet, each of them able to serve the information needs of the many more personal users—an estimated 79 million in the United States and Canada alone—who connect on a daily basis.

The World Wide Web

And what of the World Wide Web, the famous "www" represented in so many Internet addresses? In actuality, the Web is only part of the Internet, albeit the part that most users consider the whole thing. Perhaps best described as the graphical, mouse-oriented, *hyperlinked* face of the Internet, the Web was invented by Tim Berners-Lee in 1989, at the CERN particle physics laboratory in Switzerland. Whereas the "original" Internet was and still is text based and primarily devoted to e-mail, file transfers, and newsgroups, Berners-Lee created a graphical *browser*/editor that used hyperlinks to allow people—scientists at that point—to collaborate. They did this by accessing computers and documents stored on computers through the use of Universal Resource Identifiers (later renamed *Universal Resource Locators*, or *URLs*). To this "universe" of stored and shared information, which included links to graphics and sound files as well as text documents, he gave the name the World Wide Web.

Thus the Web was born—to make it easier for scientists to collaborate and share information. Perhaps more important, it allowed people to work naturally, to jump from idea to idea (or from document to document) in whatever random pattern they choose, rather than by wading sequentially through one document after the other in order to reach the information they want or need. It is a way of working that resembles the way a computer accesses information on a disk drive. It is also the way of working embodied in the Web browsers so much in use today.

The Future

And what of the future? Where are networks, from LANs to the Internet, headed? Obviously no one knows for sure, but here are some of the major directions underway.

On Earth (and yes, there are plans afoot for networks in space), developments are tending somewhat toward the idea of network computers, or at least toward server-based applications, as well as toward distributed computing, intranets, and extranets. In addition, the United States government, along with research institutions and universities, is working on a next-generation Internet that is intended to be faster and to offer the kind of *bandwidth* needed—indeed demanded—by people who are frustrated with current connection and download times on the "World Wide Wait."

In terms of developments closer at hand, network computers, as you probably know, are intended to be inexpensive, low-maintenance desktop stations that rely heavily on server computers within the organization for applications and data storage. Although they have processing ability of their own, these machines are intended to have limited capacity for expansion and customization and thus to have limited needs for expensive and time-consuming support. They are relatively new, and they face obstacles from two primary directions: (1) competition from the rapidly dropping cost of standard desktop computers equipped with both expansion capability and local storage, and (2) reluctance from users to give up their current ability to store whatever they want—including sensitive documents—on their own machines. In certain circumstances—for example, in offices where people require a limited number of applications and where they need to share information—network computers seem to offer a viable solution. They are, in a sense, smarter versions of the dumb terminals of old. In other cases, say for people who work independently or creatively on a large number of projects requiring multiple applications, the value of network computers seems more doubtful. How and to what extent they will replace desktop computers as network resources remains to be seen.

Distributed computing refers to a networking environment in which processing can be performed by different computers within the network, while the actual location of the machine(s) doing the "thinking" remains invisible to the user. The network, its operating system, and its applications are responsible for determining which computer performs a particular task and for fetching, updating, and saving the files needed for the job. In order to do all this, the computers within the network (as opposed to the clients accessing them) must be able to communicate freely among themselves and to collaborate in the sense of either sharing the workload or taking on different tasks in order to contribute to the end result. Distributed computing thus represents a different way of using a network. Whereas most current networking requires users to handle file management themselves, the computers in a distributed system essentially take more of the burden on themselves and, in the process, they reduce the burden on their users.

As for intranets and extranets, both are based on Internet technologies—the Web lifestyle—but instead of making information available to the world, they restrict access either to an organization's employees (intranets) or to employees and selected business partners, such as resellers and vendors (extranets). Both are based on hyperlinked Web pages. Both are moves toward greater efficiency. Both make information broadly available. Both are intended to cut costs or keep them down. Extranets, in particular, are increasingly being seen as promising ways to improve communication with business partners and to eliminate delays and costs associated with purchasing and delivery; they can move transactions on line instead of relying on paper-based ordering and tracking. Both intranets and extranets will doubtless become a fact of life in *enterprise computing*.

And finally—the space thing. Yes, NASA announced in August 1998 that it plans to begin exploring the development of an "Interplanet," an Internet-like network between planets and among the stars for supporting future missions and, perhaps, even colonization on planets far from the

Earth. It's an intriguing thought, especially when combined with the viewpoint of Vinton Cerf, one of the developers of the packet-switching technology so basic to the Internet and to networking in general. His concern: it's time to start thinking about naming domains in space—domains such as .mars, for instance.

Well, this is the world you propose to enter. It's an exciting one with a most interesting past, present and, it seems, future.

A Network Does…

…the dishes. No, no. All right, then, what does a network do? Well, as Chapter 1 kept reminding you, a network enables communication and sharing between and among computers and, in the process, it enables communication and sharing between and among people. This is its job.

But interaction of this sort, whether human or machine, takes different forms, exists for different reasons, and often has different requirements. In the non-computerized world, for example, both telephones and letters enable interaction and sharing, yet one form of interaction requires hardware (the telephone) and an elaborate, technically sophisticated communications infrastructure, while the other requires pen, paper, stamps, and logistically complex but technically less challenging ground, air, and sea support for mail delivery. This chapter provides an overview of the basic ways communication and sharing take place, as well as some of the broad concerns related to entire networks, in terms of supporting that capability.

Communication First

Before turning to networks themselves, think for a moment about the process of communication and about how and when it happens. Sometimes, for example, folk gather around the water cooler, swap stories around a campfire, or chat over the back fence. Although each of these situations is different from the others, in all cases the people involved are—aside from enjoying themselves—sharing information in *real time*. That is, they are broadcasting and receiving, so to speak, in the same time frame and in a synchronized way that depends on the participants taking turns (usually politely) on center stage.

But people don't always communicate in this way. Sometimes they sit down to write letters. Or they compose, publish, and distribute newsletters. Or they hop in the car with an index card and pen, and they go to post an advertisement on the grocery store bulletin board. In these instances, people are still communicating and sharing information, but their interactions are delayed, or *asynchronous*. The "broadcast" goes out, to be sure, but the response might come hours or days later...or it might not come at all. Communication of this type does not rely on, or even require, that sending and receiving be "in sync." In terms of timing, the two are completely independent of one another.

But even though timing is considerably different in real-time and asynchronous communication, both types of interaction are equally important in allowing people to share information. Networks, existing as they do to support all kinds of communication and information distribution, naturally support both styles.

Networking in Real Time

Real-time communication over a network happens in different ways. Consider, for example, Internet chat rooms. They represent a recent and enormously popular innovation, and one that enables people literally worldwide to comment back and forth, on subjects ranging from the righteous to the risqué, as if they were all sitting in the same room together. No matter how far apart the people are geographically, all they need do is connect via telephone to a virtual meeting room on the Internet at the same time in order to chat in real time.

Business networks, too, support such real-time communication. For example, when employees in different offices collaborate on a report with the help of videoconferencing software, they are relying on the network to help them interact in real time. In the case of software such as Microsoft's NetMeeting, it's the network that even allows group members to share an application installed on one participant's computer. Similarly, when the

CEO delivers a lunchtime speech that the company broadcasts to desktops throughout the organization, she is using the network to communicate in real time. When your colleague takes an interactive training course via the company network, he, too is working with the training materials in real time. And even the employee who accesses the corporate intranet to record vacation time in a database located somewhere on the network can be thought of as communicating in real time, even though the "communi-cation" is between a living, breathing human and a mass of records on a hard disk. Why? Because most likely the employee's vacation database is updated immediately or as soon as possible—if the update is delayed, for example, because the record is already in use or because a large number of simultaneous connections have slowed the system slightly.

As you can imagine, such real-time use of a network relies on the interaction of many technologies ranging from a network operating system to power-ful server software, audio- and video-enabled client software, databases and other applications, and intranet support. It also relies on sophisticated communications capabilities and various transmission methods and pro-tocols that ensure smooth, even delivery of information to one or many cli-ents at the same time. You'll be looking into these matters in later chapters.

Networking Asynchronously

Even though real-time networking, especially as it is related to the Internet and Internet-based intranets, is gaining in popularity, far more interaction currently happens through asynchronous communication. For example, anyone who has been frustrated by telephone tag or has run up and down the hall leaving messages on someone else's chair can appreciate the time savings and convenience offered by the ultimate in asynchronous net-worked communications: e-mail. Pound out a message to a colleague, and continue working while you wait for a response. You might hope for an immediate reply, but even if you don't receive one, the consequences— and the effect on your temper—are less extreme than with other alterna-tives. In addition, your colleague now has the luxury of responding whenever doing so fits his or her schedule, perhaps allowing the person to take needed time to gather information, to mull over an issue that requires some thought, or to postpone handling a situation better dealt with later.

Similarly, asynchronous networking comes into play when you use your word processor to route a budget or a report to various people for their comments. Each person can work independently on the document and, when finished, simply send the document back to you electronically. With the help of the network, you can even take this scenario one step further by sending the edited document over the network to a shared printer. And even this bit of human/hardware interaction might well happen asynchronously if the printer is busy and your job must join the tail end of a queue of documents, all of which are scheduled to be printed in the order received.

Like real-time networking, asynchronous networking relies on the interaction of unseen hardware, cabling, and software ranging from client and server operating systems to both server-based and client-based applications that are designed to recognize the network and to shunt information along its wires. In addition, with people routing information back and forth to one another, the network requires technologies that support not only the transfer of files from place to place, but also the use of "convenience" items, such as the *directories* that keep track of people's names and the network addresses of their computers. These, too, you'll be meeting in later chapters.

Sharing and Distribution

Where person-to-person communication is concerned, e-mail messages form a large and important part of the traffic that moves from place to place on a network. E-mail alone, however, does not a network make, even though some people live by and for their electronic messages. In addition to human collaboration, networks support two different types of sharing: file sharing and resource sharing.

File sharing

File sharing covers any kind of *content* that has been named and saved for future use. Document files, such as letters and reports, are obvious examples of content. Just as legitimate, however, are graphics, Web pages, database records, spreadsheets, slide presentations, and any other named collections of information. If a file can be stored on a network and either routed from one computer to another or accessed by any computer given permission to do so, it is fair game for file sharing. The information it contains might be made available to all, restricted to a small group, or even placed on the network for use by one person. In terms of networking, none of that matters. What is important is that, through the network, it's possible to communicate, share, and distribute information in the form of files between and among computers.

From ARPANET till now, this file sharing has been the primary function of a network and a driving force behind the technologies developed to make computer-to-computer communication happen as smoothly as possible, even between incompatible hardware and software *platforms* such as Macintosh and Windows/Intel ("Wintel") machines. The ability to transfer information is the reason the protocols, networking models, communications technologies, and other matters covered in the rest of this book were invented.

Resource sharing

In addition to sharing files, however, networks also provide one additional—and in some cases economically needed—benefit: the sharing of *resources*, which are typically understood to be pieces of hardware that are set up for use over the network. A network hard drive, for example, is a resource that—when shared out—can be used for storage by people assigned their own portions of space on it. Or it can be used as a temporary home for files being transferred from one computer to another:

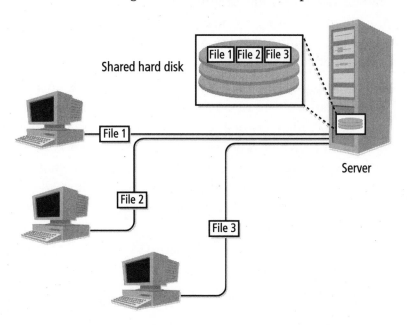

Shared hard disk

File 1 File 2 File 3

File 1

File 2

File 3

Server

Similarly, a network printer is a resource that can be used and shared by any-one who knows how to specify its network location to the Print command in his or her word processor, spreadsheet, database, or other application program:

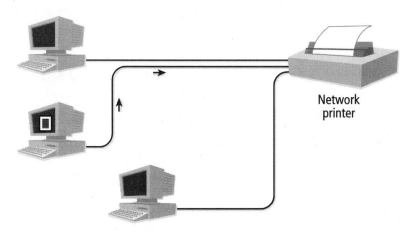

Network printer

Broadcasts and push technology

You might have noticed that the preceding descriptions and illustrations of communication and file and resource sharing had one thing in com-mon: all are dependent on the person wanting to communicate or share. That is, the user of the network instigates the activity. Whether it's finding and using a shared file, sending an e-mail message, locating a Web page on the intranet, saving a file on a network hard disk, or printing a document on a shared printer, the action always starts with the person wanting to use the network.

But these days, the burden isn't always on the user. Fueled by the increas-ing popularity of and reliance on Internet technologies, networking has, in part, turned into more of a two-way street. Thanks to the development of "Webcasting," which relies on Internet technologies and a service known as *push*, a network server can, under certain circumstances, take an active role in delivering information to a network user instead of waiting until the user has the time or the inclination to search out and "pull" the same information to the desktop.

Push was developed to provide network users with an automatic means of receiving periodic updates on information they want or need to keep abreast of. By "subscribing" to certain services that periodically push information to its subscribers, network users can keep up with information as varied as stock reports, sports scores, news, or—closer to the business of business—reports on production, sales, inventory, and other frequently changing corporate statistics. The same technology, by the way, also serves for real-time transmissions, such as audio or video broadcasts and live, online training, and it can—and is—used by network administrators for delivering application programs and updates to an organization's desktop computers.

How Communication Needs Affect a Network

As already mentioned, numerous technologies—both hardware and software—underlie the ability of a network to deliver both real-time and asynchronous transmissions. You'll begin to delve into the details in later chapters, but for now assume you have a bird's-eye view of an entire, functioning network with all its pieces nicely integrated and humming along. From this high-flying point of view, you can imagine the network as being something like a Tinker Toy concoction of cables and nodes like this:

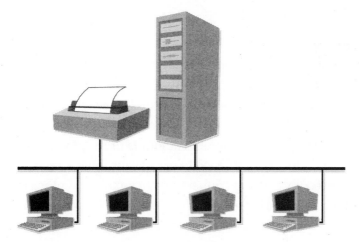

Looking down on this hard-working collection of computers, you might wonder about what broad communication/sharing/data transfer issues affect not only the administrators of the network, but even more important, directly affect its end users. It's not hard to think of all kinds of issues that can impact individual computers, but what about those that affect the usability of the network as a whole?

The following sections attempt to provide you with a broad overview of these issues by grouping them into a few not-very-scientific but perhaps helpful categories. These sections also, and not incidentally, introduce you to some terms that are frequently bandied about in reference to networks in general.

Note, however, that the following sections simply provide an overview of these concerns. Although the most important of the technologies and topics described here are also covered in more detail later in the book, none of the information below is intended to provide advice on who, what, where, why or, especially, how. That job belongs to much more detailed books, white papers, product suppliers, and consultants, as well as to research, strategizing, and cost analyses based on a particular network's hardware, software, configuration, and user needs.

So what types of things affect whole networks and their ability to support human and machine communication and interaction? Some of the most important, visible to administrators and users alike, are reliability, scalability, security, and speed.

Reliability

A network that doesn't work, or that doesn't work reliably, is in some respects worse than no network at all. As an organization becomes more and more dependent on networking, it naturally becomes more dependent on having a functioning network. As a network is entrusted with the storage and transmission of considerable amounts of information, down times become less and less tolerable. Network *storms* (bursts of excessive traffic) frustrate users by making connections to e-mail and other resources either difficult or temporarily impossible. Too little bandwidth (and, thus, too slow a network) raises everyone's blood pressure.

But what does reliability mean, other than "a network that doesn't fail"? The term actually covers a range of issues related to both hardware and software. On the hardware front, for example, reliable network servers are assumed to be computing workhorses able to handle the tasks required of them both consistently and with as few mechanical failures as possible. Electrically, power to those servers must remain continuous and stable in order for the network to be considered reliable. Even the shape, or *topology*, of the network can come into play, because a network that is ring-shaped (logically, if not physically) is considered more reliable than other layouts.

Where software is concerned, reliability demands (of course) stable operating systems and applications that support the various transport methods and protocols in use on the network. The *network operating system*, the *OS* in use on the network servers, for instance, must be as *fault-tolerant* as possible; that is, it must be designed to remain unfazed by application and other "glitches" and must be able to recover quickly from more serious errors.

Similarly, because many different programs run on and over a network, operating systems and applications—whether "out of the box," developed internally, or purchased from a third-party provider—must be able not only to work on their own but also to communicate and transfer information between and among themselves to the extent required to support the tasks demanded of the network. E-mail clients on the desktop, for instance, must be able to work with e-mail servers on the network in order to send, receive, download, and store mail messages.

And, of course, these days there's the Millennium Bug problem, the Y2K issue that, more than any other aspect of computing, has tended to define the word *reliability* in the late 1990s. Although the actual extermination of that particular "insect" is a job requiring the technical skills provided by programmers, the Millenium Bug is an equally big concern for the network administrators, technicians, and other support staff responsible for the servers and other hardware that make up a functional—and functioning—network. Because so many critical (and non-critical) systems depend on computers representing the date accurately, enormous resources, both financial and professional, are dedicated to ensuring a smooth transition to the next millenium.

Such are some of the issues that fall into the "reliability" category.

Scalability

Scalability, although it somehow seems to refer to how easily you can clean a fish for dinner, is obviously not used in such a way in the networking world. Instead, scalability refers to how well a network or its software can grow (scale) up or down to meet an organization's needs. There are different ways in which a network and its software can scale, however. Some ways are hardware-related, while others are dependent on the capabilities of its software.

The most immediately obvious way in which a network can scale upward—grow—is by adding nodes to support more users. It can also grow, however, by adding more server power. For example, by using servers with multiple processors, the network can rely on a feature known as *symmetric multiprocessing*, or *SMP*, in which the processors work as a team, each performing whatever task needs doing in order to improve performance (see Figure 2-1). Such capability must, of course, be supported by the network operating system running on the server, because it is the operating system and not the processors that determines how the tasks are parceled out.

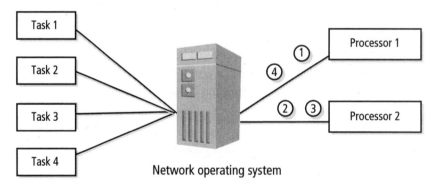

Figure 2-1.   *How SMP works.*

Likewise, a network can scale upward by *clustering* multiple servers, joining them in a group that acts like a single system and appears to be one as far as clients on the network are concerned. One of the advantages of clustering—a serious one economically—is that it allows a network to grow incrementally. As more power is needed, more servers can be connected to the cluster. Figure 2-2 shows how clustering works.

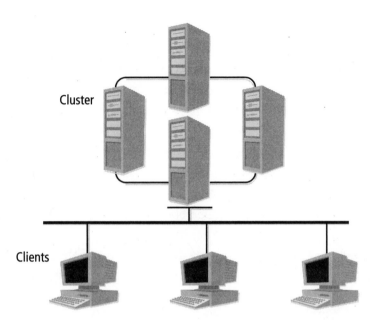

Figure 2-2.   *A server cluster appears to be a single system to its clients.*

Of course, scalability doesn't apply only to hardware. As already noted, the network operating system must support the capabilities of the server hardware, whether those capabilities involve SMP, clustering, or any other means of processing information.

Other types of software can be scalable, too. The software that provides mail service to clients can be designed to scale upward with increases in number of users and, consequently, the load it must handle. Similarly, the server software that provides access to databases on the network can support scalability to meet changing requirements in the network population, the size(s) of databases, the complexity or number of transactions taking place, and so on.

Organizations don't usually grow to their optimum size, implement a network, and then stay the same size forever after. That's why scalability, in both hardware and software, is an issue that affects both the entire network and its users.

Security
Security covers a range of issues. Some of them are software-based and relate to maintaining the integrity of the network, its resources, and its devices.

Security in this sense means ensuring that programs cannot inadvertently access memory they are not cleared to use by the operating system and that one program cannot tamper with or even damage the data belonging to another. Other issues involve caring for the physical well-being of the network and its data through measures such as fireproofing and regularly scheduled data backups.

Other aspects of security, such as the multi-level set of strategies known as *RAID* (Redundant Array of Inexpensive Disks), concentrate on protecting the data on network disks—the repositories of everything important that travels over, or is stored on, the network. RAID, which comes up frequently in discussions of network integrity, basically protects data by *mirroring* (duplicating) data or by *striping* data across multiple disks, as shown in Figure 2-3, to ensure that all won't be lost if one of the disks fails.

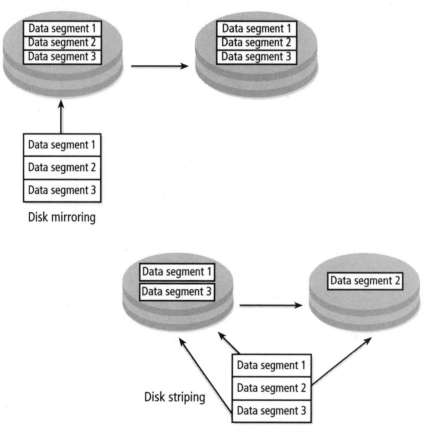

Figure 2-3. *Two strategies used in RAID: (a) disk mirroring and (b) disk striping.*

More commonly, however, security is usually thought of as keeping unauthorized users from accessing the network and its resources. This is the type of security that networks deal with head on through the use of passwords and permissions, firewalls, proxy servers, and other strategies that help identify the good and corral or filter out the bad and the ugly.

Accessing the network itself

As most everyone knows, authorized users gain access to network services and resources by *logging on* at the start of a network session. Part of the logon process involves providing the network with a *username* (the person's friendly, widely distributed network name) and a *password* (the private, not-to-be revealed code word or name that verifies the individual to the network). Whereas usernames can be, and are, freely distributed, passwords represent the network's first and, from the end user's point of view, best defense against unauthorized entry. Although they are not impossible to *crack* or steal, passwords are so important that they are never displayed on a monitor, even while being typed, and they are commonly stored in *encrypted* (unreadable) form to help preserve security.

Accessing resources

But even if everyone who logs on to a network is a true-blue, genuinely authorized user, there still remains the question of what files, resources, and even servers "everyone" can connect to. The network must also be able to discriminate among its users to determine whether Mr. X can access the payroll files, or whether Ms. Y can make changes to the company's price list.

To control access among authorized users, networks can rely on either of two devices: password-protected resources and *access permissions*. By assigning a password to a resource, such as a folder or a printer, the owner or manager of the resource can control access by limiting distribution of the password to selected individuals who want or need to use the resource. In addition to (or instead of) assigning a password, the resource owner might also rely on access permissions, which provide users with read, write, or full (read, write, and delete) access to information. In some cases, people who know the password granting access to the resource might also be restricted to, say, only read access. Or, if the resource is not password-protected but users are granted access singly, one by one, each user might be given a different type of access permission. Joe, for instance, might only be able to read documents in the shared Contracts folder, but Jean might be granted the ability to both read and modify those documents.

Controlling access from outside the organization

If network use were confined to computers physically cabled to one another, passwords and controlled access would be admirable champions of security. These days, however, networks often need to be accessed from outside, via modem and telephone. Someone telecommuting from home, for example, might need to connect frequently in order to send and receive e-mail. Complete strangers might need to search for information on the company's Internet site. Or semi-outsiders—vendors and business partners, for example—might need to use network resources as they and their businesses work with the organization.

In the first case, an authorized network user dialing in from the outside, security can be implemented through the setting up of one or more dedicated servers that represent the only "doorway" through which such users can gain access to the network. These servers can be provided with special methods for authenticating the caller. One such method involves a *callback* mechanism in which the server authenticates the caller's username and password, disconnects, and then returns the call at either a predetermined number or, in the case of individuals who call from many different locations, at a number provided by the user during the initial connection. For security to be extended in this situation, transmissions—including the user's password—can be encrypted for travel over phone lines.

In the case of strangers accessing an organization's Internet site, the recommended means of protection is known as a *firewall*. Like a physical firewall that is intended to keep a fire from spreading from one part of a building to another, a network firewall forms a barrier between the network and the Internet. The firewall, which can be hardware, software, or a combination of the two, monitors messages traveling into the network, rejecting those that are unauthorized while passing the authorized messages along. In this way, a firewall allows communication to flow freely while keeping the network completely separate from the Internet.

Not all traffic between an internal network and the Internet passes from outside to inside, however. More and more, network users access the Internet from within the network. To ensure security in these cases, organizations can rely on a form of firewall known as a *proxy* server, which filters traffic in the opposite direction by literally standing in for the computer requesting the Internet connection. So, for example, a computer on the network "connects" to a particular Internet site by relaying the request to the proxy server. The proxy server, in turn, relays the request to the site and then relays the response back to the requesting computer. As in the case of a firewall sifting through incoming transmissions, a proxy server provides network users with access to the Internet while it keeps the world outside at bay.

Speed

Ah, speed. Where network users are concerned, speed has only one meaning: the faster the better. But what constitutes fast? That depends. On a small, peer-to-peer network consisting of a few computers physically cabled together, fast is generally not much of an issue unless too many computers (more than five to ten) are linked together. After all, the range of transmission is limited, and electricity does travel quickly over the *coaxial* or *twisted pair* (telephone wire) cabling generally used, both of which typically transmit at the rate of about 10 Mbps (megabits, or millions of bits, per second). That's certainly fast enough for the small office.

On larger networks, however, speed counts. So the question becomes, what contributes to a network's speed? The number and power of its servers, of course, and whether or not the network is being asked to support too many nodes. Where network speed is concerned, however, people usually think of the speed of transmission over the network cabling.

Typical LANs, as you recall, are mixtures of desktop computers (the clients) and high-performance servers, which are the parts of the "digital nervous system" that collect, store, and dish out shared (or shareable) resources, including files, printers, and applications. These clients and servers are generally connected by cabling. (Wireless connections, though not as common, can also be used.) Like most products, cabling comes in different varieties that have different capabilities and are often best suited to different jobs. Later chapters go into the gory details, so at this point, where you're just looking at the speed of transmission, it's enough to say that there are three basic types of cabling: coaxial and twisted pair (the same types used in peer-to-peer networks), and fiberoptic. Coaxial cabling and twisted pair cabling transmit messages electrically and, as already mentioned, typically transmit at about 10 Mbps. Fiberoptic cabling, which uses light for transmission, typically moves information 10 times faster than coaxial or twisted pair wiring, that is, at about 100 Mbps, although the speed can reach 1 Gbps (billion bits per second) or even more.

WANs, which are often made up of scattered LANs linked by communications devices, rely on cabling locally, but they add communications and advanced networking technologies to the mix in order to transfer messages across sometimes vast geographic distances. WANs can rely on telephone connections, but more sophisticated—and faster—networks rely on digital connections, such as *T1*, which transmits at 1.544 Mbps, or on microwave, cable, or satellite communications. The defining aspect of a WAN, however, is less in its cabling and communications than in the technologies it uses to transmit messages.

Just as with the ARPANET of thirty-some years ago, WANs typically rely on packet switching, which divides messages into small, usually equally sized *packets* of information that are then forwarded to their destination. The various packet-switching technologies aren't often rated precisely in terms of speed, but rather are described as "high-speed" or "very high-speed," presumably leaving the rest to your imagination. All, however, are characterized by some type of "smart" routing. Some, such as the technology known as *frame relay*, rely on permanent, dedicated lines to achieve rapid transmission. Frame relay theoretically can reach speeds up to 100 Mbps. More typically, however, it runs over connections such as T1 that operate at 56 Kbps to 1.5 Mbps. Other packet-switching technologies, such as the up-and-coming *asynchronous transfer mode*, or *ATM*, rely on commercial communications services and small, fixed-size packets known as *cells* to achieve transfer rates that range from a typical 155 Mbps to 622 Mbps or more. Given the rapid and ever-changing advances in communications technology, network speed, not to mention reliability, will no doubt continue to increase.

In thinking about speed, however, do note that the rate at which information *can* travel over a network isn't necessarily the rate at which it *does* travel. The performance of a network is also related to its bandwidth, or *throughput*, which refers to its capacity to handle traffic. Network throughput is not necessarily the same as the transmission rate of the cabling over which the traffic moves. On an idle network, for example, a single message can obviously speed along to its destination. However, on a congested network that is already handling about as much traffic as it can bear, messages must wait to be transmitted, and so the speed of the network, in terms of throughput, slows down.

Networks, Networks Everywhere

Chapters 1 and 2 introduced you to networking in general and to the types of traffic that normally travel over a network. Now it's time to start getting down to the nitty-gritty, to begin poking into what a network is made of and how it works. This is the fun part, and it's what the rest of the book will cover.

Networks As a Whole

At first glance, networks appear to be a tangled web of hardware, software, protocols, activities, transmission speeds, bandwidth, and other niceties, all of which interlock to the point that you might wonder how to find the one piece that can help you begin untangling the various technologies to see how they all fit together.

Finding a starting point is actually not as difficult as it might seem. After all, when confronted with a mass of green growing things crowding in and competing for your attention, you know it's often helpful to just step back a little to get some perspective—to see the forest rather than the individual trees. You can use the same approach here. Instead of looking at a network as a high-tech mass of disparate though integral pieces, step back and look at it as an entire entity. Start by looking at the way it functions—its modus operandi, or MO, so to speak.

Types of Networks

Different networks can be described functionally as belonging to one of three broad categories: *centralized networks*, *peer-to-peer networks*, and *client/server networks*.

Centralized networks are built around terminals and mainframes. They are based on direct cabling from the terminals to the mainframe and on processing housed in the main—central—computer. They are also, obviously, in wide use today and remain a valuable and highly reliable means of creating a community of users within an organization.

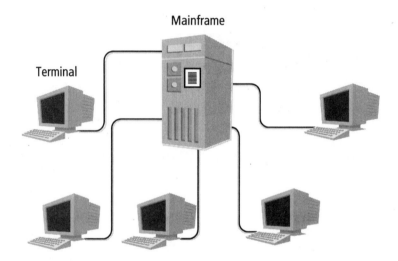

Centralized networks are costly and not as scalable as the client/server networks currently implemented in many large and small corporations, so growing the network can mean replacing expensive hardware. Mainframe-based networks can, however, interoperate with client/server networks with the help of mediating software such as Microsoft's SNA Server.

To move on...in order to provide networking functionality, but with greater scalability and cost effectiveness in mind, emphasis in the 1980s and especially in the 1990s has been turning to the networking models built around microcomputer technologies. These models, which assume both desktop processing capability and access to network resources, include the peer-to-peer and client/server designs that form the basis for local area networks and wide area networks. These types of networks are not only a mainstay of business, government, and education; they are, frankly, where most of the "action" is these days, in both microcomputer and software development. How, then, do they differ?

Peer-to-peer

Peer-to-peer, as defined in this book, is a highly democratic form of microcomputer-based network in the sense that all the computers in the network are peers, equals, "buddies." Any or all of them can act as a network resource, providing files, printers, and even disk storage to the others. At the same time, all are also capable of working on their own, because they have the internal resources—disk storage, sufficient memory, and processing power—to act as stand-alone computers.

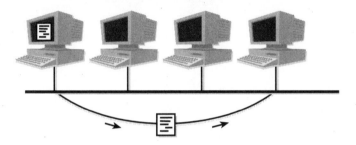

Peer-to-peer networks are recommended for small groups of five to ten workstations located in the same area, as in a small office. Although they do not offer the sophistication of larger networks in terms of security, centralized management, and expandability, peer-to-peer networks offset these limitations with ease of installation, relatively low cost, and ease of administration (which, incidentally, boils down to each user determining how, when, and with whom the resources on his or her computer will be shared with other members of the group).

In a peer-to-peer network, there is no central authority figure, no network administrator who handles security, user accounts, passwords, management, and so on, although there might well be one individual who knows more about networked computers than anyone else and so becomes the network guru through either design or default. Regardless, in this kingdom of peers, all members give and take, and all are responsible for maintaining their own resources and (password-based) security. The (human) members control access to their resources on either a user-by-user or a share-by-share basis. With a user-by-user basis, individuals are granted read, write, or other controlled access; with a share-by-share basis, a drive (bad idea if you're talking the computer's main or only hard drive), folder, subfolder, or device is shared out for use by those who need it.

In a nutshell, then, here are the advantages and disadvantages of peer-to-peer networks. The main advantage is that peer-to-peer networks are not only inexpensive, but they are also easy to implement. Each computer in the network simply needs a network card that enables it to communicate with the others, TV-type coaxial or telephone-type twisted pair wiring to link it with its peers, and an operating system, such as Windows 98 or Windows NT Workstation, that has been built to support peer-to-peer networking. And the disadvantages? Peer-to-peer networks are limited in size and scope, and they are not designed with security in mind. Each user must take responsibility for the security and management of his or her own machine.

Client/server

Client/server networks are far more powerful and wide-ranging than peer-to-peer networks. They can support thousands of clients, and they can link multiple computing platforms, such as Windows 95/98, Windows NT, and Macintosh. Like mainframe-based, centralized networks, client/server networks are built around one or more centralized servers and are administered from a central location. Unlike mainframe-based networks, however, client/server networks are based on less centralized hardware—often, minicomputers and high-performance microcomputers—and on server-oriented operating systems. Except in environments relying on thin-client computing (see the "Clients" section of this chapter), they also differ from mainframe-based networks in assuming that the clients have independent processing power and local storage of their own and thus are functional workstations in their own right.

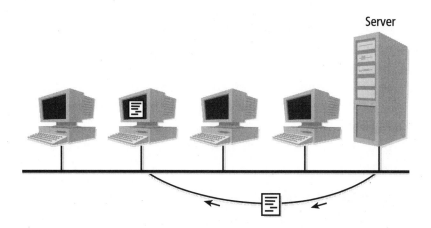

Whereas peer-to-peer networks consist of computers linked to one another, client/server networks consist of computers linked—again by means of cabling—to a centralized server. In addition, because different servers can be dedicated to different functions, a client/server network opens the door to additional capabilities, including remote access, such as when a worker telecommutes from home, and the hosting of a Web site separate from an organization's internal (not open to the public) resources. In addition, whereas peer-to-peer networks are limited in size, client/server networks are highly scalable. As demand or the number of users increases, additional servers can be tossed into the mix to spread the load and support the increase in traffic. In line with this, a client/server network can also be used to provide connections with other networks, either to create a larger LAN or WAN or to provide network users with access to "foreign" networks or systems, including mainframes.

The hardware, software, and administrative skills required to implement a client/server network successfully are considerably more sophisticated than those required for a peer-to-peer network. The servers, for example, must be capable of running a network operating system (NOS), such as Windows NT server, UNIX, or Novell Netware. Such NOS are much more complex than a typical desktop operating system. The desktop operating system, for instance, is responsible for managing the applications and data on a single computer. It is beholden primarily to its own user and is therefore most concerned with efficiently allocating processing time, memory, and other resources for an audience of one. In contrast, the NOS must answer to the demands of many users and must do so in the fastest, most effective way possible. Because so much of value in terms of both productivity and information depends on it, the NOS must offer, among other things:

- Fault-tolerance—that is, it must be as "bullet-proof" as possible against data loss and down times

- Security

- Different levels of access—comparable to different security clearances for individual users

- The ability to validate any of hundreds or thousands of users

- Backup capability

- Centralized monitoring and administration

- The ability to manage multiple applications as well as the traffic generated by security needs, messages, and access limitations of numerous clients yapping at it simultaneously

This is not a trivial task by any means. That such operating systems exist at all is a great credit to their developers.

In a nutshell, then, here are the advantages and disadvantages of client/server networks. The advantages: Client/server networks are scalable and they are less expensive than centralized networks. They support many more users and provide considerably more power than peer-to-peer networks, and they provide the benefits of controlled access to resources. Client/server networks are more secure than peer-to-peer networks and allow for centralized security and administration. They can also be set up to communicate with other networks, and they can support remote access, Internet sites, and multiple computing platforms. Disadvantages (if such they are): Client/server networks are more expensive and complicated to set up than peer-to-peer networks, and they require dedicated administrative personnel.

A note about peer-to-peer and client/server

Although this book, like most networking books, distinguishes between peer-to-peer and client/server networks both for clarity and because they do, in fact, differ considerably, you should *not* think of these two types of networks as mutually exclusive. They are not.

Think, for example, of a typical client/server network. The servers on the network run a network operating system such as Windows NT server. The desktop computers run a client operating system such as Windows 98 or Windows NT workstation. Because these client operating systems have built-in peer sharing capabilities, the desktop machines are fully capable of making their own resources available to their peers without requiring direct intervention or support from the servers. Within a workgroup, for instance, the desktop PCs can share resources as peers, yet they can also take advantage of the server-based resources offered by the larger network.

The primary distinction to keep in mind is that a purely peer-based network is one in which each computer can be both a client and a server within a network that does not itself include any centralized servers to which the clients connect. A client/server network is one built around one to many centralized servers, but it can also support client-to-client sharing if the desktop operating systems support the capability.

LANs vs. WANs

In addition to classifying networks by the way they enable communication, you can of course classify them according to their scope. Those that are relatively limited in size are LANs. Those that cover more geography are WANs. Although both are based on the same underlying technologies, they do differ in the technologies required to help them do their jobs. A WAN, for instance, needs communications hardware and software, message-routing capabilities, and long-distance transmission technologies that a localized LAN does not.

Local area networks

Both peer-to-peer and client/server networks can be LANs. Indeed, because of its small size, a strictly peer-to-peer network can't be anything else. It is limited geographically and in the number of nodes it can support. A client/server network, on the other hand, is such a flexible beast that it can be a standalone LAN in a single building, or it can be a link in a chain of networks spread across the country or around the world.

Wide area networks

WANs, in contrast to LANs, cover much more ground and rely on communications of some sort to enable computers to interact. The communications part can be provided by modems and telephones or, in situations in which more bandwidth and speed are needed, by advanced digital technologies, such as the ISDN and T1 lines you've probably heard much about.

Depending on the amount of ground they cover, WANs are often categorized in subgroups including CANs (campus area networks), DANs (department area networks), MANs (metropolitan area networks), and GANs (global area networks).

Everything Starts with Computers

Even though their work revolves around people and their needs, networks of any kind begin and end with computers. Because this book is primarily about client/server networks, what better place to start than with the clients and their servers?

Clients

Network clients are typically desktop computers with their own local storage and their own processing power. There are, however, less powerful, less expensive, and more easily managed *thin clients* available for client/server networks. These thin clients do not have local storage, and so they rely on network servers for applications, data, storage, and other resources.

In order to communicate, both client computers and servers must be equipped with a network adapter card, or network interface card (NIC), which is usually installed in one of the expansion slots inside the machine. The network adapter card is responsible for both sending messages and for monitoring—"listening" to—the network for incoming messages addressed to the client. To actually connect the client to the network cabling, the network adapter includes a *port* that accepts a cable ending in one of several types of connectors. Depending on the type of network, the connector can be a round plug known as a *BNC* (British Naval Connector); it can be a 15-pin *attachment unit interface* (AUI) connector—a typical "computer"-looking connector; or it can be an *RJ-45* jack similar to, but larger than, the connector on a telephone wire.

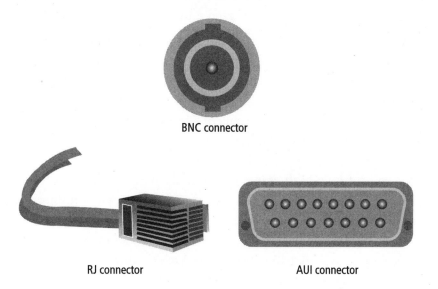

BNC connector

RJ connector   AUI connector

Servers

Network servers are the behind-the-scenes workhorses that provide services requested by the client computers (desktop machines and workstations). The servers themselves can be categorized in different ways, depending on the type of work they do.

Dedicated and nondedicated servers   First of all, servers can be classified as either *dedicated servers* or *nondedicated servers*.

Dedicated servers are the (usually) quite powerful machines that power the network and provide resources but are never used for the tasks performed by the client desktop PCs and workstations that request their services. These machines must be fast enough and powerful enough to handle multiple simultaneous user requests and to run a network operating system that provides for network security, administration, and management.

Nondedicated servers, typical of peer-to-peer networks, are machines that are set up so they can both provide (serve) resources and do the work required of a client machine. These machines can, in fact, be normal desktop PCs in their day-to-day lives, as long as they run an operating system, such as Windows 98 or Windows NT Workstation, that gives them the ability to share files and resources. Specialized services, such as high-level security and centralized administration and management, are not required on a nondedicated server.

As for the actual hardware.... A nondedicated server requires less processing power, memory, and disk storage than a dedicated server so, typically, it can be a machine along the lines of a Pentium-class desktop computer with, say, a standard serving of 32 to 64 MB of RAM and a hard disk of 3 GB or more. In contrast, a dedicated server, such as one running Windows NT Server, can be (and in large enterprises usually is) a much more powerful machine. In high-demand situations, as when such a server hosts a popular Web site or provides database access to a large number of people, the server might even contain eight or more Pentium II processors, or it might be based on a *RISC* (*Reduced Instruction Set Computing*) chip such as the Sun SPARC (Scalable Processor Architecture). It almost surely has large quantities of RAM—128 MB or more—and it might have multiple disk drives. It is also certain to be protected by some type of backup power supply and to be carefully monitored both in terms of performance and stability.

Specialized servers   Dedicated servers can further be classified by the type of work that they do. Although it's tempting to picture servers as simply sitting in the middle of the network somewhere, dishing up whatever flavor of data their clients request, such a picture would be more than just a little oversimplified. It's far better to think of these servers as specialized "chefs" in a blue-ribbon kitchen. Instead of concentrating on sauces, desserts, and main courses, however, these servers are equipped with specialized software *services* (often, though confusingly, also called servers) that enable them to concentrate on serving up access to: files, printers, applications, mail, faxes, communications, and even backup services to guard the network's invaluable data stores. Here's a closer look at these jobs and what they entail:

- **File servers store whole files.** When a client requests a particular file from a file server, the server transfers the entire document to the client. Note that the server does no processing of its own; all the processing is done by an application running on the computer that requests the file. In other words, processing is done at the *front end* (the desktop), rather than the *back end* (the server). As shown in Figure 3-1, the file server in effect serves as a document library, one that "checks out" files to its clients when asked to do so.

- **Print servers provide access to one or more attached printers.** Sometimes, the same server acts as both a file server and a print server. In other situations, which may be based on the networking software that oversees these services, the print server is a machine dedicated solely to printing.

- **Application servers have a somewhat misleading name.** Although it sounds as though they're dedicated to handing out applications to clients, in fact they are not. Their job is to store information, such as databases, and to perform back-end processing on that information

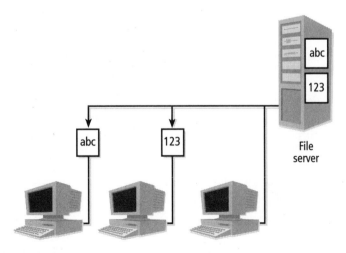

Figure 3-1. *A file server delivers whole documents to its clients.*

in order to deliver only the portion of data the client requests. In other words, the application server runs an application to sift through the entire mass of data it holds and find what the client wants. The server then delivers just that portion of the data to the client's desktop. As shown in Figure 3-2, the fact that an application server processes information *before* delivery to the desktop distinguishes it from a file server.

■ **Mail servers operate as the network postal service.** They provide a centralized *post office* for message handling and storage, and they work to deliver mail messages to network users, either immediately or, as in the case of remote users, on a "when I ask for it" basis. Depending on the size of the installation, a mail server can be dedicated only to messaging or (in smaller environments) it can perform other duties as well.

■ **Fax servers are computers equipped with fax/modem boards.** As you would imagine, they handle incoming and outgoing faxes for the organization.

■ **Communication servers coordinate traffic.** Although their name suggests some type of messaging service, communication servers actually handle traffic between the network they serve and other locations, including other networks, mainframe computers, and users dialing

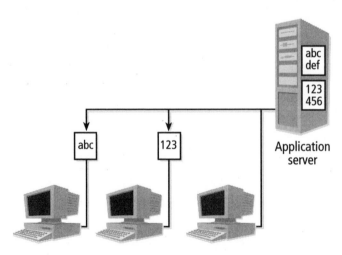

Figure 3-2.   *An application server delivers requested portions of its data to its clients.*

into or out of the organization. Gateways, which you'll meet later, are a type of communication server.

- **Backup servers concentrate on preserving data.** With the help of backup software and storage media, such as disk or tape, they have the ability to perform regularly scheduled backups to archive data and thus safeguard the network's store of information.

The Shape of a Network

The shape, or more technically the *topology,* of a network refers to the way the computers are cabled together. There are three basic designs that networks follow, known as *bus* (essentially a straight line), *ring*, and *star*. Although the actual, physical shape of the network might not bear much, if any, resemblance to a line, a ring, or a star if you could peer down on them from above, the actual connections *logically*, if not *physically*, correspond to these shapes. That is, network traffic does, indeed, travel in a line, a loop, or outward in a starlike pattern. To help you see how this works, the following illustration shows a network based on a ring topology in which computers are connected one to the other in a closed loop. If you imagine these computers as being in different offices or even on different floors of a building, you can see that the network might not physically resemble a ring, but the logical connections do, indeed, form a closed circle.

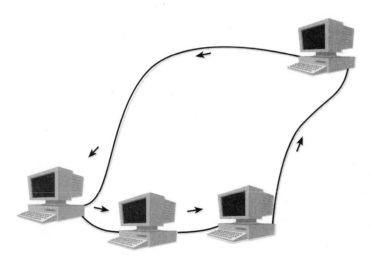

Bus

The simplest and easiest topology to implement, a bus network (also known as a *linear bus*) consists of a single cable to which the client computers and servers connect, somewhat like socks hanging from a laundry line. (Well, perhaps a zero-gravity laundry line in the following illustration.)

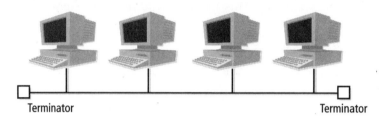

Terminator   Terminator

At any rate, on a bus network, the nodes are *passive* participants, "listening" in on the line and waiting for messages addressed to them. They do not, as do nodes on ring networks (described in the next section), take active part in moving messages from node to node through the network.

In terms of the transmissions themselves, any node on a bus network can transmit to any other node whenever it wants. Each message is broadcast, along with the recipient's unique network address, to the entire community, but only the node to which the message is sent can actually intercept and read it. Transmissions are limited to one computer at a time, so at any given time, one computer is master of the network and any other one wanting to transmit must wait until the line is free.

To avoid *contention*—multiple nodes trying to transmit at the same time— the network relies on some type of arbitration. The Ethernet standard (the most well-known type of bus network) manages contention by a technique known as *carrier sense multiple access with collision detection*, or *CSMA/ CD*, which stipulates that each node must wait for the line to be free before attempting to transmit. If, as sometimes happens, two nodes transmit at the same time, both must back off and wait a random length of time before trying again.

Messages on a bus network travel in either direction ("left" to "right" or "right" to "left"). Because the network is based on a single cable, also called a *trunk* or *backbone*, the ends of the cable must be equipped with a device called a *terminator* that absorbs signals and keeps them from bouncing back along the cable, where they could create havoc by interfering with other signals.

Bus networks are easy to implement and require less cabling than other topologies. In addition, nodes are relatively easy to add and remove. On the negative side, problems can be difficult to pinpoint on such a network, and a break in the trunk cable means a breakdown in the entire network. Also, the number of nodes supported by the bus can affect network performance. Too many nodes slows the network, because the nodes must wait for longer periods before being able to transmit over an open line.

Ring

A ring network, as you would imagine, forms a circle, at least as far as the nodes are concerned. Network transmissions travel from node to node, in one direction only, in a closed, round-robin loop. When a transmission has traveled the full circuit, it has moved from the node that started the transmission, to the computer connected to that node, and so on until it has gone around the loop and returned to the starting node. The following illustration shows how a ring topology is usually diagrammed.

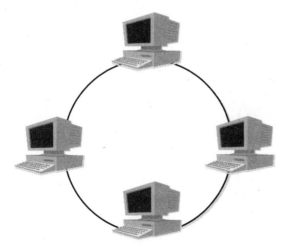

Notice that each node communicates directly with only two others: the node that transmits to it and the node it transmits to. Also, unlike the nodes in a bus network, the nodes in a ring network participate actively, not only in sending and receiving messages, but also in sending the signal around the ring and in some cases even *boosting* (strengthening) the signal before passing it on to the next node.

To avoid contention, ring networks typically rely on a well-known method of transmission called *token passing,* which resembles a relay in that the computers pass a *token*, a small collection of bits, around the ring. When a node has some information to transmit, it waits until it receives the token. It then modifies the token, in effect "stamping" it to inform the other nodes that the token is in use, and it then passes the token and its message along to the next node in line. When the token (and message) arrive at the recipient, that node acknowledges receipt of the message and creates a new, available-for-use token, which it then sends on its merry way around the ring.

Ring networks don't require massive amounts of cabling and fancy hardware to implement, and one of their great advantages is in giving each node an equal opportunity to transmit. As in bus networks, however, problems can be difficult to pin down, and a break in the cabling brings down the entire network.

Star

A star network, like the arms of an octopus, stretches out in different directions from a central location. This location is occupied by physical equipment known as a *hub* (for obvious reasons, as you can see in the following illustration).

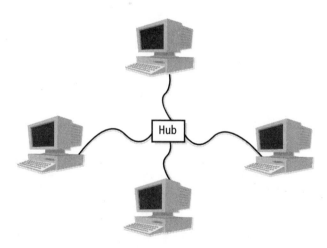

The hub itself can participate actively in the network by boosting signals as they pass through, or it can be a passive wiring panel that simply relays transmissions through the network. Regardless, the hub (or hubs in larger networks) forms the centerpiece, the distinguishing feature, of a star-wired network.

By way of example, the form of network known as low-impedance ARCnet—popular for small networks—is based on a star topology that can include both active and passive hubs. The passive hubs, which connect to active hubs, serve as "plug-in" points for groups of nodes; the active hubs serve as central gathering points for passive hubs, nodes, and servers. This same form of ARCnet, by the way, relies on token passing to maintain order. In this case, because the nodes do not form a logical ring, the token passes from one node to the next in a preassigned order—node 1 to node 2 to node 3, and so on.

Star networks are often hybridized with other topologies. Another form of ARCnet (high-impedance ARCnet), for instance, is based on active hubs and a bus topology. However, high-impedance and low-impedance ARCnet can be combined in the same network in a combination star and bus topology.

One advantage of star networks is that the ease with which more nodes can be added makes them easily expandable. Certain types of hubs, called hybrid hubs, can also support the use of more than one type of cable in the network. In addition, because the cabling in a star network extends from hub to nodes, problems are easier to isolate, and a break in the cable brings down only the node directly affected by that cable. (If the network depends on a single hub, however, a breakdown in that hub does, of course, affect the entire network.)

How Network Traffic Gets from Here to There

Now that you have a rough idea of what a network "looks like" as a whole, the next step is to examine how all the traffic it handles manages to move to and from the various nodes on the network and, in some cases, between one network and another.

Data Packets

Networks are fast. Very fast. Compared to the speeds at which they operate, humans are somewhere between slo-mo and no-mo. But networks, like the highways they conceptually resemble, have an upper limit to the amount of traffic they can bear. They do not have infinite bandwidth (that capacity to carry information that everyone talks about and wishes they had more of). Given that the laws of physics—and the demands of its users—put some constraints on a network, how can it (a) move traffic as quickly as possible and (b) provide fair, if not equal, access to all users? The answer is: by breaking traffic into small pieces known as *packets*.

Imagine, for example, a situation in which one computer needs to send a multi-megabyte file to another—say, a text document with embedded graphics. If that computer were allowed to swamp the network cable for the entire time it took to send the file, other computers with traffic of their own would need to wait until the transmission was complete. Imagine, too, that a temporary glitch, a hiccup somewhere in the network, caused an error in transmission. The same big file would have to be resent. Sigh.

To avoid both unhappy situations, networks break their transmissions into packets. The large file thus becomes a large number of small packets that, instead of blocking access, can merge into the traffic flow along with packets from other computers. In addition, because the large file has been broken into pieces, the error caused by the network hiccup affects only a small part of the file, and only that part needs to be retransmitted. Thanks to packets, everyone wins.

Anatomy of a packet

Packets are chunks of data, but that's by no means all they are. They must also include information on where they came from, where they're going, how they should be checked for errors, and how they should be reconnected to form the original file or message. To contain all this information, a packet consists of three parts: a *header*, the data itself, and a *trailer*.

Header   Data   Trailer

The header, as you would expect from the name, precedes the chunk of data in the packet and includes the source and destination (network) addresses as well as control and timing information to ensure that the packet is transmitted appropriately.

The data section contains the actual chunk of information being transmitted. Depending on the network, this portion of the packet is typically between 512 bytes and 4 KB in size.

The trailer is more or less the "mop up" section of the packet and contains, among other things, the error-checking information that enables the receiving computer to verify that the data arrived intact.

Error checking

To verify the accuracy of a transmission, networks commonly rely on an error-checking method known as a *cyclical redundancy check* (*CRC*), in which the sending computer calculates a value based on the information in the packet and includes that value in the packet. The receiving computer then recalculates the same value. If the results match, there is assumed to be no error in the transmission.

Packets and the network adapter

With all manner of information whizzing through a network, you might wonder how it manages to get neatly chunked, addressed, and delivered, even with the recipient's address attached to each packet. Much of that job is handled by the network adapter card in each computer connected to the network.

Let's start from the *very* beginning. Within the computer, information travels between devices and the processor along pathways known as *busses*. Like freeways, these busses consist of multiple "lanes" (wires, actually) set side by side. And, like freeway traffic, information travels these lanes side by side—in today's microprocessor-based computers, typically in groups of 16 or 32 related bits (and in the near future, 65 related bits) representing, say, a text character or a memory address. This orderly march of data through the computer is known as *parallel* transmission, because the bits are transferred in groups. And as you are probably aware, the larger the number of bits in a group, the more information the computer can move at one time and, hence, the faster that information travels from place to place within the machine.

When information moves out of the computer onto a network cable, however, the signal must change. Even though the bits transmitted still represent the same data, the groups of bits can no longer travel in parallel. Unlike computers, network cables require information to travel bit by bit, as *serial* transmissions. In effect, the multiple lanes of the freeway must feed their traffic onto a single-lane road—one with a very high speed limit to be sure, but a more constrained channel nonetheless.

Bits, however, being mindless entities, cannot make the decision to travel single file. Nor can they decide to get off the computer's bus to board a network-bound packet. They need help, and that help is provided by the network adapter card. It is the card that converts the computer's parallel transmission to serial form. It is the card that requests the data from the computer. It is the card that addresses and packages the data. It is the card that moves the packet onto the network and coordinates transmission size, speed, and timing to ensure a successful data transfer.

And on the receiving end, the network adapter handles the reverse. It listens to the network, watching for and intercepting packets sent either specifically to its address or broadcast to the network as a whole. It strips addressing and other travel-related information from the packet. It converts the data from serial to parallel form. And finally, it passes the data to the computer for use by whatever application requested it or is designed to use the information.

All that sophisticated activity goes on in a paperback-sized card like this:

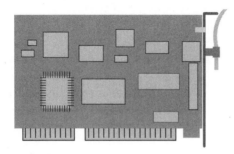

Transmissions

And what of the transmission itself? There are two basic forms of transmission, baseband and broadband. Both are largely defined by bandwidth, that bugaboo of networking in its present state.

Bandwidth

And what exactly is bandwidth? Everyone, especially on the Internet, complains that there's too little of it, but what is it? Put simply, bandwidth is the maximum speed at which a particular communications medium can transfer information. From here, however, the situation becomes a little confusing because the way bandwidth is measured depends on the type of signal, analog or digital, used to carry the information. Ready?

Analog   In an analog signal, such as the kind used for radio and voice telephone, information travels as a continuously variable wave, as shown in the following illustration:

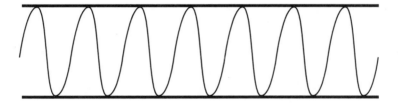

As you can see, the signal cycles up and down, with a single cycle being the distance between wave top and wave top (crest to crest) or between dip and dip (trough to trough). As you can readily imagine, the closer the cycles are to one another, the more frequently they occur in a given amount of time. This frequency, which is measured in Hertz (Hz), or cycles per second, is the basis for measuring analog bandwidth.

So far, so good. Now, think about the electromagnetic spectrum, that stuff you learned about in school that includes everything from subsonic waves to radio and X-rays. As you recall, this spectrum covers a continuous range of frequencies. At the low end of the spectrum, you have long, slow, lazy waves. Moving up, you have more active, higher-frequency waves like those used for radio and television. And at the top of the spectrum, you have extremely high-frequency waves like X-rays and gamma rays. Because this range of frequencies is so vast, people refer to subsets of frequencies. For example, AM radio is defined as the range of middle frequencies roughly between 500 and 1600 kiloHertz (thousands of Hertz, or kHz). The difference between the top and bottom frequencies in this range is the AM radio bandwidth.

Analog bandwidth, then, refers to the spread between the highest and lowest frequencies in a communications channel.

Digital   When you deal with digital signals, which are typical of modems and are becoming more widely used in voice telephone as well, you are dealing with a simpler signal in the sense that information travels in discrete on/off pulses over the communications medium. A digital signal thus looks more like this:

It's much easier to understand, and so is the way in which bandwidth—here in the sense of speed—is measured: *bits per second,* or *bps.* That's it. No ranges of frequencies, no continuously variable signal. Just number of bits per second. The greater the number of bits, the greater the bandwidth.

Digital bandwidth is what you see referred to in discussions of advanced modem technologies, such as ISDN and ADSL, as well as network architectures from ARCnet and Ethernet to the more advanced ATM and FDDI networks. Because these and other technologies rapidly transfer huge quantities of bits, most measurements you see will refer to Kilobits per second (Kbps), Megabits per second (Mbps), and sometimes even Gigabits per second (Gbps).

 OTE   Modem technologies are discussed in Chapter 7, ARCnet and Ethernet in Chapter 5, and ATM and FDDI in Chapter 8.

Now, here's how these analog and digital signals relate to network transmissions.

Baseband vs. broadband transmissions

Baseband transmissions, which are typical of most current LANs, send digital signals over a single channel. In other words, one signal at a time travels over the network cable, and the entire bandwidth is assigned to that signal. Although only one signal at a time is transmitted, however, that does not mean that a single message "hogs" the network's entire bandwidth for the time it takes to travel from sender to receiver. Multiple transmissions can be sent through the channel at the same time through a technique known as *multiplexing*, in which separate transmissions are interleaved on the signal and kept separate by some means, such as time (time division multiplexing) or space (space division multiplexing).

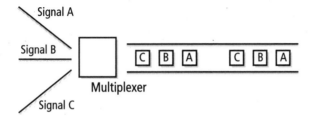

Because a baseband signal tends to degenerate the farther it travels, networks relying on baseband transmissions sometimes use devices called *repeaters* which, like electrical transformers, revitalize the signal before sending it on its way. Well-known network architectures that rely on baseband transmission include Ethernet and Token Ring, both of which are described in Chapter 5.

In contrast to baseband transmission, broadband transmission relies on an analog signal, a range of frequencies, and a communications medium—either coaxial (electrical) or fiberoptic (light-transmitting) cable—that can be divided into multiple channels separated by small bands of unused frequencies to avoid one channel interfering with the signal being transmitted on its neighbors. Also unlike baseband transmission, broadband moves in one direction only—it is unidirectional. To provide for both sending and receiving, the communications bandwidth can be divided into two channels, one for each direction, or two separate cables can be used for transmission and receiving. The bandwidth of a broadband transmission can also be reserved for separate channels carrying voice, data, and video. Cable television is based on broadband transmission, as is the wide area networking technology (described in Chapter 8) known as ATM, or Asynchronous Transfer Mode.

Next stop: network models and network etiquette.

Standardizing Networks

Going from the more or less general to the increasingly specific, we move on now to a look at the standards that define—and drive—the way network hardware and software work, both alone and in partnership. These standards are the "rules of the road" that guide the design and operation of every part of a network, from its cables to its hardware to its application software. They are also what enable different networks built on different architectures to find common ground and to communicate with one another. Without standards (both those that have already been defined and those that are continually evolving for the future), networks could, and possibly would, devolve into a polyglot collection of islands unable to see, hear, or interact with any but those that were built like them and that spoke the same communications language.

Network Models

A functional network relies on many components, all of which must fit together like the pieces of a well-designed jigsaw puzzle. Not only must these pieces be able to work smoothly together, they must also be able to rely on one another for different services. Applications, for example, must be able to trust that the network's underlying cables, communications hardware, and networking software will send and receive information accurately between client and client, client and server, or server and server.

Similarly, the network's hardware infrastructure—its cables, servers, transmission facilities, and so on—must be able to trust the network's communications software and services to break information down into data packets suitably addressed and sized for transmission.

To help guarantee that these disparate parts and pieces work together, the makers of networking hardware and software follow sets of guidelines as they design and build their products. The most well known and most widely used of these guidelines is a set of specifications developed by the *International Organization for Standardization* (ISO) in 1978. These specifications, revised and rereleased in 1984, are known as the *Open Systems Interconnection Reference Model*—a jawcracker often shortened to *OSI Reference Model* or, more simply, the *ISO/OSI model*.

OTE   Here's one for collectors of verbal hairballs: Even though ISO and OSI represent vastly different abbreviations, they contain the same letters and, when put together, they form a palindrome—a "word" that reads the same backward and forward. That's both an interesting coincidence and a possible source of confusion, at least at first, when it can be difficult to remember whether it's the ISO/OSI model or the OSI/ISO model. The solution is easy, though: the order is I before O, just as in the alphabet.

What Open Systems Interconnection Means

At first glance, tagging something as fundamental as a network specification with as weighty a name as Open Systems Interconnection Reference Model might seem somewhat ponderous or overly technical. It really isn't, though. The ISO designed this set of specifications as a blueprint of sorts that describes a network architecture. Any manufacturer of hardware or software networking components can use this blueprint to create products that do two things:

■ Communicate with one another

■ Slip neatly into a *layered* architecture in which elements in one layer can rely on services provided by each of the other layers without having to deal with the actual way in which those services are implemented

In other words, the OSI Reference Model describes a pattern, a model, for building components that can work together in an open, interconnected communications network. It is a "reference model" because, even though it describes how the parts of the network should function, it leaves the details of the actual implementation to the manufacturer.

The Seven layers of OSI

The OSI model is built around a set of seven protocol layers. Each layer is responsible for some action or service that helps prepare information for transmission over the network. Each layer interacts only with its immediate neighbors, and each relies on a clearly defined *interface* that determines both how it offers its own services to the layer above it and how it accesses the services of the layer below it. Figure 4-1 diagrams the seven OSI layers. As you can see, the layers define successive layers of abstraction (roughly, distance) from the hardware, starting with the physical means of transport at the bottom and ending with application software at the top. Notice also that the layers are numbered 1 through 7, starting at the bottom.

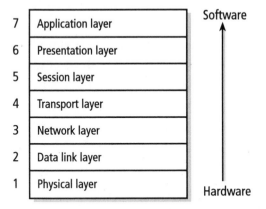

7	Application layer
6	Presentation layer
5	Session layer
4	Transport layer
3	Network layer
2	Data link layer
1	Physical layer

Software ↑ Hardware

Figure 4-1.   *The seven layers of the OSI Reference Model.*

So how does it work?

Describing a network in terms of the seven OSI layers is all well and good, but the question arises: how, exactly, does a packet get from computer A to computer B? The diagram in Figure 4-2 outlines the process.

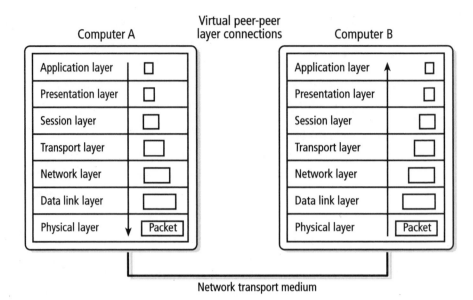

Figure 4-2. *Packet formation and delivery in the OSI Reference Model.*

And here, in words, is what the diagram shows:

1. First of all, as you can see, computer A and computer B both implement the seven OSI layers.

2. When computer A readies a transmission for computer B, each layer on A assumes it will be communicating with its equivalent layer, its peer, on computer B. Although no *actual* communication occurs between levels, the various levels on both computers assume that they "speak" the same language and follow the same rules (protocols) that ensure that each layer on the receiving computer receives exactly the same data package put together by its peer on the sending computer.

3. Actual packet formation begins at the top level, the application level, on computer A and moves downward toward the physical level at the bottom. As the packet passes from one level to the next, each adds the transmission information—addressing, formatting, and so on—for which it is responsible. The process thus resembles an assembly line in which each station adds to the emerging "product."

4. When the packet reaches the physical layer (which includes the network adapter), it is converted to a serial bit stream and sent over the

transmission medium (cable, for example). It is through this, and only this, layer that computer A actually communicates with computer B, although even here, A and B communicate only indirectly in the sense that they are both linked by the same transport medium.

5. When the transmission reaches computer B, the process begins in reverse, with the packet essentially "bubbling up" through the seven OSI layers.

6. First, the physical layer on computer B converts the serial bit stream back to packet form and hands the result to the next higher layer, the data link layer.

7. As the packet now travels upward through the various layers, each layer strips away the addressing and formatting information added to the packet by its peer on computer A, until the application layer at the top receives the original information sent by the application layer on computer A.

Now for what those layers represent and what they do. Because it's easier to envision the complete data transfer process by starting with the sending and receiving applications, the following sections describe the seven layers in reverse order, from top to bottom.

Layer 7: the application layer   The application layer of the OSI model is the part that deals with providing network access to application software. This is the level occupied by such varied applications as e-mail software, file transfer software, database access software, and even network management software. The application layer is also what enables such network-related functions as file and printer access, resource sharing, and the use of *directory services*, that is, use of information databases (directories) that identify all the users and resources on the network.

Application layer	Provides applications with network access

Because there are so many network-related applications, the application level is a many-splendored thing, reflecting the many different ways in which programs access and use the network. Both file transfer programs and e-mail, for example, gain access at this level, but the file transfer program is concerned primarily with moving files from one place to another, whereas the e-mail program needs services related to message handling, storage, and delivery. In both cases, the programs rely on application-level protocols, among which are the e-mail specifications known as X.400, the directory services specifications known as X.500, and the file transfer protocol known as FTP (short for, of course, File Transfer Protocol). These and others are described in more detail later in the chapter.

Layer 6: the presentation layer   The presentation layer is an easily understood, rather likeable layer. Its primary job is to ensure that information transmitted between two computers is encoded in the same...alphabet. As you probably know already, computers don't always use the same coding scheme for text and other characters. Most, for example, use the *ASCII* (*American Standard Code for Information Interchange*) character set, but a computer "speaking" ASCII might, at some time, need to communicate with a computer—an IBM mainframe, most likely—relying on a different character set known as *EBCDIC* (*Extended Binary Coded Decimal Interchange Code*). Although ASCII uses either 7 or 8 bits to represent up to 256 characters and EBCDIC uses 8 bits to represent 256 characters, the numeric value assigned to a given character in each coding scheme is not necessarily the same. The lowercase letter *a* in ASCII, for example, is decimal 97; in EBCDIC, the same letter is decimal 129.

Application layer	Provides applications with network access
Presentation layer	Adds common format for data representation

What this all boils down to is that it's the responsibility of the presentation layer to ensure that both computers use the same representation for data. In addition, the presentation layer handles any encryption or compression of data required.

Layer 5: the session layer   So far, you've seen that in the OSI model, the job of the application layer is to provide access to the network and to hand off information to the presentation layer, which ensures that the information is represented in a form understood by both sending and receiving computers. What's next? The information now moves downward to the session layer, which is responsible for enabling applications on the sending and receiving computers to establish a connection known as a *session*. A session is, in many respects, comparable to a telephone conversation:

Application layer	Provides applications with network access
Presentation layer	Adds common format for data representation
Session layer	Establishes communication session

First of all, remember that the overriding responsibility of the session layer is to establish communication between two parties. These parties are known as *application entities*, or *AE*s. You can think of these AEs as being comparable to two human "entities" who want to talk on the phone.

To begin the process, the session layer on the communicating computers establishes the connection. If required, the session layer also takes care of security measures, such as validating passwords. This part of the process is similar to dialing the phone at one end, having it answered on the other and, if necessary, asking whether the person speaking is the one you want to talk to.

Once a connection is established, the session layer then ensures that the conversation, or dialog, goes smoothly. It does this by monitoring and synchronizing the data flow, controlling who transmits, when, and for how long. This part is comparable to having a third party "referee" a phone conversation, so that the two people on the phone take turns at controlling the line and don't speak at the same time.

When the data transfer is complete, the session layer then takes responsibility for ensuring that the session ends smoothly—that both parties "hang up."

As in every other layer of the OSI Reference model, the session layer includes protocols for handling the services provided at this level. One that you might encounter is the *NetBEUI* protocol (short for NetBIOS Extended User Interface) implemented in Microsoft-based networks. NetBIOS, by the way, is an application programming interface, or API, that enables application programs to request session-level services.

Layer 4: the transport layer   The transport layer is, in a sense, the shipping company of the OSI Reference Model. It doesn't actually move the "freight," but it *is* responsible for ensuring error-free delivery—what's referred to as quality of service, or QOS. Essentially, the transport layer ensures that information is neither lost nor duplicated. As part of its responsibilities:

Application layer	Provides applications with network access
Presentation layer	Adds common format for data representation
Session layer	Establishes and monitors communication session
Transport layer	Provides quality of service

- The transport layer on the sending computer breaks down the information (which so far has been passed from layer to layer in whatever-sized chunk it was originally) into packets of the size required by the network layers below it. On the receiving computer, the transport layer then reassembles the packets into the original chunk of information.

- If using *connectionless communications*, in which packets can be sent over different routes and arrive out of order, the transport layer on the sending computer sequentially numbers the data packets making up a complete transmission, to guarantee that they can be delivered and reconnected correctly.

- The transport layer provides for *end-to-end* delivery, including acknowledgment from the receiving computer that the message arrived without error.

- If the frame buffer, the temporary storage area on the receiving computer, is full, the transport layer orders the sending computer to wait before sending more.

■ The transport layer might also be responsible for multiplexing messages or sessions and for keeping track of which is which.

Essentially, the transport layer sits between the application-related layers above it and the *subnet*, the network/hardware-related layers below it. The intermediary between the two, the transport layer is the guarantor of reliability to the application-related layers above, no matter how reliable (or unreliable) the subnet layers below happen to be.

Layer 3: the network layer   The network layer is the topmost of the three subnet layers of the OSI Reference Model. It is, in fact, the controller of the subnet in that it takes responsibility for routing and addressing messages both within and between networks. Just as the transport layer guarantees reliability to the higher layers, the network layer relieves all the layers above it, including the transport layer, of the need to "know" anything about the actual transmission and routing technologies used by the subnet.

Application layer	Provides applications with network access
Presentation layer	Adds common format for data representation
Session layer	Establishes and monitors communication session
Transport layer	Provides quality of service
Network layer	Addresses and routes messages

As part of its routing duties, the network layer on the transmitting computer determines which route to use in sending the message, basing its choice on a number of factors, including network conditions—traffic load—on the network or, in network-to-network transmissions, on various intermediate segments. In the course of routing a transmission, the network layer can, if necessary, transfer a packet (technically referred to at these lower networking levels as a *frame*) to a router, a piece of hardware that acts as a transfer point between networks based on different architectures. Because frame size, known as the *maximum transmission unit*, or *MTU*, varies on different networks, the network layer on the sending computer also takes responsibility for allowing the router to break the frame into smaller units if the current frame size exceeds the size that the router can handle. Conversely, the network layer on the receiving computer takes responsibility for reassembling frames that have been broken into smaller pieces.

In the addressing area, the network layer on the sending computer is in charge of resolving—translating—logical and physical network addresses. That is, it must accurately convert between a node's network address (the logical address) and the physical address that is literally "burned in"— hardwired to its network adapter card.

Among the protocols that operate at the network layer are the IP (Internet Protocol) and the X.25 protocol used on packet-switching networks. Both are described later in this chapter, and they're also covered in later chapters dealing with WANs (Chapter 8) and the Internet (Chapters 9 and 10).

Layer 2: the data link layer   The data link layer lies between and communicates with the physical layer below it and the network layer directly above it. Although "data link" isn't as intuitive a description as "physical" or "application," the function of the data link layer is reasonably easy to understand, in that it deals with data and with links between computers. Its job is therefore based on two activities:

Application layer	Provides applications with network access
Presentation layer	Adds common format for data representation
Session layer	Establishes and monitors communication session
Transport layer	Provides quality of service
Network layer	Addresses and routes messages
Data link layer	Packages data in frames and establishes sessions

■ The formation of the data packets, or frames needed by the network architecture (there's the data part)

■ The creation and termination of logical links between network nodes and the transmission of those packets over the physical layer (there's the link part)

In doing its job, the data link layer doesn't just "packetize" data and establish links between computers. In order to ensure that the network layer, as well as all the other layers above it, can rely on error-free transmission, the data link layer is also responsible for controlling the flow of frames, for acknowledging transmission, and, when necessary, for retransmitting frames that have been damaged en route.

Layer 1: the physical layer   And finally, you come to the physical layer, the layer where the hardware's at. This is the layer at which a stream of 1s and 0s is zapped across the network from one computer to another. As such, the physical layer is concerned with the guts of a network: its cabling, connectors and pins, adapter cards, and electrical signals. Numerous specifications exist that define each of these elements. There are, for example, specifications for the number and function of pins (pin assignments) in a connector. There are specifications for the type and kind of cables and specifications for how those cables are connected to the network adapter.

Application layer	Provides applications with network access
Presentation layer	Adds common format for data representation
Session layer	Establishes and monitors communication session
Transport layer	Provides quality of service
Network layer	Addresses and routes messages
Data link layer	Packages data in frames and establishes sessions
Physical layer	Defines hardware and transfers data as a serial bit stream

In addition to these very physical—touchable—components, the physical layer also addresses the less visible but equally important aspects of signaling itself: the encoding and decoding of the bit stream, as well as the crucial timing and synchronization methods required to ensure that information is transmitted accurately, so that each bit departs and arrives in exactly the same condition.

The physical layer encompasses a veritable alphabet soup of specification letters and numbers. Two that you will encounter in Chapter 5 include the Institute of Electrical and Electronic Engineers, or IEEE (pronounced "eye-triple-eee"), 802.3 specification for Ethernet networks and the IEEE 802.5 specification for Token Ring networks. Another, covered in the section on modems in Chapter 7, is the RS-232-C standard for serial communications issued by the Electronic Industries Association (EIA).

Other Networking Models

The OSI Reference Model is the one most commonly referred to in descriptions of network layering and, for that matter, in discussions of the various networking protocols. ("The *XX* protocol runs at the *YY* layer.") OSI isn't the only networking model, however. Two others, also layered, tend to pop up in descriptions of network architectures: One is IBM's network architecture, known as *SNA*, and the other is an Internet-related model known as the *TCP/IP Reference Model* or, alternatively, the *Internet Reference Model*.

The five To seven layers of SNA

SNA, which is shorthand for *Systems Network Architecture*, was designed by IBM in the 1970s as a means of enabling IBM products—mainframes, terminals, and printers—to communicate with one another and exchange data. SNA was originally designed around the mainframe/terminal relationship but was later modified, in a specification known as *APPC* (Advanced Program to Program Communications), to include minicomputers and personal computers.

The SNA model, which preceded the ISO/OSI Reference Model, is IBM-centric, but roughly comparable to the later, open-to-all-comers, ISO version. The basic SNA model consists of five layers. An extended version adds two more to complement the ISO/OSI model. These basic and extended layers are illustrated in Figure 4-3.

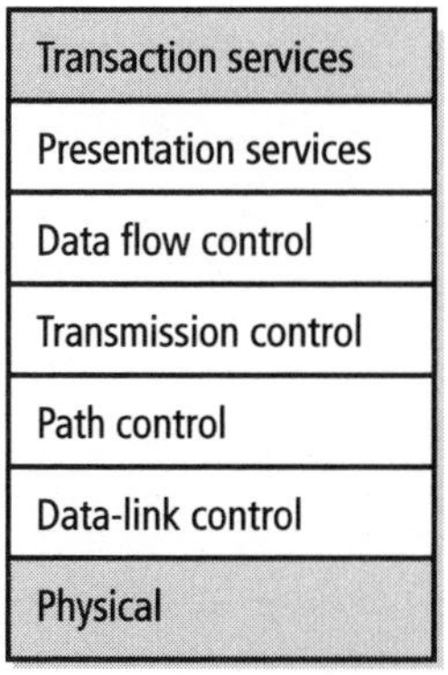

Transaction services
Presentation services
Data flow control
Transmission control
Path control
Data-link control
Physical

Figure 4-3.   *The basic (unshaded) and extended (shaded) layers of the SNA network architecture.*

The following list describes these layers and compares them with comparable layers in the ISO/OSI Reference Model:

■   The topmost layer, transaction services, includes the protocols responsible for application-to-application communication. As such, it is comparable to the ISO/OSI application layer.

■   The next layer, presentation services (or function management), handles formatting, compression, and data translation, as between ASCII and EBCDIC. As you recall, this work is directly comparable to the responsibility of the ISO/OSI presentation layer.

■   Moving downward in the SNA model, you next encounter the data flow control layer. This layer describes, but does not actually implement, the rules to be followed during a communications session—for example, error recovery and whether information will be transferred in two directions at the same time (full duplex) or in one direction at a time (half duplex). This layer is partially comparable to the ISO/OSI session layer.

■   The next layer, transmission control, handles sessions between communicating nodes. It starts, stops, and maintains sessions, routes data over the network, and ensures that the data arrives correctly. In part, this layer is comparable to (once again) the ISO/OSI session layer. In terms of routing and ensuring accurate delivery, however, the transmission control layer also blurs into the transport and network layers of the ISO/OSI model.

- The path control layer in the SNA model takes on the tasks of linking nodes, managing the links, and routing data. In terms of function, this layer is more or less comparable to the ISO/OSI transport and network layers.

- The lowest of the five basic layers in the SNA model is the data link control layer. Like its "peer" in the ISO/OSI model, the data link control layer is responsible for ensuring reliable data transfer over the actual, physical, network hardware.

- The physical layer of the SNA model is the second of the two extensions to the basic five layers. It is not directly implemented in SNA but, like the physical layer in the ISO/OSI model, it encompasses the physical infrastructure and electrical signaling used on the network.

Unlike the ISO/OSI Reference Model, SNA is based on a number of different network units, each of which serves a different function. At its core, SNA is based on a host mainframe, which, in a mainframe/terminal environment, is in charge of creating every communication session. Communication sessions extending beyond this core rely on additional controllers known as Network Control Programs, or NCPs, which take on the burden of routing and path control through intermediate nodes on the network. In addition, the APPC enhancement of the original SNA model provides for two different kinds of nodes: end nodes (ENs) that connect to and use the network, and network nodes (NNs) that both connect to the network and perform routing and management duties.

By the way, the SNA model is even more filled with abbreviations than the ISO/OSI version. The SNA abbreviations include not only those described here, but also things like PU (physical unit, that is, devices and their software) and LU (logical unit, that is, an application or end user). Detailed descriptions of these and other aspects of SNA are available if needed, most especially in the substantial amount of documentation created by IBM.

The TCP/IP, or Internet reference model

Whereas SNA was originally concocted to define and describe communications in a mainframe-based, IBM environment, the birth and evolution of the Internet gave rise to yet another model, the TCP/IP Reference Model, often referred to as the Internet Reference Model.

Unlike both the ISO/OSI and SNA models, the TCP/IP model is *not* based on the idea of a communications session, a clearly defined link between communicating nodes. In other words, the TCP/IP model reflects the world of internetworking, the transfer and routing of information between and among varied workstations and networks. This is quite different from the world of mainframe/terminal or relatively constrained client/server data transfer, where establishing, maintaining, and terminating sessions is important enough to warrant an entire protocol layer in its own right. Figure 4-4 shows the difference between the TCP/IP and ISO/OSI reference models, as well as rough—not exact—equivalents between the layers in the two models. Note that the illustration draws no relationship between the TCP/IP internetworking layer and any layers in the ISO/OSI model—for the reasons explained above. Note also that the TCP/IP model does not include an equivalent to the physical layer although, obviously, any type of network relies on hardware and signaling standards.

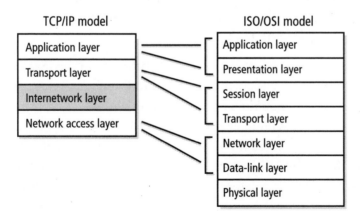

Figure 4-4.   *The different layers in the TCP/IP and ISO/OSI reference models.*

So what are these TCP/IP layers, and what do they do? Here's a brief rundown:

■ The network access layer, which would lie just above the physical layer (if the model included it, that is), includes the protocols required to transmit and deliver data frames. This is the layer that contains the protocols required for determining how frames are transmitted and how they are passed to, and transmitted on, the actual physical network. For its job in delivering data frames, this layer relies on the addresses hardwired into network adapter cards. In brief, the network access layer is the part that contains the protocols responsible for interacting with the physical network, as well as those responsible for knowing the details necessary for creating and addressing data frames.

■ The internetwork layer, which has no equivalent in the ISO/OSI and SNA models, is the part of the TCP/IP model that includes the protocols responsible for routing messages from sender to receiver—a process that can require packet forwarding that can include *hops* through intermediary networks or network segments. In this layer, packets are commonly referred to as *datagrams*, which are essentially data packets with header and trailer information attached. The routers and gateways used to actually shuttle datagrams from here to there are included in this level.

■ The transport layer, like the transport layer in the ISO/OSI model, is responsible for ensuring reliable end-to-end datagram delivery and for helping communicating computers establish a *connection*, or *virtual circuit*. A connection is like an ISO/OSI "session" in that it begins with a command to open and ends with a command to close and provides the sending and receiving computers with a defined path over which data is to be transmitted. In the TCP/IP world, however, not all transmissions require an actual connection. In many cases, packets are routed from source to destination along the best route available at the time. These transfers are known as *connectionless*.

■ The application layer, unlike the other layers in the TCP/IP model, can be clearly equated with the application and presentation layers of the ISO/OSI model. The TCP/IP application layer contains the various—and varied—protocols that provide applications with network access and services (as in the ISO/OSI application layer), as well as those that ensure a standardized and mutually comprehensible method of representing data (as in the ISO/OSI presentation layer).

The ISO/OSI, SNA, and the TCP/IP models are, as you've seen, different in the layers they define. They are not, however, mutually exclusive. Modern networks and internetworks can and do rely on protocols and services that fit more than one model. A LAN running the TCP/IP protocols, for example, can be based on a network operating system designed with the ISO/OSI model in mind. And, further, that LAN can, given the appropriate "translation" software and gateways, communicate with an IBM-based SNA mainframe network.

Network Models and Protocols

So. Knowing that network models exist is fine and dandy, because viewing networks in terms of self-contained layers makes it much easier to sort out and understand the relationships between and among the numerous tasks and services provided by a network. Throughout the descriptions of these models, however, you've put up with references to this or that protocol running on this or that layer.

So what's the relationship between a model and a protocol? After all, a model is a conceptual description that slices and dices the idea of a network into multiple layers, whereas protocols are embodied in the actual software that makes a real, live network work. In actuality, however, the relationship is pretty simple: The model describes what needs to be done, and the protocol makes it—whatever the "it" is—happen.

Furthermore, thanks to the layered model, protocols that are concerned with a particular service, such as providing network access or addressing a data frame, can assume that other protocols, operating on other layers, are taking care of services needed to ensure that the entire communication process happens correctly. That is, a protocol addressing a data frame doesn't have to give a hoot about how that data frame will actually be loaded onto the cable, whether that data frame will be transmitted correctly, and whether it will be retransmitted if necessary. Other protocols on other layers take care of that. The frame-addressing protocol only has to worry about doing its job correctly. Through layering, protocols are given the luxury of developing tunnel vision, of concentrating on their own work and assuming that everything else will be taken care of properly.

What this all boils down to is that a protocol, any protocol, on the sending computer needs only to concern itself with communicating with its peer on the receiving computer. It does, of course, have to be able to accept information from the layer immediately above it (when sending) or below it (when receiving), and vice versa. But otherwise, a protocol just needs to worry about, and correctly handle, its part in the whole process of sending or receiving data.

Where protocols rely on models, such as the ISO/OSI Reference Model, is in the area of standardization. By breaking out and standardizing the services to be provided at each layer, the models effectively describe standardized protocols for each layer. The models don't themselves define the actual protocols. That is, ISO/OSI model doesn't define, for example, any application-level protocols, such as those used by file transfer applications to gain access to a network. What the model does, instead, is standardize the services and interfaces provided by protocols running at the application level and, in this way, it provides a standardized protocol "blueprint" that applications can rely on.

Protocol Stacks and Suites

ISO/OSI and other networking models define clear-cut layers related to packaging, sending, and receiving transmissions. Now, what about the protocols that provide the necessary services at each level? Is there a single protocol that runs at all levels, handling the tasks appropriate for each? No. Is there a single set of related protocols, each running at a different level, that *together* handle all the tasks required in packaging, sending, and receiving transmissions? Yes. Is there more than one such set of related protocols? Yes, again.

Enter, now, the world of protocol *stacks* and *suites*. Although the terms are often used interchangeably, there is a somewhat subtle difference between a stack and a suite:

- A stack refers to a complete set of protocols, usually one for each layer, running on a network. A network can rely on more than one stack of protocols—for example, it can run the Novell Netware stack and a TCP/IP stack. The stacks are, however, independent. That is, the protocols in each stack are designed to interact with and rely on their own stack brethren, rather than on those in the "foreign" stack.

- A suite, in contrast, refers to a set of protocols designed and built (again, usually one for each layer) as complementary parts of a complete, smoothly functioning set. Thus, a set of TCP/IP protocols designed by a particular vendor would represent a suite. When running on a network, that vendor's TCP/IP suite would become the network stack.

Clear as mud? Try this. Think of a stack as being the layered set of protocols running on a network or network computer. ("My computer runs the the Netware [or AppleTalk or SNA] stack.") Think of a suite as being the set of protocols created by a particular vendor or organization. ("My network uses the Microsoft TCP/IP suite for Windows NT.")

A Quick Look at a Protocol Stack

These days, with the explosion of the Internet and the growth of internetworking, TCP/IP has largely taken the place of the ISO/OSI model, even though the latter is still a foundation stone in descriptions of network structure, and even though the OSI protocol suite (which includes protocols that correspond directly to each of the seven OSI levels) runs on many networks. Because such emphasis is now placed on TCP/IP, this section uses the TCP/IP model as the basis for a simplified example of a protocol stack and what it contains.

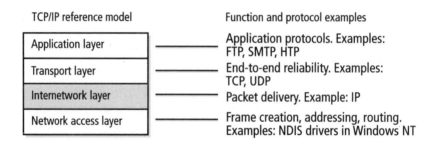

Starting from the top, where data transmissions originate (at least on the sending computer), here are the four TCP/IP layers and brief descriptions of the protocols shown in the illustration above:

■ The application layer, as already explained, is the highest, most abstract layer in terms of its "distance" from the physical network. This is where applications access the network using protocols such as FTP, the Internet's famous File Transfer Protocol; SMTP, the Internet's Simple Mail Transfer Protocol for e-mail message delivery; and HTTP, the Internet's very famous HyperText Transfer Protocol, on which browsers depend for the delivery of Web pages containing a mixture of text, graphics and, these days, sound, animation, and video.

■ Protocols in the transport layer mediate between the application layer and the internetwork layer, accepting data from the former and passing it to the latter. TCP (Transmission Control Protocol), the protocol from which the model takes part of its name, belongs in the transport layer, as does UDP (User Datagram Protocol), the other example shown in the illustration. TCP is a connection-based protocol that connects sending and receiving computers and, if necessary, provides for retransmission in the event of a transmission error. By way of example, TCP is used in Microsoft networking for file and printer sharing. UDP, in contrast, is a connectionless transport protocol, and one that is often referred to as *unreliable* because it does not provide for any means of verifying that transmitted data arrives correctly at the other end. (Applications are responsible for verification.) Real-world uses for UDP include browsing, logon, and broadcast or multicast transmission to many recipients at the same time.

- The internetwork layer, the "information superhighway" of the Information Superhighway, is where packets are sorted, routed, and delivered via packet switching. This layer is also home to the other half of the TCP/IP model, the Internet Protocol, or IP. Like UDP, IP is a connectionless protocol that does not check for errors in transmission. IP is primarily concerned with routing datagrams, which it does by checking the sending and receiving addresses attached to each datagram and comparing the destination to a *routing table* that helps it determine where to forward the datagram—for example, to a particular computer or to another network. In addition, if a datagram must be broken into smaller units, the jobs of fragmenting and reassembly fall to the Internet Protocol.

There are, of course, many more protocols than those described here. In terms of networks alone, there are protocols that deal with applications, those that deal with transport, and those that deal with enabling sessions and transferring data to the physical network. When broadened to include communications in general, there are also protocols related to modems, data encoding, routing, file transfer, and so on and so on. Where appropriate, the most important of such protocols will be defined and described in later chapters. For now, however, since protocols (and network models) are so firmly grounded in the idea of standardization, take a quick look at some of the industry organizations involved in evaluating and standardizing network-related hardware and software.

Where Standards Come From

Standards in the computer industry evolve in different ways. At times, especially in the early days of computing, certain products would become so widely used as to evolve into de facto (after the fact) standards. Where communications is concerned, one early and well-known example would be the modems made by the Hayes Corporation. As Hayes modems grew in popularity, they eventually came to define (at least around the mid to late 1980s) modems, and those produced by other manufacturers commonly advertised themselves as "Hayes-compatible."

More often, however, an idea for a standard is presented by a business or a technical group to a well-known standards body for consideration, refinement, and eventual approval. Currently, many such ideas—specifications—related to Internet technologies are evolving from just this type of beginning. Web-based authoring tools such as dynamic HTML (dynamic Hypertext Markup Language) and the user-definable XML (eXtensible Markup Language) are two such examples, and so is the Java language specification submitted by Sun Microsystems to the ISO/IEC (International Electrotechnical Commission) standards bodies.

Because standards bodies play an important role in creating the playing field for computer technologies, and because the names and acronyms of many standards bodies appear frequently in descriptions of networking technologies, the following sections describe, in alphabetical order, some of the most important network-related and Internet-related standards organizations and the work they do.

ANSI

ANSI, the *American National Standards Institute*, is a voluntary, non-profit organization composed of business and industry groups in the United States. Founded in 1918 and headquartered in New York, New York, ANSI is dedicated to supporting U.S. business in the global environment through the development of U.S. standards and adoption of international standards when appropriate. ANSI also represents the United States in the International Organization for Standardization (ISO) and the International Electrotechnical Commission (IEC).

ANSI is known for its recommendations for programming languages, including ANSI C; for commands, such as the escape sequences embodied in the ANSI.SYS device driver that provided MS-DOS users with a means of controlling and customizing the screen; and for various networking technologies, including the high-speed, fiberoptic SONET networking specification.

EIA

EIA, the *Electronics Industries Association*, is another U.S.-based organization. Founded in 1924, it is headquartered in Washington, D.C., and takes its membership from electronic equipment manufacturers.

EIA is hardware-related and works on the development of industry standards dealing with telecommunications, data processing, and computer communication. Among the many standards developed by EIA is the RS-232 interface specification that defines the connections—pins, lines, and signal characteristics—in the connectors commonly used to connect devices for serial transmission. (The RS in RS-232, by the way, stands for Recommended Standard.)

IEEE

IEEE ("eye-triple-eee") is the acronym for the *Institute of Electrical and Electronics Engineers*, a society of technical professionals founded in 1884 and based in the United States, although its membership includes individuals from about 150 countries around the world.

The IEEE is focused on electrical/electronics matters and computer engineering and science. In the area of networking standards, it is renowned (among other things) for the specifications produced since 1980 by twelve subgroups known as the 802 committees. These specifications, some of which are described in later chapters, deal with aspects of the physical and data link layers of the ISO/OSI model. Different aspects of networking are assigned to decimal "subsets" within the 802 standards specifications. Among the better known are: 802.3, which defines Ethernet networks; 802.4, which defines bus networks that rely on token passing; and 802.5, which defines ring networks that rely on token passing.

IETF

IETF is the *Internet Engineering Task Force*, a worldwide group of individuals interested in networking and the growth and evolution of the Internet. Membership in the IETF is open. The work performed by this organization is parceled out to various Working Groups, which focus on topics such as routing, security, transport, applications (searching and indexing directories, faxing, multicasting, and so on), and various Internet-related subjects. The Dynamic Host Configuration Working Group, for example, is charged with developing a protocol dealing with the allocation and management of IP addresses, the numeric "tags" that identify computers on the Internet.

In terms of general networking and the Internet, the IETF is the organization that developed and published the specifications known as RFCs (Requests for Comments) for the TCP/IP protocol standard.

ISO

The ISO, or International Organization for Standardization, is a federation of national standards organizations from 130 countries worldwide. Although often referred to as the International Standards Organization (to match the letters in ISO), the International Organization for Standardization in fact takes the "ISO" from the Greek word *isos*—equal—as in *isosceles* (the triangle with two equal sides) and *isopod* (the invertebrate critter with two legs per body segment). In terms of the work the ISO does, *equal* is a reference to equalization, or *standardization*.

At any rate, the ISO is nongovernmental and is focused on promoting international standards related not only to technology and communications, but also in other areas that concern trade, commerce, and products as diverse as photographic film, wire ropes, freight containers, and screw threads. In terms of networking, of course, the ISO stands out as the originator of the seven-layer ISO/OSI Reference Model.

ITU

The *ITU* is the *International Telecommunication Union*, an international organization based in Geneva, Switzerland. The ITU concerns itself with matters related to telecommunication, producing recommendations and standards related to telephone and data communications networks. The organization itself is divided into three sectors known as the Radiocommunication Sector, the Standardization Sector, and the Development Sector.

Of these three, the one most relevant to this chapter is the Standardization Sector, which goes by the abbreviation ITU-T and—this is important—was formerly known as the CCITT (Comité Consultatif International Télégraphique et Téléphonique). Although the CCITT became part of the ITU in 1992 and no longer exists as a separate body, its initials live on in a number of specifications and recommendations related to networking and modem communications. There are, for example, the recommendations known as the CCITT V series, which define modem design and operation, and the CCITT X series, adopted by the ISO, that define networking specifications, including the ISO/OSI model itself (X.200), e-mail message handling (X.400), and connecting a computer to a packet-switched network (X.25). The CCITT V and CCITT X series are described in more detail in Chapter 7 of this book.

W3C

Finally, although this is hardly the last of the many standards organizations in existence, there is the *W3C*, the *World Wide Web Consortium*. As you would expect, the W3C ("double-yew-three-see") focuses on the World Wide Web. Founded recently, in 1994, the W3C has bases in the United States, Europe, and Japan. Its goal is to provide information about the Web to both developers and interested end users (though some of that information might be just a bit technical) and to promote the development of open Web standards.

Among the recommendations considered and released by the W3C are specifications designed to standardize the markup and display of Web pages (cascading style sheets, XML, HTML, and so on). Although these specifications are not network-related (at least not in the sense of plugging together a LAN or a WAN), businesses of all sizes are increasing their dependence on Internet technologies in networking. So even if the specifications themselves have little to do with establishing and maintaining a functional network, the W3C and its work are noteworthy in and of themselves.

One of the leaders of the W3C, by the way, is none other than Tim Berners-Lee, the person who actually sat down and *created* the World Wide Web.

LANs

Wide area networks and internetworks are essential in connecting widely separated parts of an organization, but where basic client/server networking is concerned, the core of any network is the LAN, first described in Chapter 1. After all, a client/server network limited to a department or building is, in fact, a LAN. Beyond this, LANs are the building blocks from which larger, interconnected networks can be formed. And it's LANs speaking to other LANs through long-distance communications, and LANs "learning" how to route packets (through hardware and software, of course), that form the core of a wide area network.

LANs, then, are important. How important? Take a look at all the things they can do:

- They can form standalone networks in small-to-medium-sized businesses.

- They can serve as links to a mainframe-based network.

- They can be LANs in their own right at the the same time as they're also forming segments of larger networks.

- With the help of routers and gateways, they can transmit information, even if they're based on different network architectures.

- And as of 1998, they can be used in the "automated" home to connect multiple PCs and devices (such as printers), to turn the lights on and off, to control heating and cooling, and even to let the dog in.

Imagine today's world without LANs—a world in which:

- Snail mail rules

- Appointments are made (a) in person, (b) by mail, or (c) via phone tag

- Voice mail and telephone menus don't exist (hooray, say some...)

- Price lists, inventories, and product catalogs are available only on paper

- Anyone who wants to print a document must find a computer connected to a printer

- Files must be copied to disk and walked from person to person

- Purchase orders, bills, and sales reports cannot be linked and made available to multiple departments at the same time

- Employee schedules, meetings, and personnel records cannot be automated

- Reports and other documents must be photocopied and distributed for review

- People cannot telecommute

- Your auto dealer cannot access your car's service record from a keyboard

- Products from books to T shirts are sold only through stores or by telephone or mail order

- And...good grief, where stock reports and sports scores must wait for the evening newspaper

No, thanks.

Variations on a LAN

A basic LAN is a self-contained network of servers, nodes, and assorted devices such as printers and fax machines. The LAN itself, as described in Chapter 3, can take the shape of a logical (not necessarily physical, re-member) bus, ring, or star, or it can be a combination, such as a *star bus* or a *star-wired ring,* as shown in Figures 5-1 and 5-2.

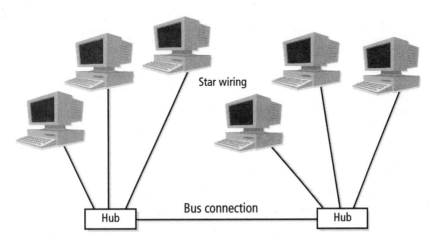

Figure 5-1. *A star bus topology. Note the linear (bus) connections from hub to hub.*

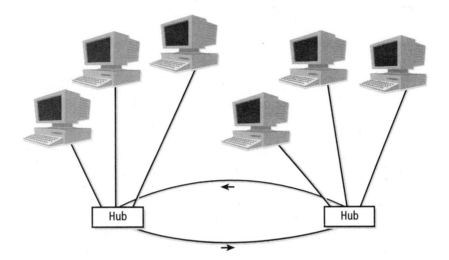

Figure 5-2. *A star ring topology. Note that the clients are wired to the hubs in a star pattern, and that the ring is formed by the connections between the hubs.*

As network traffic begins to increase and network response slows down due to added traffic and nodes, LANs must eventually either expand or be reorganized to handle the additional load. This is when network administrators begin to examine other options, including:

■ Adding more nodes, although this is a finite solution

■ Segmenting a larger LAN into two smaller ones

■ Joining separate LANs—something of a corollary to the preceding option

■ Creating an internetwork

All of these solutions, however, evolve from some basic LAN configurations and require additional pieces, such as routers and gateways, as well as (in WANs) modems or other communications technologies. Those technologies are covered later in the book, in Chapter 7. For now, it's time to concentrate on LAN essentials, starting with the standards, known as *IEEE 802.x*, that define the behavior and protocols of a network at its lowest levels, the physical and data link layers of the ISO/OSI Reference Model.

IEEE 802.x

IEEE 802.x (the *x* stands for a decimal number, as shown in the table on page 96) is named for the year (1980) and month (February) in which the IEEE launched what it called *Project 802*, an ambitious attempt to define networking standards. Through the efforts of various working groups and the publication of technical papers, Project 802 resulted in numerous recommendations, specifications, and standards.

LLC and MAC

Although the 802.x standards and the ISO/OSI Reference Model were developed separately, the two complement each other nicely, with just two differences: first, as mentioned earlier, 802.x limits its concerns to the physical and data link layers; second, and more important, 802.x divides the data link layer into two sublayers known as *Logical Link Control* (*LLC*) and *Media Access Control* (*MAC*), as shown below:

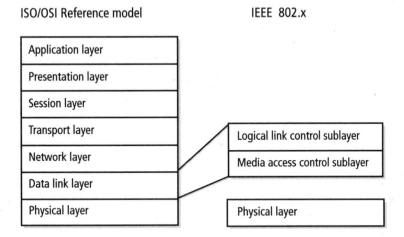

The Logical Link Control sublayer:

■ Manages—establishes and terminates—links

■ Sequences and acknowledges frames and controls frame traffic

The Media Access Control sublayer:

■ Manages access to the physical network

■ Is responsible for delimiting frames and error control

The Standards Themselves

And for the standards themselves: The 802.x committee, known officially as the IEEE 802 Local and Metropolitan Area Network Standards Committee, includes thirteen different working groups, some of which are currently inactive. These working groups focus on six basic standards categories, as shown in the table on the next page. (Do not be concerned if some of the terms are unfamiliar; they are explained later. At this point, the table is intended simply to make the 802.x standards categories a little easier to distinguish from one another.)

IEEE Committee Working Groups and Their Areas of Responsibility

IEEE 802 working group	Standards category and current group status	
802.1	Internetworking	
802.2	Logical Link Control (currently inactive)	
802.3, 802.4, 802.5, 802.6, 802.9, 802.11, and 802.14	Access and signaling for different types of local area and metropolitan area networks, as follows	
	802.3	Bus topology with Carrier Sense Multiple Access/Collision Detection (CSMA/CD)
	802.4	Token Bus topology
	802.5	Token Ring topology
	802.6	Metropolitan Area Networks (MANs) based on Distributed Queue Dual Bus (DQDB) architecture (currently inactive)
	802.9	Integrated voice and data—isochronous—networks
	802.11	Wireless networks
	802.12	Demand Priority Access LAN, known as 100BaseVG or, in an extended form, as 100VG-AnyLAN
	802.14	Cable television/cable modems
802.7	Broadband advisory group (currently inactive)	
802.8	Fiberoptics advisory group	
802.10	Security	

Today, the IEEE 802 committee is *the* standard-setting body where the physical layer and the LLC and MAC sublayers are concerned. As you can see in the "clump" of LAN standards in Table 5-1, the efforts of this group have resulted in multiple standards that define families of LAN architectures, including Ethernet, Token Bus, Token Ring, and others.

IEEE 802.3: Ethernet

If there is such a thing as an ancestral LAN technology, it's probably the one known as *Ethernet*, in that many, if not most, of the LANs in use today are based on this technology. Named after the "ether" that in olden days was thought to be the medium that conducted electromagnetic energy, Ethernet was developed in the early 1970s at the famed Xerox Palo Alto Research Center (Xerox PARC), which was also the birthplace of the laser printer, the mouse, and the graphical user interface (GUI).

There's a saying, however, that "if I see farther, it is because I stand on the shoulders of giants." In other words, scientific (and technological) advances seldom spring up in complete isolation. They are built upon work that has gone before. Ethernet is no exception to that rule. Although Ethernet's cabling and signaling were invented at Xerox PARC, it was based on an earlier network—a WAN, actually—implemented at the University of Hawaii in the 1960s. This earlier network, named ALOHA, was notable in using *CSMA/CD* as its means of controlling network access and contention. And CSMA/CD is characteristic of Ethernet networks.

CSMA/CD

So what is CSMA/CD, other than a particularly cryptic abbreviation? As mentioned earlier, the letters stand for Carrier Sense Multiple Access [with] Collision Detection. It functions on the MAC sublayer and is the means relied on by network nodes in Ethernet and certain other LANs to:

- Gain access to the network when they have packets to transmit

- Ensure that two nodes do not try to transmit at the same time

As for the actual meaning of those words, here's how to break them down in a way that makes the technology itself both memorable and easier to remember. The *Carrier Sense* part means that the nodes on the network "listen" for—are able to sense—a carrier signal on the line that indicates the network is busy. The *Multiple Access* part means that more than one node might want to transmit at the same time. If, in fact, that is the case, and two nodes actually do transmit simultaneously, the nodes rely on *Collision Detection* to resolve the situation.

In operation, CSMA/CD turns the network into something like a telephone party line on which all of the nodes are comparable to people wanting to (or waiting to) participate. Like conversations on the line, transmissions travel in both directions. And, like nosy neighbors on the line, all of the nodes "listen" for the carrier signal at all times. When one node has something to transmit, it waits until the line is free, meaning that it does not sense the carrier signal. At that time, it puts its transmission onto the cable. If the node is the only one transmitting at that time, all is well and the other nodes wait until the transmission reaches its destination before trying to transmit any data of their own.

Sometimes, though, two nodes can simultaneously assume that the line is free and try to transmit at the same time, much as two people on a party line might start talking when the line is temporarily free. When this happens on a CSMA/CD network, the result is a data collision in which signal activity rises and the data itself is corrupted—rather like the noise level rising and words becoming difficult to understand, if not unintelligible, when two people speak simultaneously. On the network, the nodes are able to detect this increased activity and to interpret it as a data collision. When this happens, the nodes cancel their transmissions (the equivalent of saying, "oops" or "excuse me") and—again, like two parties on the telephone line—both back off for a random period of time before trying to access the network again and transmit. The amount of time the nodes wait is called the *deferral time;* it works on the assumption that both will back off for different periods of time and that one or the other will thus be able to transmit successfully the second time around.

CSMA/CD is also notable for being labeled a *contentious* means of gaining network access. Unlike the more polite nodes on a token passing network that take turns transmitting, as described later in this chapter, nodes on a CSMA/CD network are scrappier individuals that contend with one another for the right to transmit. The first node to pop its data onto the cable is, in effect, the "winner" of the moment.

Although CSMA/CD sounds like a brawling free-for-all and a rather clumsy way to regulate network transmissions, it works, as the popularity of Ethernet networks indicates. As an access and control method, CSMA/CD works best on networks that don't carry a lot of traffic or numerous small transmissions, any of which might be responsible for a data collision. On busy networks with numerous nodes exchanging large numbers of packets, probability alone increases the number of possible—and actual—collisions. The very acts of detecting and avoiding transmissions on such networks can slow the network.

Features Common to Ethernet Networks

As described in the following sections, Ethernet networks vary in topology, speed, and the types of cabling they use. In addition to CSMA/CD, however, Ethernet networks also have certain elements in common:

■ All are defined in the IEEE 802.3 specification.

■ All rely on broadcast transmissions that deliver signals to all nodes at the same time. This broadcasting is, in fact, necessary for CSMA/CD to work.

■ All are baseband networks. (Well, this is not *quite* true. All the widely known and used forms of Ethernet are baseband. There is one broadband variant known as 10Broad36, which is built around coaxial cable-television, or CATV, cable. More about standard Ethernet cabling later.)

In addition, Ethernet networks all use the same Ethernet-unique format for transmitting information. This format, known as a *frame*, ranges from 64 bytes to 1,518 bytes in size. Regardless of length, however, all frames are built of the following pieces:

■ An 8-byte preamble that marks the beginning of the frame

■ A 14-byte header that contains the source and destination addresses

■ A 46-byte to 1,500-byte data section

■ A 4-byte trailer that includes a cyclic redundancy check (CRC)

Variations on the Ethernet Theme

In other respects, Ethernet networks can be quite variable. Or at least they can be variable enough to cause some mental overload at first, especially in terms of the names used to describe them and the ways in which different names can sometimes refer to the same network. To start off with, however, here are the basic areas in which Ethernet networks differ:

■ Topology. Although all Ethernet networks are based on a linear bus topology, they can be based on a star bus topology as well.

■ Speed. Ethernet networks traditionally operate at either 10 Mbps or 100 Mbps (megabits per second). Technology does march on, however, and as of 1998, a much faster form known as *Gigabit Ethernet* has also been added to the mix. Operating at 1000 Mbps, or 1 Gbps, Gigabit Ethernet is under development primarily as a high-speed backbone for existing LANs.)

- Cable type. Ethernet networks can use *coaxial*, *fiberoptic*, or *unshielded twisted-pair* (*UTP*) cable. (These cable types are described in more detail in Chapter 6; here, you'll simply be introduced to the distinctions among them in terms of Ethernet networks.) In addition, networks based on coaxial cable are further categorized as Thin Ethernet (3/16-inch cable) or Thick Ethernet (3/8-inch cable).

It does get confusing. The following sections try to sort things out for you. The sorting begins by grouping different Ethernet networks into two basic groups: those that run at 10 Mbps and those that run at 100 Mbps.

10 mbps Ethernet

Baseband Ethernet networks running at 10 Mbps can be divided into four types, each of which has some variation of the name 10BaseX. Although the name at first doesn't seem particularly descriptive, it becomes so when you realize that it is composed of three parts, each of which describes an important feature of the network:

- The *10* stands for the speed of the network.
- The *Base* portion tells you the network is a *base*band network.
- The *X*, used here as a placeholder for an identifier that differs for each type of network, describes cable length or cable type.

These three elements are combined to produce the following four basic names for 10 Mbps baseband Ethernet networks: *10BaseT*, *10Base2*, *10Base5*, and *10BaseFL*. These different forms of Ethernet are described in the following sections. To help you distinguish one from the other, their differences are also summarized in the following table.

Feature Summary of 10BaseX Ethernet Networks

Network	Also known as	Cable type	Segment length	Comments
10BaseT	Twisted-pair Ethernet or UTP Ethernet	Twisted-pair wiring	100 meters	Popular, inexpensive; supports up to 1,024 nodes
10Base2	Thin Ethernet or ThinNet	Thin (3/16-inch) coaxial cable	185 meters (roughly 2 times 100 meters)	Relatively expensive, popular; supports up to five segments, with 30 nodes per segment
10Base5	Thick Ethernet or ThickNet	Thick (3/8-inch) co-axial cable	500 meters (5 times 100 meters)	Generally used for network backbone; supports up to five segments, with 100 nodes per segment
10BaseFL	10BaseF	Fiberoptic cable	2000 meters (2 kilo-meters)	Valuable in spanning distances, e.g., for connecting repeaters in separate buildings

10BaseT, or twisted-pair Ethernet 10BaseT describes an Ethernet network based on twisted-pair (telephone cable) wiring. The wiring can be either shielded (STP) or unshielded (UTP) twisted-pair wiring, but it is generally the latter. Widely used and inexpensive, a 10BaseT network is built around hubs to which nodes connect in a starlike pattern via a network adapter and telephone-like RJ-45 jacks. A 10BaseT network can include up to 1,024 nodes. The maximum length of the cable connecting a node to a hub can be no more than 100 meters (328 feet).

10Base2, or thin Ethernet Sometimes also known as "CheaperNet," 10Base2, or *Thin Ethernet*, is characterized by the thin (3/16-inch) coaxial (cable-TV) cable used for the network backbone, or trunk segments—the ones that, like your own backbone, hold the network together. The 2 in 10Base2 refers to the maximum allowable length of a cable segment—185 meters, or roughly 2 times 100 meters.

A 10Base2 network is based on a bus topology. It can support up to 30 nodes per trunk segment and can include a maximum of five segments covering a total distance of 925 meters. Of the five segments, however, only three can have attached nodes, so a 10Base2 network supports a maximum of 90 stations, rather than the 150 (five segments x 30 nodes per segment) that you might assume.

10Base5, or thick Ethernet   Also known as "standard" Ethernet, 10Base5 is based on thick (3/8-inch) coaxial cabling. Because this type of cabling is more difficult to handle than thin coaxial cabling, 10Base5 is generally used for network backbones rather than for entire Ethernet networks.

Like Thin Ethernet, *Thick Ethernet* is based on a bus topology and can support up to five segments, three of which can have attached nodes. The cabling, however, can be much longer—up to 500 meters—and can support 100 nodes per segment. Thus, the maximum length of a Thick Ethernet network is 2,500 meters, with a maximum of 300 nodes.

The nodes in a Thick Ethernet network, by the way, attach to the trunk by means of a cable known as either a *drop cable* or a *transceiver cable*. (A *transceiver*, which takes its name from the words *transmitter* and *receiver*, is the device on a network adapter that, no surprise, transmits and receives signals and does the actual conversion of data from parallel to serial and vice versa before and after the data travels over the network.)

 OTE   Here's a particularly memorable note for future network gurus who are also science-fiction fans. The transceiver connects to the Thick Ethernet cable by means of a connector known as a *vampire tap*—so called because it uses a pin to pierce the cable partway, passing through the outer insulating layer in order to connect directly with the copper core over which the signals travel. (Shades of Dracula in the information age...)

Because thick coaxial cable carries signals over longer distances and is thus desirable for network backbones, whereas thin coaxial cable is more manageable and thus desirable for connecting nodes to the network, many large networks combine the two in a hybrid thin/thick Ethernet network.

10BaseFL   The 10BaseFL Ethernet specification covers networks using fiberoptic cable, a safe and reliable medium that can, in this type of network, carry signals over distances as great as 2000 meters, or 2 kilometers.

Because of the distances it can cover, 10BaseFL is used primarily to connect hubs or repeaters (devices that strengthen signals by regenerating them before passing them along to the next network segment).

100 Mbps Ethernet The 100 Mbps Ethernet networks fall basically into two groups. One is known as *100BaseVG* (for Voice Grade), which was developed by Hewlett-Packard and accepted for ratification as a standard by the IEEE in 1995. The other, known as *100BaseX*, includes three 100 Mbps specifications distinguished by the type of cabling used in the network. The following sections describe these in a little more detail.

100BaseVG - AnyLAN The 100BaseVG specification, defined in IEEE 802.12, covers networks that run ten times faster than any of the 10BaseX networks and are based on voice-grade (known as Category 3) twisted-pair wiring. Unlike other Ethernet networks, a 100BaseVG-AnyLAN network is distinguished by:

- Its support for both Ethernet and Token Ring (covered later in this chapter) message frames

- A topology known as *cascaded star*, in which nodes are connected to hubs and hubs can be connected to other hubs in a parent/child relationship in which the parent hub controls the transmissions of the child hubs

- The ability of hubs to filter message frames for privacy

- A network access method known as *demand priority*

This last feature, demand priority, makes a 100BaseVG–AnyLAN network a little bit of an oddball in the Ethernet world of contentious CSMA/CD. Whereas CSMA/CD allows nodes to transmit when they sense that the network is free, demand priority gives the hubs, rather than the nodes, control of network access. Thus, instead of simply attempting to transmit when the line is free, a node on a 100BaseVG–AnyLAN network sends a request to transmit to the hub. To help the hub figure out when to pass the transmission along on the network, this request also includes a transmission priority level, which can be either low or high. The node waits until the hub gives permission and then transmits its information to the hub, which then sends the transmission along to its destination—immediately if the node has requested high priority, or when network traffic allows if the node has requested low, or regular, priority service.

The 100BaseVG–AnyLAN specification is designed to ease the process of upgrading from a slower Ethernet network or connecting to an Ethernet or token ring network. Although the cabling in a 100BaseVG–AnyLAN network can consist of either unshielded twisted-pair wiring or fiberoptic cable, the network adapters in the nodes and the network hubs must be designed for a 100BaseVG–AnyLAN network.

100BaseX, or *fast Ethernet* Getting back to a more "traditional" Ethernet, there are three 100BaseX specifications that, except for speed, resemble their 10BaseT cousins. All three 100 Mbps versions are based on a star topology, all three rely on CSMA/CD for network access, and two of the three specify some form of twisted-pair wiring. The three specifications are as follows:

- 100BaseT4 uses four pairs of medium-to-high grade (Category 3 to Category 5) twisted-pair wiring. (Note: The down and dirty details of wire pairs and grades, or categories, of twisted-pair wiring come in the next chapter. For now, Ethernet varieties should be enough to handle.)

- 100BaseTX uses two pairs of high-grade (Category 5) twisted-pair wiring.

- 100BaseFX uses two strands of fiberoptic cable.

These three variants of 100 Mbps Ethernet are defined in a recent (1995) IEEE 802.3u specification.

Buses, Rings, and Tokens

Although Ethernet is widely used in LANs, it is not the only LAN architecture in town. There are others, two of which crop up often in descriptions of networking: token bus and token ring. The first of these, token bus, corresponds to the IEEE 802.4 specification. The second, token ring, is described in all its glory in the IEEE 802.5 specification. The networks differ in topology and other features, but in both forms, the network nodes use a small electronic "baton" known as a token to gain network access.

Tokens and Token Passing

Unlike the contentious (and as it's also described, probabilistic—meaning whoever gets there first) CSMA/CD method of gaining network access, *token-passing* networks rely on a more harmonious, deterministic (meaning everybody gets a chance to play) method in which the nodes themselves take an active role in managing access and avoiding collisions. At the heart of this access method is a small, special data frame only a few bytes in size, the *token*.

This token is a unique frame—there is only one on the network at any given time. Like the baton in a relay race, it is passed from node to node in the network, always moving in the same direction and in a predetermined order that forms a logical, if not physical, ring. So, for example, if a network consists of nodes 1 through 25, node 1 passes the token to node 2, node 2 passes it to node 3, and so on. When the token reaches node 25, that node passes it back to node 1, thus completing the "circle" and forming a logical ring no matter how the nodes are actually distributed on the network.

As you would imagine, the token is not just a trinket that nodes pass among themselves for the heck of it. Its function is, in fact, critical to maintaining order on the network, because only the node that currently holds the token is allowed to transmit. To make matters even more equal among the nodes, the holder of the token can transmit only a single packet before being required to pass the token along to the next node.

In operation, if the network is very quiet and none of the nodes has any information to transmit (an unlikely situation), the token simply circulates over and over. On the other hand, if a node has information to transmit, it waits until it receives the token. It then temporarily takes the token out of circulation by marking it "busy," attaches its packet of data, and then passes the token and data frame to the next node in line. This node, noticing that the token is "busy," passes the package along to the next, which does the same. And so it goes, until the package reaches the intended recipient. At that point, the recipient strips the data from the frame, marks the frame as having been read, and sends it on its way. When the sender receives the frame once again, it checks to see whether the data was received, marks the token as "available for use," and sends it to the next node in line.

If that node has information to transmit, it repeats the process of marking the token as "busy," transmitting its data, waiting for the frame to return with a "read it" acknowledgment, and once more passing the token along. In this way, each node on the network is given an equal chance to transmit whenever it receives the token, and, because only one node at a time holds the token, the network manages to avoid collisions.

Figure 5-3 diagrams the token-passing process.

Now, on to the IEEE token-passing specifications. Here, although the token bus specification, IEEE 802.4, comes numerically before the token ring specification (IEEE 802.5), you'll meet token ring first, because it is far more common on PC-based networks.

IEEE 802.5: Token Ring

When you think about token ring, there are two different "forms" to keep in mind. One is the IEEE specification, which is spelled with a lowercase *t* and a lowercase *r*. The other, spelled with initial capital letters—*Token Ring*—is an IBM-designed architecture created to aid in connecting PCs with IBM's larger midrange and mainframe computers. Although the IEEE token ring specification was developed before IBM developed its Token Ring architecture, and even though there are some differences between the two, the IBM Token Ring architecture is so successful and so widely used that descriptions of token ring architecture generally talk about the IBM implementation. That said...

Token Ring (capital letters) is based on a ring topology, as its name indicates. However, because a break in the ring cabling can bring down the entire network, Token Ring networks generally rely on a safer, more reliable star-wired ring in which nodes are connected to one or more hubs called *Multistation Access Units*, or *MAUs*. The connections within (or between) the hubs form a logical ring.

A Token Ring network can include up to 33 MAUs, each of which is equipped with 10 connectors (ports). Computers can be connected to eight of these ports on any MAU, but the remaining two ports, known as ring in (RI) and ring out (RO), are reserved specially for connecting one MAU to another.

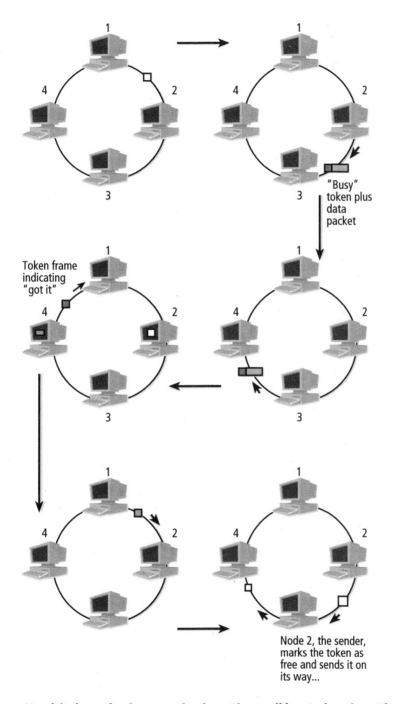

Figure 5-3. *Simplified travels of a network token. The small box is the token. The larger box represents a data packet. For easy visualization, the network is shown as a ring topology.*

Because of the ring topology, MAUs are a little picky about how they are connected to each other: The ring out port on one must be connected to the ring in port on another in order to preserve the logical ring. Because the connections can be a little difficult to visualize, Figure 5-4 shows multiple connected MAUs in which the ring in and ring out ports preserve the ring topology.

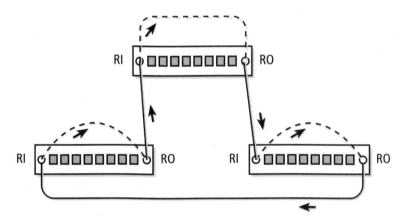

Figure 5-4.   *A logical ring in a MAU-to-MAU-to-MAU connection.*

In addition to using token-passing for both network access and contention control, a Token Ring network:

- Typically transfers information at 1 Mbps or 4 Mbps per second (in the IEEE specification) or at 4 Mbps or 16 Mbps (in the IBM version)

- Uses baseband transmission

- Is based on twisted-pair or fiberoptic cable

(Like Ethernet, however, Token Ring refuses to stand still. In 1998, it evolved into a 100 Mbps specification, and a 1 Gbps Token Ring architecture is expected in 1999.)

IEEE 802.4: Token Bus

Token bus, although it more or less corresponds to the LAN known as ARCnet, is used primarily in manufacturing situations. In fact, the specification was originally designed to suit the need for automation in factories like those belonging to General Motors.

On a token bus network, the trunk is either linear or tree-shaped (as shown in Figure 5-5), but the nodes send the token to one another in a predetermined order—in this case, from the node with the highest network address to the node with the lowest—that forms a logical ring. For example, as shown in Figure 5-6, node E sends to node D, which sends to node C, and so on down the line. When the token reaches A, the last node on the bus, node A transmits the token back to node E.

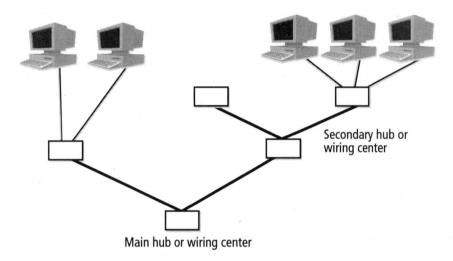

Figure 5-5. *A tree topology in which hubs or wiring centers "branch" from a main "root."*

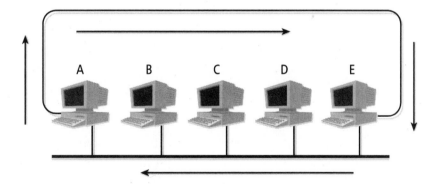

Figure 5-6. *The ring-shaped path taken by a token on a token bus network.*

In addition to token-passing and a bus or tree topology, token bus networks are characterized by:

- Coaxial or fiberoptic cable

- Speeds of 1 Mbps to 20 Mbps, depending on the type of cabling used

ARCnet: Token Bus for LANs

Although the token bus specification was designed with factory automation in mind, there is a PC-based LAN architecture that corresponds, at least in its topology and reliance on token passing, to the IEEE 802.4 specification. That architecture is known as *ARCnet*, which stands for *Attached Resource Computer Network.*

ARCnet has actually been around since before the IEEE formalized its specification for the token bus architecture. It was developed in the late 1970s by a company called Datapoint Corporation, and it has become popular for smaller networks, in part because its components—including network adapters—are inexpensive and because it is both flexible and relatively easy to set up.

An ARCnet network is built around either a bus or a star topology and can support up to 255 nodes. The original version of ARCnet transfers information at a rate of 1.5 Mbps; a new form, known as ARCnet Plus, runs at 20 Mbps, and a third form can reach a speed of 100 Mbps.

ARCnet networks are built around three types of hubs:

- *Passive hubs*, which connect to either active hubs or nodes, simply pass the network signals along.

- *Active hubs*, which connect to other active hubs, passive hubs, or nodes, both regenerate and pass the signals.

- *Intelligent hubs* are active hubs with additional "smarts" that enable them to monitor the network or perform diagnostic tasks.

Other ARCnet components include network adapters, connectors for joining cabling, and coaxial cable, twisted-pair wiring, fiberoptic cable, or a combination of cable types. The maximum length of a cable segment is a little confusing, because it depends on the type of cabling, the type of hub, and the topology (bus or star) of the network. For example:

■ A network using coaxial cabling, in a bus topology with no hub, has a maximum segment length of about 300 meters (1000 feet).

■ A network based on twisted-pair cabling and a bus topology has a maximum segment length of about 120 meters (400 feet).

■ A bus network built around active hubs and coaxial cabling can have a maximum cable length of about 300 meters between nodes and about 600 meters (2000 feet) between hubs.

■ A star-wired network including active and passive hubs can have cables up to about 600 meters between active hubs and/or nodes and about 30 meters (100 feet) between active hubs and passive hubs and/or nodes.

Other IEEE LAN Specifications

Ethernet, Token Ring, and—to some extent—token bus and ARCnet are the primary LAN architectures, at least in terms of popularity and reknown. The IEEE 802 specifications do, however, cover a few more, including metropolitan area networks (currently handled by an inactive committee) and two others that are beginning to crop up more frequently: *isochronous networks* and *wireless networks*. The following two sections briefly describe each of these.

IEEE 802.9: Isochronous LANs

Isochronous LANs...well, the LAN part is easy to understand, but *isochronous*? That's quite a word. According to Webster's dictionary, it comes from the Greek *isochronos*—equal (iso) and time (chronos). In networking terms, it means that these LANs are time-sensitive. In terms of the IEEE 802.9 specification, *isochronous* refers to the blending of *ISDN* (*Integrated Services Digital Network*) and LAN technologies, specifically at the—you guessed it—physical and LLC/MAC network layers.

Often referred to as *Integrated Services LAN* (*ISLAN*), isochronous LANs are aimed at enabling multimedia capabilities on a network. The specification itself began with an IEEE study group that started investigating Integrated Voice/Data (IVD) networks in the mid-1980s. The work involved developing an integrated standard based on unshielded twisted-pair wiring that complemented both the IEEE 802 specifications at the MAC sublayer and the ISDN standards set by the *CCITT*. (CCITT stands for a mouthful of an organization, the Comité Consultatif International Télégraphique et Téléphonique, which was eventually folded into an equally long-winded standards body known as the International Telecommunications Union-Telecommunication Standardization Sector, or ITU-T). Eventually, this effort was renamed Integrated Services LAN (ISLAN) and a specification was approved by the IEEE in 1993.

The ISLAN specification revolves around devices collectively referred to as Integrated Services Terminal Equipment, or ISTEs. Despite the somewhat forbidding moniker, ISTE is just a general name for multimedia-related devices, for example, telephones (voice TEs) and computers (data TEs). The specification itself describes a star topology in which these devices connect to an Access Unit (AE) and, thence, to the network backbone via twisted-pair wiring.

In terms of ISDN technology, IEEE 802.9 supports both Basic Rate Interface (BRI) and Primary Rate Interface (PRI) ISDN. Duh.... All right, in brief: ISDN, which is described in more detail in Chapter 7, is a means of delivering different types of information—voice, data, video—in digital form over standard telephone wiring. One of the hallmarks of ISDN is its division of the signal into two primary types of channels known as B and D channels. The B channels carry data at the rate of 64 kilobits per second (Kbps); the D channel carries signaling and other control information at the rate of 16 Kbps. In the form of ISDN known as BRI (Basic Rate Interface), there are two B channels and one D channel. In the more expansive form known as PRI (Primary Rate Interface), there are either 23 (in the U.S., Canada, and Japan) or 30 (Europe) B channels and, again, one D channel.

As to what this all means and why IEEE 802.9 is called *isochronous*, well, just think for a second. Data, such as text, can be sent in intermittent bursts in packet form, and the packets can be reconstituted at the receiving end to deliver a smooth, coherent whole. The same is not true of multimedia-type information, including audio and video. Both must be delivered smoothly and at very constant, very specific time intervals. Video, for example, must be delivered at a certain number of frames per second. If the delivery were interrupted or the frames were to arrive whenever they felt like it, the transmission would be distorted at best and unwatchable at worst. The same is true with digital audio—deliver me correctly, or don't bother. In other words, audio and video are time-dependent, and the network must support that requirement. It must be isochronous.

IEEE 802.11: Wireless Networks

References to wireless LANs or LAN connections can be a little bit ambiguous. On the one hand, they can refer to, say, a portable PC equipped with a radio-based network adapter that connects to a similarly radio-based access point that, in turn, connects to a standard wired network. In such a hybrid situation, wireless and "wired" equipment communicate with one another. On the other hand, a reference to a wireless network can actually refer to a completely "unwired" LAN. This is the type of network described here, as laid out in the IEEE 802.11 specification.

The IEEE 802.11 specification defines wireless networks that are roughly comparable to Ethernet networks, in that these LANs rely on a technique related to CSMA/CD for network access and contention control at the MAC sublayer. Wireless LANs differ, however, in using a method known as *CSMA/CA*, or Carrier Sense Multiple Access with Collision *Avoidance*, rather than CSMA/CD—Carrier Sense Multiple Access with Collision *Detection*. Although CSMA/CA is much like CSMA/CD in that nodes are required to "listen" to the transmission medium and transmit only when it is free for use, in CSMA/CA, the node doesn't simply grab the open "line" and transmit. Instead, it first does the equivalent of holding its hand up in the air by sending a short message known as a request to send (RTS), which specifies the intended recipient at the same time as it warns all nodes in the vicinity to back off for a time. In return, the recipient sends clear to send (CTS) back to the initating node. Once this is done, the node transmits its data. If the data is correctly received, the recipient finishes the process by sending an acknowledge (ACK) message to signify "A-OK." At this point, the medium is free for another node to use.

At the physical layer, wireless LANs rely on two different methods of wireless transmission:

■ Light, specifically, diffuse infrared light, in which a light signal is "broadcast" and receivable by any node in the area. Diffuse infrared signals essentially bounce around, off walls, floors, and ceilings, until they reach the recipient. In this, they are unlike the kind of infrared signal known as line-of-sight, in which a beam of light must shoot straight and true into the waiting (red) "eye" built into the receiving device (such as a VCR or a computer designed to work with a wireless keyboard). Although diffuse infrared allows nodes to move around wherever necessary, the signals are relatively slow and weak because of all the bouncing around that they do. Typically, diffuse infrared has a range of only about 33 meters (100 feet).

■ Radio, in which signals are broadcast over the 2.4 gigaHertz (GHz) radio band. Radio signals are, in turn, categorized as either Direct Sequence Spread Spectrum (DS) or the Frequency Hopping Spread Spectrum (FS)—a warm and fuzzy, bunnylike name if ever there was one.

  ▪ Direct Sequence Spread Spectrum uses a modulation technique—a means of "loading" data onto the radio wave—in which each transmitted data bit is broken down and encoded as part of a pattern of smaller "particles" known as chips. Although the process is difficult to picture, the end result is that the encoded data can be transmitted over a broader range of frequencies than the "unchipped" data could cover. In addition, because the actual data is embedded in the "chipping code" of mini-bits, the data stream itself is encrypted and can be decrypted only by a receiver equipped with the same chipping code.

  ▪ Frequency Hopping Spread Spectrum is much easier to understand. In this process, the transmitting and receiving radios literally hop in unison from frequency to frequency across the transmission band. At each stop, they transmit and receive before moving on to the next. The time spent at each frequency (called the dwell time) and the choice of channels are all predetermined, so that everyone on the network knows where and when to move on.

Also known as *WLANs* (*wireless LANs*), such networks are especially useful in situations in which:

- Nodes must move around freely, as in a hospital, a supermarket (noting inventory, for example), or on a factory floor

- Network connections are needed in a very busy area, such as a convention lobby

- Connections are unreliable or dependent on external (unpredictable) factors, as in military operations

- It is difficult or impossible to wire a building for a network

Wireless LANs are not currently all that common, but they probably will become more popular as time and technology march on.

Leading LAN Protocols

The network architectures you've read about so far in this chapter affect the bottom two layers of the ISO/OSI Reference Model. They describe the underpinnings of the network, the physical media involved, the layout of the network, and the methods used by network nodes to access and transfer data frames peacefully and as efficiently as possible. The IEEE 802.*x* specifications you've read about so far describe the network protocols—Ethernet, Token Ring, and other protocols at the physical layer, and CSMA/CD, CSMA/CA, and token passing at the data link layer—and the ways they operate at these low levels.

But, as you learned in the last chapter, there are another five layers sitting on top of the physical and the data link control/LLC-MAC layers. They are involved with preparing, addressing, and checking the data frames that go flying through the network. And they, too, follow rules that help deliver the network freight. The remaining sections of this chapter describe some of the LAN protocols supported by various networks and network operating systems.

Before you go on to them, however, there's a question to be answered: How does a network card know which protocol(s) it's supposed to use? The answer: binding.

Binding

Binding is the process by which protocols at the various network levels become associated with (bound to) one another and, hence, with the network adapter. That is essentially what binding means: the act of literally tying the protocols together to provide data with a route from the application level down to the network adapter. Binding ensures that the bound protocols can use and depend on the services provided by those above and below them, and that the adapter can process the traffic passing to and from the node in which it is installed.

The process of binding, however, also involves software known as the network adapter's *driver*. A driver, or device driver as it's often called, is a piece of software designed to enable a computer to work with a particular attached device. There are drivers for all kinds of devices—printers, pointing devices, disk drives, and so on. In every instance, the driver is what enables the computer's operating system to communicate with, and use the capabilities of, the device itself.

Network adapters are no different from other hardware devices in requiring drivers. These drivers inhabit the MAC sublayer and ensure that the computer can communicate with the network adapter and, hence, with the network itself. During the binding process, one or more protocols (for example, the TCP/IP and NetBEUI protocols described in the following sections) are bound to the network adapter. Once this binding takes place, the network adapter, with the help of its driver, is able to connect with, and use, the network in accordance with the protocol that has been bound to it.

Now, as for the most often-used protocols themselves...

TCP/IP

TCP/IP was used as an example of a protocol stack in Chapter 4. Here's a little more detailed look at it.

Originally developed for ARPANET, TCP/IP has, with the rise of the Internet and internetworking in the PC and client/server realm, become a hot property. It is, in fact, a networking standard these days, in part because it:

- Is robust

- Enables communication among and between different systems

- Is available on a wide variety of computing platforms

And, of course, it provides access to the Internet—increasingly, a "must have" in enterprise networking.

At heart, TCP/IP is based on the two protocols from which it takes its name:

- *TCP*, or *Transmission Control Protocol*, as described in Chapter 4, operates at the transport layer and is responsible for delivering information correctly.

- *IP*, or *Internet Protocol*, operates at the network or, in TCP/IP terminology, the internetwork layer and is responsible for routing packets, sometimes through many different networks.

TCP/IP Reference model

Application layer	
Transport layer	TCP
Internetwork layer	IP
Network access layer	

In addition to these, the TCP/IP suite also includes the transport-level protocol known as *UDP* (*User Datagram Protocol*), which also relies on IP for packet routing. Unlike TCP, which is a reliable, connection-based transport, UDP is an unreliable, connectionless transport. What that means is that TCP establishes a connection between sender and receiver before transferring data (in pieces known as segments), retransmits segments when it does not receive an "arrived OK" acknowledgment from the recipient, and can control the flow of information to ensure that the sending computer does not overload the buffers (receiving areas) of the recipient. In contrast, UDP does not include any means of guaranteeing delivery—it makes a best effort, but it is unreliable in that it does not establish a connection between sender and receiver before transmitting its information (in pieces called *datagrams*) and does not expect or require an acknowledgment from the recipient. In addition, because the datagrams transmitted via UDP are independent of one another, even when they are parts of the same transmission, they can arrive out of order. The datagrams, like the unacknowledged means of transmission, are connectionless.

These protocols are basic to the TCP/IP suite in the sense that they provide services to a number of other protocols, most of which are involved with application-related matters, and they simply assume that TCP, IP, and/or UDP will take care of the lower-level transport and network matters. Among the application-related protocols in the TCP/IP suite are:

- *FTP*, the *File Transfer Protocol* used in moving files to and from computers over a network

- *TELNET*, the network terminal protocol that people use in logging on to another computer on a network, effectively using that computer by "remote control" from the computer that they are actually working on—which simply acts as a go-between

- *SMTP*, or *Simple Mail Transfer Protocol*, which uses TCP to transfer e-mail messages

- *SNMP*, the *Simple Network Management Protocol*, which is involved in services related to managing a network

NetBEUI

NetBEUI, which is pronounced "netboo-ie" by some and "netbyou-ie" by others, is short for *NetBIOS Extended User Interface*, a protocol developed by IBM in the mid-1980s and designed for LANs of up to 200 computers. NetBEUI is a transport-layer protocol and has been used in Microsoft's networking products. Although NetBEUI is small and fast, it does not support routing and so is restricted to LANs only. With the growth of wide area networking, internetworking, and the Internet, NetBEUI has been supplanted by TCP/IP.

On Microsoft's Windows operating systems, NetBEUI is a transport go-between that communicates with higher levels (the session, presentation, and application layers) through a programming interface known as the TDI, or Transport Driver Interface. NetBEUI communicates with lower levels through an interface known as NDIS (Network Driver Interface Specification), which provides a means for network adapter device drivers to support multiple protocols at higher levels. The following (simplified) diagram shows how NetBEUI fits between the TDI and NDIS interfaces in relation to the ISO/OSI Reference Model.

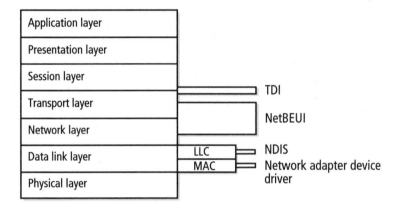

DLC

DLC, short for *Data Link Control* is, like NetBEUI, another protocol supported by Microsoft's Windows operating system—specifically, Windows NT. Unlike other protocols, DLC is designed to provide access to either of two specific types of hardware: IBM mainframes and Hewlett-Packard printers that are connected directly to the network. Because of this specificity, DLC needs to be installed only on the devices that actually access mainframes or (in the case of an HP printer—connected to the network, remember) on the print servers that send jobs from requesting nodes to the printer itself.

XNS

XNS, which originated at Xerox PARC, is short for *Xerox Network System.* It is a set of protocols assigned to five layers, numbered 0 through 4. Although XNS was developed before the ISO/OSI Reference Model existed, it corresponds well to the OSI model, as you can see in the diagram at the top of the next page.

ISO/OSI Reference model

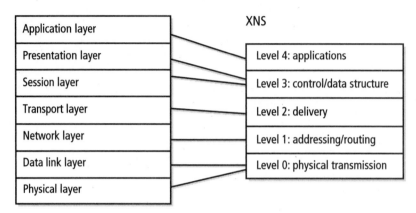

- Level 0, the lowest, corresponds to the physical and data link layers of the ISO/OSI model. Although XNS allows for these layers, it does not itself include protocols that run on those levels. Instead, it relies on the network itself to provide for data transmission in the form of Ethernet, Token Ring, or other architectures.

- Level 1, which corresponds to the OSI network layer, is represented by the XNS protocol known as IDP, or Internet Datagram Protocol. IDP addresses data packets and determines which transmission medium is to be used.

- Level 2, which corresponds to the transport layer, includes a number of protocols that, together, handle tasks such as sequencing data packets, checking for errors, retransmitting damaged packets, and controlling the rate of transmission. Among these protocols are the Routing Information Protocol (RIP), the Error Protocol, the Sequenced Packet Protocol (SPP), and the Packet Exchange Protocol (PEP).

- Level 3, which corresponds roughly to the session and presentation layers, includes protocols involved in structuring data and controlling interaction over the network. There is one protocol, the Courier Protocol, that runs at this level.

- Level 4, which corresponds to the application level, includes a number of application-related protocols, including the Printing

Protocol for printer services, the Filing Protocol for file access, and the Clearinghouse Protocol for network name services.

IPX/SPX

IPX/SPX, short for *Internetwork Packet Exchange/Sequenced Packet Exchange*, refers to two proprietary protocols based on XNS that were designed by Novell for its NetWare networks. IPX, which corresponds to the IP protocol in TCP/IP, runs on the network layer of the ISO/OSI Reference Model. SPX, which corresponds to the TCP protocol in TCP/IP, runs on the transport layer.

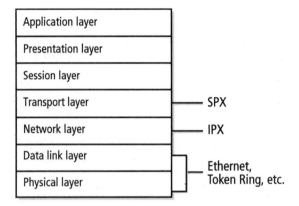

SPX, which runs at the layer above IPX, is responsible for ensuring that packets arrive correctly at their destination. As part of its job, SPX takes care of acknowledging delivery and controlling data flow. It relies on the services provided by IPX for actual routing within and between networks.

IPX is a connectionless protocol that takes care of addressing and routing data in the self-contained packets called datagrams. Because there is no direct connection between sender and receiver, the datagrams can be transmitted over different routes. To reach computer E, for example, datagram 1 might travel via a route from computer A to computer C to computer E, whereas datagram 2 might reach the same destination by shuttling from computer A to computer B to computer D and, finally, to computer E.

IPX/SPX is small, fast and, unlike NetBEUI, routable. A version of IPX/SPX called NWLink is shipped as part of Microsoft's Windows operating systems.

APPC

APPC, short for *Advanced Program to Program Communication*, is a set of IBM protocols that extend IBM's *SNA—Systems Network Architecture—* networking environment to enable applications on different computers to communicate directly, as peers, across the network, without having to rely on a mainframe host as intermediary. APPC is also known as *LU* (for *Logical Unit*) 6.2, in reference to the names (of sorts) that applications use to enable various devices to exchange information in the SNA environment.

In APPC, applications use the LU names to communicate with other systems and programs on the network. APPC operates on the transport level and is designed to allow interaction between network devices ranging from desktop workstations to host computers. It is available on numerous networking platforms, including Apple, UNIX, and Windows.

AppleTalk

AppleTalk refers to Apple Computer's local area networking hardware and software for Macintosh computers. The AppleTalk protocol stack is a set of protocols that corresponds to five of the seven layers in the ISO/OSI Reference Model, as shown in the following diagram:

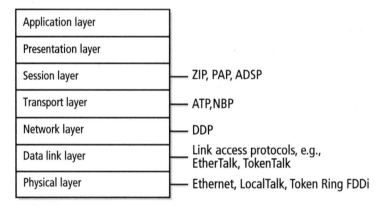

ISO/OSI Reference model

ISO/OSI layer	AppleTalk protocols
Application layer	
Presentation layer	
Session layer	ZIP, PAP, ADSP
Transport layer	ATP, NBP
Network layer	DDP
Data link layer	Link access protocols, e.g., EtherTalk, TokenTalk
Physical layer	Ethernet, LocalTalk, Token Ring FDDi

Data delivery in an AppleTalk network is based on a connectionless service (DDP described on the next page), even though the protocols at higher levels are connection-based in terms of establishing sessions between computers and ensuring reliable delivery. As you would expect, protocols in each layer provide services to the protocols above and below them. The following list briefly describes the protocols in each layer, starting from the top:

- The session layer includes:

    - The AppleTalk Data Stream Protocol (ADSP), which works with the Datagram Delivery Protocol (DDP, on the network layer) to allow computers to establish full two-way communication sessions

    - The Printer Access Protocol (PAP), which works with the AppleTalk Transaction Protocol (on the transport layer) to transmit commands from computers to servers

    - The Zone Information Protocol (ZIP), which works with the DDP to locate nodes on the network

- The transport layer includes the AppleTalk Transaction Protocol (ATP) and the Name-Binding Protocol (NBP), both of which interact with the DDP on the layer below. The ATP takes care of packet transport; the NBP takes responsibility for making the connections between devices and their network names.

- The DDP on the network layer is the protocol that takes care of network delivery, including datagram preparation and routing.

- The link access protocols at the data link layer are Apple's implementations for supporting the architectures at the physical layer. These protocols include support for EtherTalk (Apple's Ethernet), LocalTalk (a network based on AppleTalk cabling and configuration), TokenTalk (token ring), and FDDITalk (for FDDI, a high-speed ring network, described in Chapter 8, that is based on fiberoptic cabling and token passing).

OSI

The *OSI protocol stack* matches the seven layers of the OSI Reference Model. No surprise there.... What is rather surprising, given the reliance of all kinds of networking architectures on the OSI model, is the fact that the OSI protocols themselves take a back seat to other, better-known protocol stacks. The protocols are described in various numbered ISO documents, such as ISO 8473, which describes the Connectionless Network Protocol (CLNP) that operates at the network layer. The following list briefly lays out some of the OSI protocols and their positions in the OSI model:

- **Physical layer/Media access layer.** This is where you find protocols for various network architectures, such as Ethernet (IEEE 802.2) and Token Ring (IEEE 802.5).

- **Network layer.** At this layer, there are protocols for both connectionless (CLNP) and connection-oriented services. The latter is known as Packet-Level Protocol or Connection-Mode Network Protocol (CMNP).

- **Transport layer.** The transport layer is home to a number of protocols: TP0, TP1, TP2, and so on. These differ in complexity and provide such services as "packetizing" and reassembly, error recovery, and multiplexing.

- **Session layer.** The session layer protocol establishes and manages sessions, using a token to determine who can talk, and when.

- **Presentation layer.** The presentation layer protocol, which is responsible for ensuring that data is in a form everyone can understand and work with, takes the data from the session layer and passes it along to the application layer.

- **Application layer.** The application layer includes a number of application service elements, or ASEs, that are designed to provide applications with a means of communicating with the layers below. Among those that are commonly referenced are the Common Management Information Protocol (CMIP) for network management services, the File Transfer, Access, and Management (FTAM) ASE, which deals with file transfers, and the Message Handling Systems (MHS) ASE, which is involved with message transfer, such as e-mail.

DECnet

DECnet refers to both hardware and software products and to an associated protocol stack, designed by Digital Equipment Corporation (now part of Compaq Computer) for its Digital Network Architecture (DNA). DECnet was originally designed to enable Digital's computers to communicate with one another, but since its initial release in 1975, it was modified in a series of updates known as phases. The last of these updates, Phase V (five) brought DECnet in line with the OSI Reference Model.

The DECnet protocols support both the OSI protocols and Digital's own proprietary offerings. As would be expected, it supports the standard Ethernet, Token Ring, and other protocols that inhabit the physical and data link layers of the OSI model. To maintain compatibility with earlier phases, however, DECnet also supports a proprietary Digital protocol known as Digital Data Communications Messaging Protocol (DDCMP) at the data link layer.

Above this, at the network layer, DECnet includes support for both connectionless and connection-oriented services, including the ISO's CLNP and CMNP protocols, as well as for an earlier Phase IV DNA protocol called the DECnet Phase IV routing protocol.

Moving up in the OSI model, at the transport layer, DECnet includes support for both the ISO's TPx protocols and for its own Network Services Protocol, or NSP. And at the highest layers, DECnet includes support for both DNA and OSI sessions, presentations, and applications.

LAN Hardware and Software

Learning about networks in the abstract—how they're structured and how they're intended to work—is necessary to building a good foundation for dealing with their functional, real-world equivalents. But of course all the models and protocols and networking architectures in the world don't work without the two essentials that define a network: the hardware (the computers, hubs, adapters, and cabling) and the software (the operating systems, services, browsers, and other programs that make up the client and server networking software). These are the pieces that make up a working LAN, and they are what this chapter is all about.

Hardware

A network couldn't be a network without hardware. The idea itself would be ridiculous, and about as consequential as thinking of dinner as your appetite minus the food. No matter how willing the spirit, there's just no there *there.* An earlier chapter (Chapter 3) described the clients, servers, and server types that connect to one another on a network. But there are also the connectors to think about as well, the more or less invisible pieces that make up the network infrastructure.

One easy way to think about the roles played by various pieces of networking hardware is to compare what they do to the easy-to-understand, easy-to-picture situation people deal with every day: using telephones to communicate. The following table shows how the two compare.

Comparing Network Hardware to Phone Call Equivalents

Network hardware	Phone call equivalent
Clients and servers	People
Network adapters	Telephones
Network cabling	Phone lines
Hubs, routers, and switches	Call switching stations
Wireless transmissions	Cellular and satellite communications

Clients and Servers

At the top of the analogy in the preceding table are the people—or network nodes—that want to communicate. On a basic LAN these are, of course, the client PCs and the network servers. As with telephones, the clients and servers can make any of several different types of connections:

- One to one, as in client to server (phone call from Mary to Joe)

- One to many, as in client to server A, server B, and server C (phone call from Mary to Joe, Jim, and Jasmine)

- Many to one, as in server A, server B, and server C to client (phone calls to Mary from Dr. Bones, Dr. Tooth, and Dr. Vet)

To carry on with the analogy, in each of these cases the clients and the servers are comparable to people who want to communicate, and to do so they rely on their equivalent of the telephone: the network adapter, which is the hardware that actually sends and receives messages.

Adapters

Like telephones, network adapters, sometimes called LAN cards or network interface cards (NICs), are associated with a particular "number" (the computer's network address). They are also the pieces of hardware through which communication flows, and they connect one node with another via the network cabling, much as telephones connect people via telephone lines.

Physically, of course, network adapters are nothing like telephones. They are printed circuit boards. Although some come in the form of small credit card–like PCMCIA cards (which can slip into portable computers) and some are external units, typical network adapters are installed inside the computer—specifically, in one of the expansion slots inside the machine. Figure 6-1 shows what such a network adapter looks like.

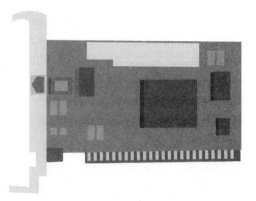

Figure 6-1.   *A network adapter, or NIC.*

Anatomy of an adapter

As you can see from the illustration, the adapter is a rectangular card with comb-like extensions along the bottom. As with other, similar circuit boards, these are the connectors that plug into an expansion slot to link the board with the computer's internal bus, its data highway.

The portion of the card that shows through the back of the computer is equipped with a port, to which the network cable connects. Most current network adapters are based on PCI (Peripheral Component Interconnect) and PNP (Plug and Play) technologies that make installation a simple matter: plug the card into an expansion slot, and then rely on software to detect and configure the card for use. Older cards, however, might include small toggles known as *DIP* (*Dual Inline Package*) *switches* for configuring the card to work with the computer and the network. The network adapter might also include the *transceiver* (*transmitter/receiver*)—the device responsible for transmitting and receiving signals and for converting the computer's parallel signals to serial form and vice versa.

How an adapter works

The chips and circuits on the board itself are, obviously, the parts of the adapter that access the physical medium and that transmit and receive data packages. There are many different adapters from different manufacturers, and each is designed in such a way that it works with a particular type of network at the lowest levels of the reference model (OSI, TCP/IP, or whatever as described in Chapter 4). That is, a network adapter designed to work with an Ethernet network will not transmit or receive over a Token Ring network because it doesn't understand the details of transmission, frame size and organization, and so on. An Ethernet card from one manufacturer can, however, communicate with Ethernet cards from other manufacturers. An adapter card's pickiness is in the type of network it works with and has nothing to do with the manufacturer of the cards it communicates with.

Small though it is—about the size of a paperback book—the adapter serves its computer in ways that seem to combine electronic miracle worker with traffic cop. For one thing, even though it might be constantly listening to the network for messages sent its way, the adapter not only works independently of the computer's processor; it also communicates with other adapters when transmitting and receiving, to ensure that both sender and receiver agree on the timing, packet size, speed, and other parameters needed for a successful transmission. Further, it is the network adapter that checks for errors in transmission and controls the data flow to ensure that the receiving computer isn't overwhelmed by too much incoming data at one time.

Even though networks generally transmit information faster than the processor can handle it, it's also the adapter that ensures information isn't lost. When it receives a transmission addressed to its computer, the adapter copies the received data into a portion of memory known as the *buffer*. So that the information doesn't just sit there, the adapter also notifies the processor of the arrival by sending it an *interrupt*, a tug-on-the-sleeve signal indicating that the transmission is in the buffer, in usable form, ready and waiting to be acted upon.

Conversely, when the computer has information to be transmitted, the processor signals the adapter and then lets the adapter take over the job of fetching the information from memory, packaging the information appropriately for the network's architecture, signaling the receiving adapter that a transmission is about to be sent, converting the data to a serial bit stream, and actually moving the data onto the network. When the transmission is complete, the adapter once again notifies the processor with an interrupt. And all this time, the processor can continue handling whatever other tasks are in progress or waiting to keep it occupied.

The whole process is really quite amazing, especially when you consider the speed at which it all takes place.

Adapter Drivers

Network adapters, capable devices that they are, are still hardware. In order to work properly with the network, they must rely on software drivers to help them work with the operating systems and network protocols involved.

In terms of drivers themselves, it's important to note that there are many different kinds of devices available for open systems, such as "Wintel" (Windows/Intel-based) machines, that are designed to work with add-ons from numerous manufacturers. Although these devices can be assigned to categories, such as printers, disk drives, pointing devices, and modems, each individual device generally marches to the beat of its own internal drum. It has its own capabilities, hardware settings, and way of working. It's the job of the device driver to "know" and work with these capabilities, as well as those of the operating systems and (in the case of network adapters) the protocols with which they run. As a result, hardware manufacturers write the drivers for their devices, tailoring the drivers both for optimum device performance and for the system(s) they want the device to work with.

NDIS and ODI

Where network adapters are concerned, two standards have been developed to help simplify the task of creating drivers to support different operating systems and the various—sometimes proprietary—protocols used on networks. One of these standards, *NDIS* (*Network Device Interface Specification*), was developed by Microsoft and 3Com. The other, *ODI* (*Open Data-Link Interface*), was developed by Novell and Apple. Both are software interfaces that define a common boundary between the network adapter and higher-level protocols. By effectively providing the adapter and the protocols with a common linkage point, these standards allow adapter drivers written to their specifications to support more than one protocol on the same card, as shown in Figure 6-2. In a sense, NDIS and ODI provide network adapters and protocol stacks with something of a generic, mutually understandable set of conventions—somewhat comparable to the conventions used in creating international symbols that can be understood by all travelers, regardless of their native language.

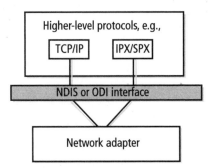

Figure 6-2. *NDIS and ODI serve as common boundaries that enable network adapters to support multiple protocol stacks.*

Connectors

Of course, a client computer (or a server), even when equipped with a network adapter, is still an island unto its networking self without a means of physically plugging in to the network. That job is done by several types of *connectors* that link one piece of the network with another to form an unbroken connection through which data can be cleanly transmitted.

Connectors in general

Basically, connectors serve two distinct purposes in a network: They connect different segments of cable, and they connect computers, via their network adapters, to the network. Anyone who has ever plugged a computer and some peripheral devices together (or even looked at the back of a working computer) can verify that connectors come in an array of shapes and sizes. There are keyboard connectors, mouse connectors, and joystick connectors. There are serial and parallel connectors for printers, modems, and other devices. There are connectors for monitors and other connectors for speakers. There are even connectors that help other connectors connect.

The connectors used on a network are not that much different. They, too, come in an assortment of shapes and sizes. In addition, like most other connectors both on and off the network, they come in two varieties, often referred to as male and female for, well, rather obvious biological reasons. *Male* connectors, also known as *plugs*, do the connecting. *Female* connectors, also called *jacks* or *sockets*, do the receiving. Since male-to-male and female-to-female connections are not possible, there are also connectors known as *gender changers* that, when needed, can be used to connect male to male or female to female.

In terms of shape, network connectors can be barrel-shaped (straight), Y-shaped, T-shaped, or angled in a shape known as an elbow. Each of these shapes serves a different purpose. Barrel connectors, for example, are used to connect two pieces of cable to create a longer segment. Y-shaped connectors are used to "funnel" two inputs into one—for example, in carrying two signals to a single device for multiplexing. T-shaped connectors attach devices, such as network adapters, to segments of cable. And elbow-shaped connectors are used to connect segments of cable going in different directions, as in around a corner.

Network connectors are also specific to certain types of cabling. Telephone-like *RJ-45* jacks, for example, are used with twisted pair Ethernet networks, whereas rounded *BNC* connectors are used with thin Ethernet networks running on coaxial cable. More about this in the next section.

Adapter to cable connectors

Unlike some aspects of networking, such as protocol stacks, adapter to cable connectors are easy to understand, because there are only three basic kinds, all very different in appearance. And, as already mentioned, each of these connectors is associated with a particular type of cabling and, thus, with a particular type of network.

For flexibility, a single network adapter can come with two or even all three types of connectors, although only one type can be used at a time to connect to the network. The choice of which connector to use is made either manually, as in flipping DIP switches, or through software-based options as is the case with Plug-and-Play–based PCI adapters.

RJ-45

The type of connector known as RJ-45 is the one most likely to look familiar. It is used with unshielded twisted pair wiring and looks very much like the plug (known as RJ-11) at the end of your telephone cable, only a little bigger because it contains eight wires as opposed to the RJ-11's four wires. Both plugs work in the same way: stick them into the socket until the small clip on one side locks into place, and off you go. RJ-45 connectors are used on Ethernet and 100 Mbps networks.

Figure 6-3 shows both an RJ-45 connector and the socket into which it fits.

Figure 6-3.   *RJ-45 connector and socket.*

BNC

This one's fun—or at least the origin of its name is. Depending on your source, the letters in this connector's name stand for:

- Bayonet Neill Concelman (Neill Concelman was the inventor of the connector)

- Bayonet Navy Connector

- British Naval Connector (after the service that developed it for communications during World War II)

- Bayonet Nut Connector

- Baby N-Connector

- Bayonet Nut Coupling

But what is all that about bayonets in the name? This is a connector, not a weapon. Well, essentially, a bayonet connector is a two-part, plug and socket contraption in which some type of connection physically locks the two together. In the case of a BNC connector (illustrated in Figure 6-4), the plug is a small, round, hollow device containing a small central pin inside a metal tube. The pin and the tube fit into the socket, and when the plug is turned 90 degrees, the two form a locked connection. T-shaped BNC connectors (shown in Figure 6-5) are used to connect coaxial cable to network adapters; barrel-shaped BNC connectors (also shown in Figure 6-5) are used to connect segments of coaxial cable.

BNC connectors are used on thin Ethernet networks. If you have cable television, you've seen a BNC connector.

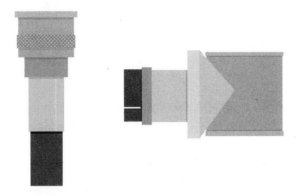

Figure 6-4. *Plug and socket for a BNC connector on a network adapter.*

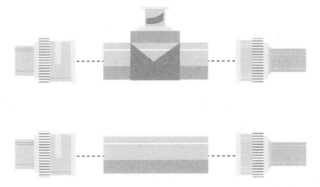

Figure 6-5. *BNC T connector and barrel connector.*

15-pin AUI

The third type of connector found on network adapters goes by the name of 15-pin AUI, or Attachment Unit Interface. Despite the somewhat ungainly name, however, it is the most recognizably "computerish" connector of the three because it looks very much like the rectangular, pin-studded connectors used on joysticks and other such devices. Also known as a *DB-15*

(Data Bus, 15-pin) connector or a *DIX* connector (after its developers, Digital, Intel, and Xerox), the AUI is used to connect network adapters to a thick Ethernet cable. Figure 6-6 shows an AUI connector.

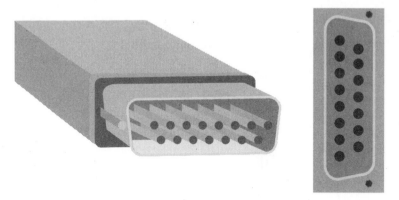

Figure 6-6. *15-pin AUI connector.*

Cables

Cables make up a wild and woolly networking topic filled with grades and standards and categories and specifications. Luckily, however, all these varied cables fall into three main categories whose names, at least, are already familiar to you. They are twisted pair and coaxial, both of which conduct signals in electrical form, and fiberoptic, which is a high-speed type of cable that uses light as the transmission medium.

At first glance, cables would seem to be fairly straightforward. After all, the electrical kind at least are, at heart, strands of wire enclosed in some type of protective covering. All, however, is not quite that simple. For instance, cables are used in many different environments, from hospitals to factories to high-tech offices. And they are used with many different types of devices, from X-ray machines and heart monitors to production-line tools that handle heavy equipment to nice, genteel computers tapping into a nice, genteel network.

In the course of doing their jobs, the cables used in these highly variable situations must deal with certain stresses, environmental factors (cold, heat, fire, water), interference from other signals, and so on. To ensure that particular types of cables meet or exceed the minimum requirements for the work that they do, cables are tested and categorized according to certain standards. Where electrical matters are concerned, one of the leading standards bodies in the United States is the Underwriters Laboratories (familiar to buyers of all kinds of electrical equipment). Another is the National Fire Protection Agency, which has developed a set of safety specifications known as the National Electric Code.

That said, herewith is a closer look at the main cable "families"—twisted pair, coaxial, and fiberoptic—and at some of the distinctions among cables within each type.

Twisted pair

Twisted pair cabling is, in one common incarnation, telephone wire—not the thin, flat, flexible cable you handle whenever you plug a telephone into the wall jack, but the cabling running inside the walls and connecting your wall telephone to the phone company. This same type of wiring, however, is also common in the cables used in Ethernet LANs.

At heart, twisted-pair wiring consists of two insulated strands of thin (1 millimeter) copper wire twisted together. Why the twisting? Because the simple act of twisting the wires shields them from interference, known as *crosstalk*, and from the resulting signal distortion generated by other nearby pairs of wires, as well as from sources of electromagnetic and radio frequency interference, such as motors and transformers. The number of twists in the wire is related to the cable's ability to withstand such interference. The twisting itself resembles what you see in a cinnamon twist donut, as shown in Figure 6-7.

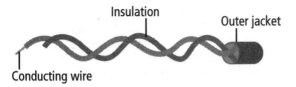

Figure 6-7.   *Twisting in a two-wire, twisted-pair cable.*

Twisted pair wiring can consist of just a single pair of wires like those shown in Figure 6-7, but it's common for two, four, or more such pairs to be bundled together and enclosed in a protective (and in some cases fireproof) jacket to form a thicker cable.

Although twisted pair wiring is simple enough to define and picture, it becomes a little more complex when you begin to look at the different forms in which it is available. To begin with, twisted-pair cabling comes as both *unshielded twisted pair* (*UTP*) and as *shielded twisted pair* (*STP*). Of the two, unshielded twisted pair is the more common. It is, in fact, the type of cable used in IEEE 10BaseT Ethernet LANs. Despite its name, unshielded twisted pair cabling is not naked. The "unshielded" part of the name simply means that the wire pairs are not further protected by a foil-coated plastic wrapper, as they are in shielded twisted pair (shown in Figure 6-8).

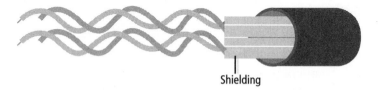

Shielding

Figure 6-8. *Shielded twisted pair wiring has an extra protective sheath around each pair of wires.*

Unshielded twisted pair is less expensive than shielded twisted pair and, being less bulky, is also easier to work with. It is, however, limited to segments no longer than 100 meters and generally does not transmit as fast as its shielded relative.

Unshielded twisted pair cabling comes in different grades that are assigned to five standards categories created by the Electronic Industries Association and the Telecommunications Industries Association. These categories, referred to as the EIA/TIA categories, are as follows:

- Category 1 covers voice-grade UTP—that is, unshielded twisted pair suitable for carrying voice, but not data. This is typical telephone cable.

- Category 2 covers data-grade UTP that transmits at up to 4 Mbps. This type of cable is used in some ring topologies.

- Category 3 covers data-grade UTP that transmits at up to 10 Mbps. This is the cable required for 10BaseT Ethernet.

- Category 4 covers data-grade UTP that transmits at up to 16 Mbps. This is used in some Token Ring networks.

- Category 5 covers data-grade UTP that transmits at up to 100 Mbps. This is the type of cable required for 100BaseX Ethernet based on twisted pair wiring.

Note that the cables in all but Category 1 are data-grade.

Coaxial

Coaxial cable, often called coax ("co-ax"), is the round, flexible cabling familiar to anyone with a cable box and cable television. This same type of cabling is also widely used in networking because it is inexpensive, stable, lightweight, and easy to work with.

If you "dissect" a piece of coaxial cabling, you find at least four separate elements, as shown in Figure 6-9. In the center, there is a copper wire, the signal conductor. Encasing this wire is a layer of nonconducting insulation (called the *dielectric*) made of PVC or Teflon. Outside the insulation, forming a protective sleeve around the conducting wire and its insulation, is another layer made of a braided mesh of copper or aluminum. This layer protects the transmitted signal from the electromagnetic interference known as *noise* that can distort the transmitted signal. Finally, outside the braided sleeve is an outer shield, or jacket, made of either PVC or a fire-resistant material such as Teflon.

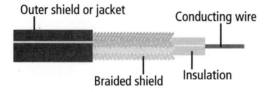

Figure 6-9. *The four basic components in coaxial cable.*

In addition to these main components, a coaxial cable can also include one or more nonconducting foil layers outside the insulation. If there is one layer of foil, the cable is referred to as dual shielded. If there are two foil layers sandwiched between two layers of braided shielding, the cable is referred to as quad shielded.

Like twisted pair wiring, coaxial cable comes in various forms. In terms of networking, the best known are the ones used for thin and thick Ethernet cabling:

- Thin Ethernet, or thin wire Ethernet, is based on the $^3/_8$-inch coaxial cabling known as RG-58. This thinnet cabling can carry a signal for about 185 meters before the signal begins to degrade (become *attenuated*).

- Thick Ethernet is based on less flexible coaxial cabling, about ½-inch thick. Also known as RG-8, thicknet cabling can carry signals farther than thinnet cabling—about 500 meters—and thus is often used as the backbone connecting thin Ethernet LANs.

In addition to the thin/thick Ethernet and RG designations, coaxial cable is categorized according to how it is constructed. Twinaxial cable, for example, contains two insulated signal wires. Triaxial cable contains an extra, non-conducting, shield between the insulation and the braided metal shield.

Coaxial cable is also graded according to its resistance to fire. PVC, or nonplenum coaxial cable, is the most common form used. There is, however, a more expensive, less flexible, fire-resistant grade known as plenum cabling (named after the space commonly found in office buildings between the ceiling and the floor above it). Plenum cabling must be certified to have a jacket that produces minimal smoke and fumes in case of fire.

Fiberoptic

Fiberoptic cabling or optical fiber, as it's also known in a little bit of name reversal, is nifty stuff. Unlike the copper-based twisted pair and coaxial cabling, fiberoptic cable has nothing to do with conducting electricity. Instead, it carries information in the form of light, as pulses corresponding to the digital 1s and 0s representing the information being transmitted. The light comes from a transmitter—ideally one using a laser as the light source—and is converted back to computer-readable information by a light-sensitive receiver. The cable itself acts as a pipe or a funnel, guiding the light from source to destination.

Physically, fiberoptic cabling consists of three layers called the core, the cladding, and the outer coat, or jacket, all of which are shown in Figure 6-10. The light-conducting core is a clear glass fiber a mere 8 to 10 microns thick, or roughly 1/25th the diameter of a human hair. Surrounding this core is a layer known as the cladding, which is also glass but with refractive (light-deflecting) properties that essentially turn it into a mirror that keeps the light signal trapped inside the core, bounding along both in straight lines and around corners. Outside the core and the cladding, which are made as a single piece of glass, is an outer plastic or plastic-like (acrylate) coat, or jacket.

Figure 6-10.   *The components of a fiberoptic cable.*

A form of fiberoptic cable known as POF (plastic optical fiber) uses plastic rather than glass for the core and cladding but otherwise has similar optical properties. POF is less expensive, easier to handle, and less fragile than the glass-based optical fiber, but it transmits signals for shorter distances.

Either type (glass or plastic) of fiberoptic cabling comes in two varieties: single mode and multimode. Single mode, the type of fiber described above, is a cable with a single fiber at its core. Multimode fiber consists of bundles of glass fibers forming a core anywhere from 50 to 100 microns thick. In multimode cable, each fiber is capable of carrying a separate signal.

Although fiberoptic cables themselves are less expensive than their copper-based equivalents, this type of network cabling is considered quite expensive overall because of costs related to connectors, repeaters (for cleaning and boosting the signal), adapters, installation equipment, and so on.

Fiberoptic cabling offers the following advantages:

- **Bandwidth.** Fiberoptic cabling offers greater bandwidth than copper-based cabling, in part because different wavelengths (colors) of light can be used to carry signals through the core at the same time.

- **Speed.** Typical transmission rates are in the 100 Mbps range. Fiberoptic cabling has, however, been shown to transmit a signal cleanly over thousands of miles at the rate of 1 Gbps (gigabit, or roughly, one billion bits, per second), and at speeds in excess of 2 Gbps over shorter distances.

- **Signal integrity.** Immunity to electrical interference is higher with fiberoptic cabling because the transmission medium is light, rather than electricity.

- **Security.** The light signal cannot be "hacked" by bad guys wanting to intercept or steal the data.

Because of its greater bandwidth and speed, and because the cabling can transmit a signal for long distances without error and without the need for refreshing and boosting, fiberoptic cable is often used as the backbone cabling connecting LANs in different locations.

Collection Centers and Shuttle Services

In addition to their normal complements of nodes, adapters, cables, and connectors, LANs also rely on devices that connect and in some cases route traffic between nodes and between LAN segments (workgroups, for example) that tie into larger LANs.

To go back to the telephone-conversation analogy at the beginning of the chapter, these devices correspond to the switching stations that route calls between parties. Like the switching stations, they are needed to connect caller A with recipient B. The two devices described here, hubs and switches, are comparable to the telephone switching technology that handles local calls. Similar devices on WANs—routers, bridges, and repeaters, described in the next chapter—are more analogous to the technologies used in long-distance telephone calling.

Hubs

Hubs are the distinguishing feature of star-based topologies. They are, in fact, characteristic of two widely used networks: 10BaseT Ethernet and Token Ring. As mentioned in the last chapter, a 10BaseT network is based on a star topology, and Token Ring is based on a star-wired ring. In an Ethernet network, the hub is just called the hub. In a Token Ring network, however, the hub is referred to as the MAU (multiple access unit).

In either type of network, the hub is central to connecting nodes and enabling them to communicate. Sitting like a spider in the center of its web, the hub forms the wiring center of the star. Each node participates in the LAN through a connection to the hub, and each node communicates with others on the LAN by means of messages transmitted through the hub. Although a typical hub and a MAU access the network differently, both collect wiring from multiple nodes in one place.

Externally, a hub is equipped with a number of ports (connectors) to which nodes and other network devices connect. As messages are transmitted by the various nodes connected to the hub, the hub ensures that the messages are copied to all of its ports, so the messages are broadcast to all attached nodes.

Beyond this, however, hubs (like most things network-related) come in different varieties. There are intelligent hubs, active hubs, passive hubs, modular hubs, and hubs that can stand alone or be stacked on (and linked to) one another. The following list describes the most common types of hubs:

■ Intelligent, or manageable, hubs are those that offer some control over the nodes connected to them. Such hubs can, for example, allow each port to be individually controlled—enabled, disabled, and managed—by the network administrator. Some intelligent hubs can also track network activities, including the number of packets they transfer and the occurrence of errors within those packets.

■ Standalone hubs are single units external to the computers they are connected to. These are what you might consider "typical" hubs, the kind illustrated in this book and elsewhere as the connecting "box" in star-shaped topologies. Standalone hubs are generally not manageable, but they often have the ability to be linked to other hubs.

■ Modular hubs are manageable hubs equipped with card slots, each of which holds the equivalent of a standalone hub. These hubs make networks easy to expand. Some of these hubs are also distinctive in being able to support more than one network type, such as both Ethernet and Token Ring.

In addition, ARCnet networks are characterized by two different types of hubs, active and passive:

- Active hubs, also called *multiport repeaters*, both pass messages along and also clean up the signal by boosting (strengthening) it and adjusting the timing. On ARCnet networks, active hubs connect to nodes, passive hubs, or other active hubs.

- In contrast, passive hubs simply pass messages for the nodes connected to them, without affecting the messages in any way. On ARCnet networks, passive hubs connect either to nodes or to active hubs, never to one another.

Switches

Instead of (or in combination with) hubs, LANs are also coming to rely on devices called *switches* to transmit messages. These devices operate on the data link layer of the ISO/OSI Reference Model—specifically, at the MAC sublayer. Unlike hubs, which "broadcast" messages to all ports regardless of the node to which they are actually addressed, switches rely on internal address tables to determine where to route packets so that they travel directly from the sender to the port associated the recipient. Although this distinction might not sound particular noteworthy on the surface, it is the means by which switches can speed up network performance.

Consider, for example, a 10 Mbps network. If the network relies on hubs for message transfer, the nodes are using a *shared medium* (the network bandwidth) because all messages are sent to all ports, and so all the nodes connected to the ports on the hub share in the total bandwidth. Thus, when a packet is sent from node A to node C, the hub copies the packet to the ports belonging to nodes B and D as well. In contrast, a switch on the same network would give each node the perception of a private LAN, in that a packet sent from A to C would travel directly between the two and thus give the two nodes the full bandwidth of the network.

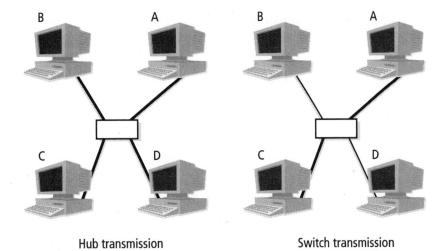

Hub transmission   Switch transmission

Figure 6-11.   *The dark lines show how transmissions are broadcast to all nodes by a hub, but routed directly between sender and receiver by a switch, effectively giving the switched nodes a private LAN when they communicate.*

In transferring packets, switches work in either of two ways known as *cut through* and *store and forward*:

- A cut-through switch, when it receives a transmission frame, simply reads the address in the frame header and then immediately routes the frame to the destination port associated with the recipient.

- A store-and-forward switch, in contrast, has more smarts. It waits until the entire frame is received and then checks for errors before sending the frame on to its destination port. In other words, it *stores* the frame momentarily and then *forwards* it to the appropriate destination.

Switches can support multiple transmissions at the same time, and the "nodes" connected to them can be single workstations, servers, or even entire LAN segments. In the last instance, in which they connect whole LANs, the switches serve as a means of dividing a large, busy network into smaller, less congested segments that can still be linked together when necessary. In such a situation, the switch or switches perform a function similar to that of a bridge (described in the next chapter), which transfers packets between the networks that form a large LAN or a WAN.

145

Wireless Transmissions

All of the LAN components described so far relate to networks that are physically cabled together. There are, however, networks using wireless technologies based on infrared, radio, and laser devices, all of which add mobility to the networking equation. *Wireless LANs*, or *WLANs*, are based on the IEEE 802.11 specification, which was described in the last chapter. The heart of a wireless LAN, according to the 802.11 specification, is a "node" known as a *station*. Because wireless stations can be—indeed, often are—mobile units, they are referred to as a *Basic Service Set*, or *BSS*, when two or more link up to communicate.

Wireless networking can be either permanent or temporary. For example, in a warehouse or building lobby, if two mobile stations are in the same range and are used to communicate with one another, they form a temporary network of two—they have access to each other, but are not connected to a wired network. In such a situation, the stations are said to form a peer-to-peer, or *ad-hoc network*.

In other cases, however, mobile or non-mobile stations can be part of a more permanent network that includes the use of resources stored on a server somewhere on an Ethernet or other wired network. In such situations, the wireless technology is used to extend, rather than replace, the wired LAN. In order to gain access to the wired network, the stations depend on transceivers (transmitter/receivers) called *access points* that are cabled to the wired network and thus provide the needed link between wired and wireless. Each access point covers a range (known as a cell) of about 160 meters (500 feet) indoors and about 300 meters (1000 feet) outdoors. In large areas, access points can be located so that their ranges overlap and provide continuous coverage for mobile stations.

Although a wireless network can rely on microwave or laser transmissions, the medium is usually either infrared or radio, and the stations in the network—laptops, handheld units, desktop computers, and even devices such as printers—are equipped with either built-in or installed wireless adapters. Here are the basic transmission media, along with their advantages and disadvantages:

- **Infrared light.** This medium provides rapid transmission (typically 10 Mbps) but is subject to interference from other light sources and cannot penetrate solid or opaque objects (walls, drapes, and so on). If an infrared signal is sent in one direction, it can transmit more than a mile outdoors. If the signal is bounced off walls, floors, and other objects, it has a broader scope but is limited in range to about 30 meters (100 feet).

- **Narrowband radio.** This is similar to broadcast radio in that it uses a particular frequency for transmission. Different frequencies can be assigned to different stations, and the transmissions can cover about 5000 meters. One significant drawback of narrowband radio, however, is that it must be licensed from the Federal Communications Commission.

- **Spread-spectrum radio.** This is the type of radio described in the last chapter, where transmissions are carried on a range of frequencies and made secure either through frequency hopping technology or direct sequence spread spectrum technology. In either case, this form of transmission is reliable and secure. (It was developed by the U.S. military.) Spread-spectrum radio is widely used in wireless networks. It does not need to be licensed, but it is not a particularly fast medium (about 250 Kbps, or kilobits per second).

Software

Ah, software. What would a network be without software? That's a rhetorical question, obviously, as the answer is "nowhere." Just as a PC is an inert collection of metal, plastic, chips, and cords without software, so a network without networking software is a collection of nonfunctioning servers, clients, adapters, cables, and connectors.

Such software comes from a number of sources. Microsoft, with its *Windows NT/2000 Server* and *BackOffice*, is one such source. Novell, with its *NetWare* operating system, is another. Others that spring immediately to mind include Artisoft's *LANtastic* software for connecting a mix of Windows-based and MS-DOS–based computers; Banyan's *VINES* networking environment; the various "flavors" of *UNIX* provided by different vendors; the open source, UNIX-like *Linux* operating system supported by companies like Red Hat; and Apple's *AppleTalk* for Macintosh networks.

N OTE This part of the chapter is partial to Microsoft's Windows NT/2000 Server and BackOffice (for some pretty evident reasons, not least of which are a fondness for and familiarity with the products). Although NT/2000 Server (primarily version 4) and BackOffice components are described briefly to provide you with some idea of the types of services required of server-based software, the book itself will not dig into the ins and outs of any of these products. Far better sources are available that deal specifically with the features and capabilities of each of these different types of networking software, besides offering step-by-step instructions in their use.

Network Operating Systems

At the heart of a functioning network there is, of course, the network operating system, or NOS. This is the software that ties everything and everyone together. Without a NOS, client machines cannot access the network. Without a NOS, servers cannot serve. Without a NOS, there is no network.

No matter which operating system a network relies on, all NOS provide certain categories of service. They must be able to:

■ Provide clients with access to network resources, including files and peripheral devices, such as printers and fax machines

■ Coordinate the activities of the various nodes and devices on the network, to ensure that communication takes place when and as required

■ Ensure the security of users, data, and devices on the network

As mentioned in an earlier chapter, NOS are also "industrial-strength" operating systems in that they must be reliable, fault-tolerant, and able to recover quickly when something goes wrong. As part of their duties, they might also be required to support multiple processors, clusters of disk drives, and data security features such as disk striping and mirroring.

In addition to these basic (though certainly not simple) tasks, network operating systems such as Microsoft's Windows NT/2000 Server have also grown to match new or evolving approaches to computing. For example, both the Internet explosion and the growth of distributed computing have affected the ways in which people use and rely on networks, and, by extension, have influenced the development of both Windows NT and, even more, Windows 2000.

The Internet, even though it is global in scope, has affected local area and wide area networks through the increasing use of Internet-related technologies, including browsers and the HTML page markup language, that enable people to access and view both local and network resources. The Internet, Internet protocols, and Internet technologies are also the forces behind the growing use of private intranets and semi-private extranets based on existing LANs.

Similarly, distributed applications are changing the way networks work. Whereas network-related computing was once clearly separable into client-based processing (front end) and server-based processing (back end), applications are now being created in which different computers carry out different tasks while contributing to the same overall goal. Typically, for example, a distributed application relies on one computer for the presentation of information, a second computer to apply the rules (business logic) that govern the manipulation of that information, and a third computer to hold the actual data that is manipulated and presented by the other two computers.

To illustrate how developments such as these are changing the face of networking, here is a list of the Internet, multimedia, and transaction-based services now offered in Windows NT Server:

- **File and print services.** (These are "traditional," but they are nonetheless present, as they are in other network operating systems.)

- **Web services.** These are managed by Microsoft Internet Information Server, which supports document sharing on both the Internet and within a company's intranet.

- **Application services.** These are related to distributing computing and are supported by Microsoft Transaction Server (for services such as application development, transaction security, and database access) and by Microsoft Message Queue Server (for enabling applications to communicate asynchronously and without error).

- **Security services.** These are related to both internal (resource) security and to Web security.

- **Communication services.** These are related to networked communications, including Internet access. Included in this category are features such as Microsoft Proxy Server, which acts as a barrier between internal users and Internet sites, and support for *virtual private networks*, or *VPNs*, which enable secure LAN-to-LAN or telecommuter-to-LAN communications over the Internet.

And, of course, these and other services are supported—indeed, extended—in Windows 2000, especially in the powerful Windows 2000 Datacenter Server designed to support such demanding work as scientific analysis, online transaction processing, and data warehousing.

All in all, the job of a network operating system is no small task, especially in large networks consisting of many hundreds or thousands of interconnected computers. That's especially the case when you consider that, at lower (code-based) levels, the NOS must also support mechanisms known as interprocess communications, or IPCs, that enable processes (roughly, applications) to communicate with one another—for example, mechanisms that enable an application on a client computer to request data from an application stored on a server, or mechanisms that enable multiple computers to work jointly on a single task, such as a mathematical calculation.

These IPC mechanisms lie squarely in the programmer's domain and are represented by such programming devices as named pipes, remote procedure calls (RPCs), and Microsoft's Distributed Component Object Model (DCOM), all of which facilitate process-to-process communication that is unseen by and undemanding of the user's intervention. Although such esoteric (and complex) matters are not the concern of a network administrator, it's good to know that they exist, the better to appreciate the software magic underlying such a seemingly simple act as requesting sales figures stored on a network server.

Administrative Tools

As part of day-to-day operations, networking software—in some cases, the operating system itself and in other cases, various tools and utilities—must be able to help with a number of administrative and management tasks, including:

- Managing users, which involves creating and deleting the network accounts through which authorized users gain access to the network, protecting passwords, and providing different levels of access for individuals

- Performance monitoring, which helps in finding bottlenecks, improving performance, and planning for the future

- Security of the network and the data stored on it

Management

Network management can be divided into three categories: management of access for authorized users, management of users and resources on the network, and management of the network itself.

User access   Each person authorized to use a particular network gains access to the network through an *account*. The account is created by the network administrator and serves to identify the individual to the network through a *username* and a secret *password*. The username is freely available to everyone else on the network and serves as the person's unique network ID. The password is, of course, the means by which the network—and only the network—verifies that the person *logging on* to the network is actually the individual associated with the username being entered.

All networks provide administrators with the means for not only creating user accounts but also inactivating those that are no longer needed. In Windows NT/2000 Server, for example, the process of adding an account for a new user is very simple—it boils down to entering information in a single dialog box:

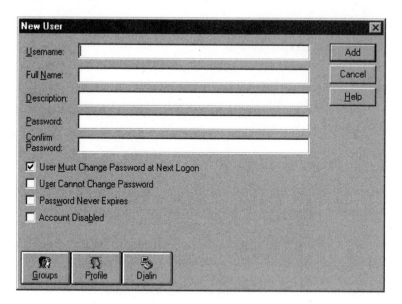

User and resource management To make servers, users, and data easily accessible and to provide security for both the network as a whole and the resources it offers, networking software tools—specifically, networking operating systems—also rely on built-in methods for management and administration of network users and network resources.

One such method, implemented in operating systems such as NetWare and Windows NT Server, is based on a feature known as *directory services*, which essentially indexes the users and resources on a network and, by serving as a central "phone book" of names and addresses, makes the network easier to administer. From the user's point of view, directory services are invaluable in eliminating the need to log on to multiple servers or remember multiple passwords. Directory services, in brief, are designed to simplify the network administration and management.

Another management approach, which is a feature of the server version of the Windows NT operating system, is the concept of *domains*. To Windows NT, a domain is a group of servers that share the same users and security information, all of which is stored in a directory services database stored on a master server known as the *domain controller*. Through domains,

Windows NT makes it possible for network administrators to organ-ize and ensure the security of a large or far-flung network.

Domains and directory services, by the way, work somewhat differently in Windows 2000. Although Windows 2000 will continue to rely on do-mains, it also implements a feature known as Active Directory. Active Di-rectory is based on Internet technologies and, unlike NT's current directory services, supports a hierarchical "tree of trees" that allows for more user accounts and also gives applications a standard means of ac-cessing components stored on remote servers.

The network itself Managing the entire network means managing the hardware and software that make up the network. What is there about all this to manage? There is hardware to track, software to track, applications to share out on servers, software to install or configure, and problems to diagnose, both on the network and on client computers connected to the network.

Various utilities are available to help with these tasks. Indeed, certain products such as the diskless network computer were even conceived with the goals of simplifying network administration and lowering the cost of managing client computers by making servers the source of both applications and data storage.

Another solution, part of Microsoft's *BackOffice* suite, is provided by a service called *Systems Management Server*, or *SMS*. SMS provides for centralized network management in several ways:

- It finds out about the computers on the network—their CPU, RAM, disk size, and so on—and stores that information in a central database.

- It does the same for software, which it can also install, configure, and upgrade.

- It can perform troubleshooting and diagnostic routines to help maintain the health of the network and its clients.

Monitoring
Whereas products such as SMS help keep track of network and client hardware and software, other types of tools built into most network oper-ating systems help monitor network performance and use.

In the Windows NT/2000 Server environment, network monitoring is performed by two utilities. One, called Network Monitor, enables the network administrator to keep tabs on the actual data streams moving to and from the server—number of frames, number of bytes, percent of buffer used, and so on.

The other, called Performance Monitor, enables a network administrator to keep track of performance data related to processors, hard disks, memory use, and the way the network is being used. With Performance Monitor, a network administrator can determine how the network normally performs, as well as find bottlenecks and keep track of usage trends that might indicate future problems or slowdowns.

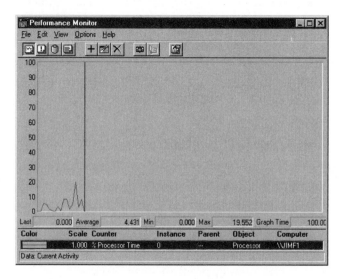

On networks that rely on the UNIX operating system, but increasingly also on PC-based networks, management software is based on a design known as *Simple Network Management Protocol*, or *SNMP*. SNMP was developed in the 1980s and has become widely used primarily because it is (as the name says) simple to implement. Because it is so popular, SNMP is also supported by numerous makers of network hardware. SNMP works through messages that can be used by a management program to gather statistical information about network devices, their status (connected or not connected), and the network traffic. SNMP, though popular, is considered to be at something of a disadvantage for network monitoring because of its very simplicity. Current networks require more detailed information than SNMP was designed to provide.

Other Server Software

In addition to the network operating system, which is essentially the conduit through which all information flows, network servers also run various types of software designed to handle various types of network-based activities related to interaction and communication. One of the most widespread types of such software is commonly lumped into the category referred to as *groupware*—software for groups of people who want or need to interact via their computers. Other server-based software is designed to help networks cope with Internet access, large-scale databases, intranets, electronic commerce setups, and so on. By way of example, the following list provides a look at various task-related services provided by network servers through the components of Microsoft's BackOffice suite—a set of services designed to work with, and complement, Windows NT/2000 Server. BackOffice includes:

■ Exchange Server, for e-mail, scheduling, and information-sharing services

■ Proxy Server, for protecting a network by creating a firewall that acts as the network's proxy—representative—for Internet access

■ Site Server, for building and managing intranets

■ Systems Management Server, for centralizing management and diagnostic services

■ SNA Server, for providing access to legacy (mainframe) systems

■ SQL Server, for building and maintaining high-performance relational databases

Client Software

Network-aware software is also required on the client side. After all, it does the user no good whatsoever to have a huge collection of servers ready and willing to dish up file and print services, mail, and other resources if the user's computer cannot even "see" the network.

One of the most important pieces of network-related software required on a client computer is known as the *redirector*. The redirector is sometimes part of the client operating system, as in Windows 95 and Windows 98. In other cases, it is part of a networking environment loaded in addition to the client operating system, as was the situation with the non-networking MS-DOS, which needed the help of networking software such as Microsoft's LAN Manager in order to connect with a network. Regardless of how it is provided to the client, however, the redirector's job is to literally intercept requests for information and then either to allow them to continue on their way or to redirect them to the network.

Applications

Although the client operating system is largely responsible for providing network access through the protocols it supports, the redirector it uses, and the adapter it communicates with, application software on the client computers must also be able to take advantage of groupware, network devices, databases, and other shared resources.

Some tasks, such as e-mail and scheduling, require interaction between the client software and a network server. With e-mail, for example, the client program, such as Microsoft Outlook, must be able to find its mail server on the network, access the user's mailbox, and manage the messages contained in it, even though some of that management might involve transferring messages from the server to various private folders on the user's own hard disk.

In other situations, applications can be primarily local but are still able to use the network when needed. A word processor, for instance, might well save most of its files on a local hard disk, but it might also be designed with the ability to access a network printer, save files to a shared network folder, or share a document with other individuals via e-mail, fax, or a document-routing feature. Here, for example, is an illustration of the document-routing menu in Microsoft Word:

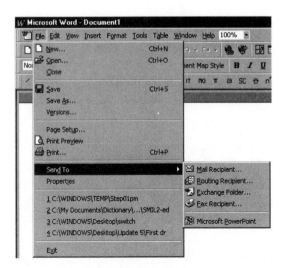

Whether designed specifically for networking or extended to take advantage of a network, client applications are, to the user, the embodiment of the network. Without these applications, the network might as well not exist. It certainly wouldn't do the user much good.

Larger LANs and WANs

LANs, like children, tend to grow and spread their wings. And eventually, the LAN that once did an admirable job for the company might need to be extended—perhaps because more nodes are needed, or because the company occupies more than one building and the LANs in each need to be connected, or because the original LAN can no longer accommodate the amount of traffic that flows through it.

When a network reaches out even farther, to geographically dispersed sites, or (in the case of the Internet) grows to cover the entire world, it comes to rely on the one characteristic that distinguishes a large LAN from a WAN: communications. This chapter begins with extending LANs and then moves on to explore the communications technologies that help LANs either merge to form a WAN or reach out to other LANs in a wide area network.

Larger LANs

Several types of hardware are designed to enable transmissions to travel within larger LANs, and these pieces of hardware fall neatly into several groups, depending on the sophistication of the work they do. One of these, hubs, you already met in Chapter 6 as the devices that link nodes and groups of nodes within a network. The devices described in the following sections range a little farther afield in their abilities to extend the reach of a network. Some of them strengthen a transmission so it can travel farther and thus increase the size of a LAN; others sort and route messages by directing them to nodes within a LAN or even to recipients on another network.

 OTE Some of the following devices are used primarily to extend LANs, but they can also be components in WANs.

Repeaters

Repeaters are the simplest devices used to extend the reach of a network. At heart, they are simply mechanisms designed to receive a signal, clean it up, strengthen it, and pass it along. Essentially, repeaters allow smaller LANs to grow into larger ones by moving transmissions from one network segment to another.

Remember that, as messages travel along a network, they tend to become attenuated—they weaken and begin to lose their "sharpness." Repeaters, which work at the physical layer, act as intermediaries by strengthening the attenuated signals before moving them along to the next network segment, as shown in the following illustration:

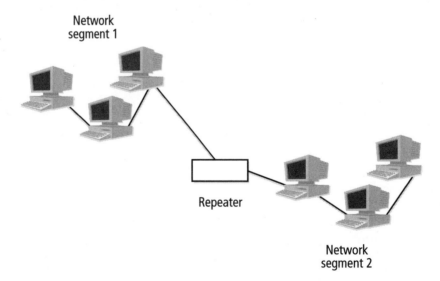

Although repeaters can increase the size of a network, note that they cannot be used to:

- Enlarge a network beyond the capabilities of its underlying architecture
- Connect network segments, such as Ethernet and Token Ring (both described in Chapter 5), that rely on different access methods

Nor can repeaters be used to filter out bad or damaged transmissions. They are not that smart.

Repeaters can, however, be used to move transmissions between different media types, such as coaxial and fiberoptic, and they do represent a simple and relatively inexpensive means of enlarging a network or dividing it into less heavily trafficked segments.

Bridges

A bridge that crosses over a wide river connects what might otherwise be unconnectable, and it provides a means of allowing traffic to move back and forth as if the geographic impasse didn't exist. Network bridges do the same thing, even though their traffic is electronic rather than animate or mechanical. Network bridges are also smarter than steel and concrete roadways, even though they might not be as beautiful as the Golden Gate in San Francisco.

Actually, depending on how you look at a bridge, it does one of two things: it connects LAN segments, or it isolates heavily trafficked segments or problematic nodes from the rest of the network.

(The latter is really just another way of saying it connects two pieces of the LAN, one too busy or too unreliable, the other not.)

Unlike a repeater, which operates at the physical layer and simply passes transmissions along between similar network segments, a bridge operates at the data link layer and both filters and passes packets between segments. Also unlike repeaters, bridges can join segments based on different architectures. They can, for example, join an Ethernet segment to a Token Ring segment and, even though the two segments follow different protocols, bridges can transfer packets between the two.

But in order to pass packets from one segment to another, the bridge must be able to figure out whether or not sender and recipient are on the same network segment:

■ If the sender and the recipient are on the same segment, there is no need to transfer the packet to another network segment.

■ If the sender and the recipient are on different segments, the bridge needs to be able to figure out where the recipient is, in order to forward the packet to the right party.

How does it do this? To begin with, a bridge operates in what is known as *promiscuous mode*, meaning that it monitors all the traffic on the segments it connects. As nodes transmit, the bridge checks the source and destination addresses of each packet.

But how does it know whether the source and destination are on the same or different network segments? It checks. Specifically, it checks a database that it maintains in memory. This database is known as a *routing table*. When a bridge first becomes operational, the routing table is blank. But as nodes transmit back and forth and the bridge dutifully checks their sending and receiving addresses, it begins to build the table by adding the *physical* address of any sending node that is not yet listed. (The "physical" is important, as you'll see in the section on routers.) At any rate, in this way the bridge builds an increasingly complete "picture" over time of the nodes and the network segments they inhabit.

So. What happens when the bridge has built a functional routing table and it receives a packet sent from node A to node B? It depends on which segments A and B happen to be on:

■ If both A and B are nodes on the same network segment, the bridge discards the packet and assumes that the network will take care of delivery.

■ If A and B are nodes on different segments, *and* if the address of node B is in the routing table, the bridge forwards the packet to node B.

■ If A and B are nodes on different segments, *but* the address of node B isn't yet in the routing table, the bridge forwards the packet to all segments except the one inhabited by node A. In other words, the bridge broadcasts the packet to all segments except the one containing the sending node, because it (the bridge) never forwards packets between nodes on the same segment anyway.

This method of "learning" which network segments the nodes are on is referred to as *backward learning*. It's something like learning your way around a new town. The more destinations you know, the more effectively you move around. It's the same with bridges: The more destinations they know, the more efficiently they can route packets and, in the process, relieve congestion by discarding intra-segment packets.

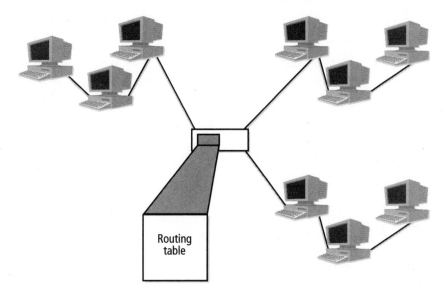

Routing
table

Bridges are clever devices. But even they are not as smart as routers.

Routers

Whereas repeaters and bridges forward transmissions from one segment of a network to another, routers take the process one giant step further by:

■ Forwarding packets from one network to another, even those separated by great distances and many networks in between

■ Figuring out the best route to use in making the delivery

Like bridges, routers can transfer packets between networks built on different architectures, but routers operate one step higher in the networking model: at the network layer.

So, how does a router route? To begin with, it communicates only with others of its own kind. That is, a router talks to other routers on other networks, but it doesn't talk directly to remote computers. In addition, a router relies on a routing table for finding other networks. However, unlike bridges, which rely on physical addresses (the addresses "hardwired" into nodes' network adapters), routers rely on network addresses, which are numbers that identify the network and, possibly, the subnetworks to which a node belongs. In this sense, network addresses are rather like the addresses that identify houses in a town.

In addition to network addresses, a router's routing table also includes other information, including the possible paths between routers, how far away they are, and how to connect to other networks. Armed with this information, a router takes an incoming packet of data and determines the best route to the destination network, based on an *algorithm* (set of steps to follow in figuring out the route) that takes into account such factors as:

- The number of *hops* (bounces from router to router)
- The line speed
- How busy the route (or segments of the route) are at the time
- Even the cost of transmission

When it determines the best route to follow, the router passes the packet along to the next router in the path, if necessary even going so far as to break the packet into smaller pieces if the original is too large to travel over the chosen route. It's quite a task, even for a piece of smart hardware.

Although routers all work in the same way, not all protocols work with routers. For instance, the older NetBEUI protocol does not, whereas IP, IPX, OSI, and XNS all do (and so are referred to as *routable protocols*). Conversely, some routers—usually older ones—support only a single protocol; others can support multiple protocols. In addition, routers used in WANs must be able to support protocols, such as those defined by the X.25 recommendations for packet-switching networks, used in long-distance transmissions.

Figure 7-1 shows two possible paths a packet could take between networks A and F.

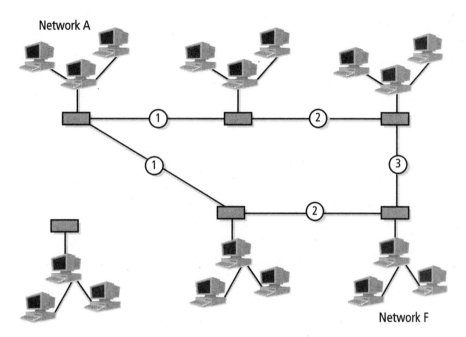

Figure 7-1. *Two possible paths for a packet traveling from network A to network F.*

Brouters

Brouters, as their name indicates, are hybrids that combine the capabilities of bridges and routers. Like bridges, they:

■ Work at the data link layer

■ Transfer and filter network traffic

Like routers, they:

■ Work at the network layer

■ Are able to route packets from one network to another

They are sometimes referred to as bridging routers. End of story.

Gateways

Whereas repeaters, bridges, and routers all deal with forwarding transmissions within or between networks, gateways have a slightly different focus, although the end result is, once again, communication between networks. In the case of gateways, the communication is between dissimilar networks, such as mainframes and LANs—say, IBM's SNA and a network running Microsoft's Windows NT/2000 Server and TCP/IP—or AppleTalk and Token Ring.

Gateways, unlike the bridges and other devices described earlier, operate at higher levels in the network model—typically at the application level, but also at the presentation and session layers and, in some cases, at all seven network layers.

Often, gateways are dedicated computers, and their job is to convert data packets to and from the protocols used by the networks they connect. In doing their work, these gateways take transmitted data packets and strip away the protocols, layer by layer, from those leaving the sending network. Before forwarding the packets, however, they repackage them in the protocol "wraps" expected by the receiving network. The whole process is somewhat comparable to changing from the day clothes expected by your everyday "network" into the uniform expected by your basketball, baseball, or soccer team.

Because of this protocol conversion, each network "sees" the other network as one just like itself, even though the architectures and protocols might be entirely different. And it's through this sleight of hand that gateways enable completely different networks to communicate.

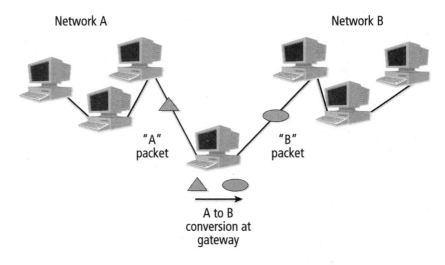

As you might expect, a single gateway isn't a one-size-fits-all model. Because of the types of conversions it performs, it handles data transfers only between very specific networks. Thus, an SNA to Windows NT/2000 Server TCP/IP gateway does not also handle AppleTalk to Token Ring, and vice versa. In this world, the motto is "to each its own." Although a gateway can be equipped with the hardware and software needed to handle more than one type of conversion, each still requires specific hardware and software for every type of conversion it handles.

More generally, and sometimes confusingly, the word *gateway* is also—especially in Internet contexts—used to refer to something other than these network gateways. Routers, for example, are occasionally referred to as gateways. Where the Web is concerned, a gateway is an access point to the Internet backbone. There are also e-mail gateways that convert messages to and from different messaging protocols, and there are gateways that support remote communications and packet switching. There are even software-related gateways of a sort. The *Common Gateway Interface*, or *CGI*, for example, is a specification designed to support interactivity between applications and Web servers. In each case, however, it's helpful to remember that the term *gateway* itself refers to some hardware or software or interface that paves the way for communication that otherwise would not happen.

On to WANs

A WAN—a wide area network—isn't just a LAN on steroids. It can cover a very large geographic area, and it often does consist of a number of LANs linked together, but a WAN is, at heart, distinguished by its reliance on communications technologies to enable computers in different cities, states, countries, or continents to transfer and share information.

Although a number of different technologies and communications media can be used to create a WAN, the signaling through which a WAN transfers information operates primarily at the physical and data link layers of the network.

WANs and Enterprise Networks

These days, with computer technology marching on and networking becoming ever more widespread, a WAN is also often indistinguishable from an *enterprise network*, which is the computing infrastructure of a large business or corporation. However, it's useful to remember that even though a WAN can be an enterprise network, an enterprise network isn't necessarily a WAN.

As described above, a WAN is a geographically widespread network that relies on telephone or other communications. Such a description obviously can also apply to the computers that form the enterprise network linking the offices of a large national or international corporation, such as Microsoft, IBM, or Boeing. In cases like these, the enterprise network also happens to be a WAN. But that isn't always the case. Although it might include more than one interconnected LAN, it isn't necessarily spread out over a large geographic area the way a WAN is. And while it might rely on communications, an enterprise network is more likely to be described in terms of the platforms and architectures (such as PC, Macintosh, and mainframe) that the enterprise relies on and that are supported and connected by the network. Thus, while a WAN can be an enterprise network, an enterprise network isn't necessarily a WAN.

Communications

But back, now, to the feature that distinguishes WANs from LANs: communications. WAN communication is based on modems and on telecommunications technologies.

The modem, of course, is the enabler through which transmissions pass from the network to the telecommunications infrastructure.

Telecommunications can involve satellites, microwave transmitters, or the endearingly named *POTS* (*Plain Old Telephone Service*), and transmissions can be either analog or digital in nature. In the former case, they are based on modems and telephone wires, at least along the so-called *local loop* running to the phone company. In digital communications, which are faster and more reliable, the transmissions might travel over cable (as in television), *ISDN* (*Integrated Services Digital Network*) lines, or the up-

and-coming *DSL* (*Digital Subscriber Line*) that provides high-speed digital transmission over existing telephone wire.

In case it isn't obvious, by the way, networking over long distances is usually dependent on the communications facilities provided by telephone companies such as AT&T. Once a transmission goes out over a communications line, most WAN connections are just as reliant on the telecommunications network—the switching systems, cabling, and communications backbones provided by phone companies—as you are when you call to "network" with a friend, whether next door or halfway around the world.

 OTE Beyond the modems and the communications infrastructure, you also encounter the far less tangible methods used by WANs to actually move transmissions around. This is where you enter the world of *circuit-switching*, *packet switching*, *frame relay*, and *dedicated connections*, not to mention the intriguing concepts behind such (mostly) recent developments as *virtual circuits*, *point-to-point tunneling*, and *virtual private networks*. These topics are covered in Chapter 8.

Modems

At the heart of computer-based communication lies a small device called a *modem*, whose name comes from the two operations it has traditionally handled: *modulation* and *demodulation* of a computer signal to enable that signal to travel over a telephone line. (More about this in the section later in this chapter titled "Standard PC Modems.")

These days, however, communications technology has caught up with, indeed surpassed, the familiar wires strung on telephone poles scattered across the landscape. Nowadays, there are cellular communications, satellite communications, and—of special interest in terms of networking—digital communications. And along with digital communications technologies have come several new types of transmission devices. These are often called modems because they serve as the interface between a computer and a communications line, even though they do not operate in the same way as the familiar, telephone-based modems installed in or on home and office PCs. Among these newer so-called modems are *cable modems*, ISDN modems, and DSL modems. Because these modems and traditional telephone-based modems differ in many respects, including speed and the communications technologies that underlie their use, each type is described separately in the following sections.

Standard PC modems

PC modems embody the computer user's idea of a typical modem: the device that connects a home computer to the Internet or to a corporate network via remote access. It is also the device from which modems take their name, the device that modulates and demodulates a transmission signal to enable two computers to communicate over a standard telephone line.

But why is a modem necessary? After all, computers come with assorted plugs and sockets. Couldn't it simply be equipped with a cable that plugs into a phone jack in the wall? Sure. But computers can't talk (yet), and so they cannot use phone lines unaided. Computers handle all information electronically, in digital (1 and 0, or on and off) form, whereas a telephone line—at least the portion running from the telephone company's central office to the home—carries signals acoustically, in analog (continually varying) form.

In order to use a phone line to communicate, both the sending and receiving computer must be equipped with a modem. The modem attached to the sending computer takes the computer's digital signal and converts (modulates) it by loading the information onto an acoustic (sound) carrier signal that travels over the phone line. When this signal reaches the recipient computer, its modem unloads (demodulates) the information from the carrier signal, converting it back to the digital form needed by the computer. The process of modulating and demodulating a signal is illustrated in Figure 7-2. To make the sequence easier to see, the modems attached to both computers are shown externally, as small boxes. In real life, a modem can be either an external, boxlike unit or (as is more often the case) it can be an internal card fitted into one of the computer's expansion slots.

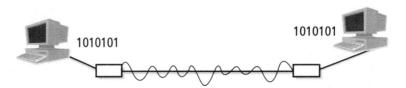

1010101

1010101

Figure 7-2. *Modems modulate and demodulate computer-to-computer transmissions by converting digital (1010101) signals to analog (wavy line) form, and vice versa.*

The connection between the computer and the modem is usually based on the RS-232-C standard, which defines the interface between the two. In RS-232-C lingo, the modem is known as the *DCE* (*Data Communications Equipment*) and the computer is known as the *DTE* (*Data Terminal Equipment*). RS-232-C, which defines connections at the physical layer, long ago became a de facto standard for modem and printer communications. It was later expanded as the RS-232-D standard, which specifies additional test signaling between modems, as well as a particular connector type. RS-232, as the standard is usually called, is approved by the EIA and is equivalent to the ITU's V.24 and V.28 modem specifications.

Modulating the wave   Since the mid-1980s, modems have become increasingly faster, going from a low of 300 bps (bits per second) to today's current maximum of 56 *K*bps (*thousand* bits per second) over the roughly 3000 Hz (hertz) that represents the bandwidth allotted for voice communications over a telephone line.

Part of the increased modem speed (though not all of it, as you'll see in the later section on 56 Kbps modems) results from new and more sophisticated ways of modulating the carrier signal so that more and more bits could be loaded onto it. These different forms of modulation are fascinating. And they are complex. Basically, however, what they all do is modify the carrier wave in some way so that the modification represents the value for a single bit, a 1 or a 0. The way in which the wave is modified is what determines how much information can be carried by the wave at a particular moment in time.

To visualize how modulation actually works, picture a wave like the endlessly repeating wave that snakes across the screen of an oscilloscope. It moves up and down, up and down, over and over again, maintaining the same size, or amplitude, and recurring at regular intervals, or frequency, like this:

Now, picture that wave being changed in some way:

- The peaks and troughs come closer together or farther apart. That's modulating the frequency of the wave. On an acoustic signal, frequency shifts would be heard as changes in pitch.

- The peaks and troughs are higher and lower. That's modulating the amplitude (height) of the wave. On an acoustic signal, amplitude shifts would be heard as changes in volume.

Both of these are methods used by modems in modulating a signal. *Frequency modulation*, also known as *frequency shift keying*, or *FSK*, uses different frequencies to represent 1 and 0. *Amplitude modulation*, or *AM* (or *ASK* for *amplitude shift keying*) uses different wave heights to represent 1 and 0. Both of these forms of modulation can be used in transmitting up to 2400 bps.

More complex techniques than these are used by modems transmitting at higher speeds. In one such technique, called *phase shift keying* (or *PSK*), changes (shifts) in the phase of the wave—the part of the wave on the way up, down, in the middle, and so on—represent information. A variation on this, known as *differential phase shift keying* (*DPSK*), relies on phase shifts in which each change is relative to the preceding state of the wave. Relying on phase shifts, a modem can transmit 2 bits per phase change, for a speed up to 4800 bps.

Beyond this are techniques such as *quadrature amplitude modulation* (*QAM*), in which both the phase and the amplitude of the wave are used to create what is known as a constellation of points. The constellation looks like the following illustration, where the inner and outer "rings" of dots represent two different amplitudes and the lines at 45-degree angles represent phase changes:

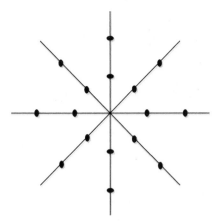

As you can see, a QAM constellation contains 16 distinct signal points. Though you might not be able to visualize them very well, these signal points can be used to represent four distinct bits of data.

Modulation techniques like QAM are used by standard, telephone-based modems transmitting at 4800 bps to 9600 bps. The same technique is also used by the much faster cable modems that use cable television as the transmission medium.

For speeds beyond 9600 bps, modems "up the ante" so to speak, by increasing the number of signal points in the constellation. At 14,400 bps, for example, the modem uses a constellation with 64 signal points. Because the constellation for speeds at and above this level consists of so many signal points, some modems rely on a variation of QAM known as *trellis-coded modulation*, which allows for error checking as well as encoding data.

Modem transmissions   In addition to their primary task of modulating and demodulating signals, modems communicate in one of three different ways, known as *simplex*, *half duplex*, and *full duplex*:

- Simplex refers to one-way only transmission. As you can imagine, this is limited to situations in which information needs to be received but not sent, and so it isn't a viable option for two-way communication.

- Half duplex refers to two-way transmission, but with the sender and receiver taking turns. Half-duplex transmission is equivalent to a polite conversation between two people.

- Full duplex, which allows for faster transmission, allows for transmission in both directions at the same time. This is analogous to two people talking at the same time—assuming both could hear and speak simultaneously. The process sounds chaotic, but it's not.

In addition to operating in some form of simplex or duplex mode and transmitting at various speeds, modems also have some "smarts" in that they understand and use certain commands to indicate their status—for example, when they are ready to receive or ready to send, activating error control, and so on. The most common set of such commands is known as the *Hayes command set*, after the name of the modem manufacturer that created what has become the de facto standard for modems. When displayed for people, as they sometimes are in communications programs and on the front panel of external modems, these commands look like the following:

- CD for carrier detect, meaning that the modem is on line and ready for use

- CTS for clear to send, meaning that the modem is ready to receive data from the computer to which it is attached

- RD for receiving data, meaning that the modem is receiving transmitted data

- SD for sending data, meaning that the modem is in the process of transmitting data to another modem

Both RD and SD are accompanied by flashing lights, either on the modem or, in Windows 95 and Windows 98, by a flashing icon and indicator on the taskbar.

Modem standards   In the time they've been associated with PCs, modems have been identified with two different sets of standards. Early on—in the late 1970s and early 1980s—they were associated with a set of de facto standards developed by AT&T. Known as the Bell standards, these applied to modems operating at 300 and 1200 bps. (Yes, they were pathetically slow and antique, but people who have been around PCs for some time can remember being completely dazzled by the thought of a high-speed, 1200 bps modem. Truly.)

At any rate, the standards for these slowpokes and the much faster modems that superseded them eventually came under the wing of the CCITT (now part of the ITU), which developed and published a series of recommendations known as the *V series*. These are the standards that are now bandied about in reference to modems designed for use over the public phone network. Some of the more notable of these recommendations are:

- V.21, which defines 300 bps duplex modems

- V.22, which defines 1200 bps duplex modems operating over both the public phone network and leased lines

- V.26bis, which defines 1200/2400 bps half-duplex modems

- V.26ter, which defines 1200/2400 bps full-duplex modems

- V.27ter, which defines 2400/4800 bps modems

- V.32bis, which defines modems operating up to 14.4 Kbps

- V.34, which defines modems operating up to 28.8 Kbps

- V.35, which defines the data communications interface on modems operating at 56 Kbps or more

- V.42bis, which defines the data compression used by high-speed modems

- V.90, which defines 56 Kpbs transmission, as described in the next section. V.90, by the way, combines the two technologies used in 56 Kpbs transmission: x2 from 3Com/U.S. Robotics and K56flex from Rockwell."

> **NOTE** The *bis* or *ter* after some of these recommendations indicates that the number refers to a revision (bis) or a revision of a revision (ter) of the original recommendation. The words are French, derived from the Latin for second (*bis*) and third (*ter*).

56 Kbps modems   Currently, the fastest PC modems designed to work over analog telephone lines are capable of receiving information at 56 Kbps, even though the fastest practical rate over phone lines is supposed to be 33.6 Kbps. How is this possible? In large part, the credit goes to changes made by telephone companies.

Over the past few decades, telephone companies have steadily been moving to digital technologies where feasible, meaning within the telephone exchange and switching infrastructure. Today, much of the telephone network is digital, and the only place where analog copper lines are the norm is in the portion of the phone network called the analog local loop—the stretch of wiring from the phone company's central office to the home.

Because of the phone companies' internal digital connections, 56 Kbps modems operating through an end-to-end 56 Kbps connection (one in which 56 Kbps technologies are supported at both the sending and receiving end) can depend on receiving a data stream that has traveled from a network server (say, an Internet server) through the phone network in purely digital form. That is, the data requires only a single analog-to-digital conversion in its travels from the server to the recipient, even as it moves through the phone network. Only when the transmission leaves the phone company is it converted from digital to analog, and this takes place as a "clean" conversion, in which the digital signal is turned into a corresponding analog signal consisting of a clearly delimited number—255—of analog values. This type of conversion does not result in loss of speed. And it is in this form that the signal then travels over the connection from the phone company to the end user's desktop, where the single analog-to-digital conversion takes place.

Because of the nature of 56 Kbps transmissions, however, the 56 Kbps speed can occur in only one direction: *downstream*. That is, the flow of information from the telephone network to the modem can occur at 56 Kbps, assuming that 56 Kbps technologies are implemented throughout the connection. In contrast, the flow of information *upstream*, from the modem to the phone network and beyond, cannot be faster than 33.6 Kbps. Why is this? Because the flow upstream involves more than a single digital-to-analog conversion, and these conversions are subject to an effect called "quantization noise" that degrades the efficiency of the signal conversion and reduces the speed of the transmission.

56 Kbps technologies are effective as long as:

- 56 Kbps technologies are in effect from end to end

- The transmission involves only one analog-to-digital conversion

- The connection to the server is digital

- The phone line isn't a noisy one

Cable modems

Unlike standard modems and their speedier 56 Kbps brethren, cable modems do not rely on the telephone system at all. Instead, they use cable television connections as their means of transferring information. Far faster than typical telephone-based modems, cable modems can download information at rates of 10 Mbps (megabits per second) to about 36 Mbps.

Typically, a cable modem connects to a PC at one end and to a cable wall outlet at the other. Although it is actually a modem in that it modulates and demodulates a transmission signal, a cable modem is also in part other things too, including network card, in that it connects to a 10BaseT Ethernet card installed inside the PC.

A cable modem, like a 56 Kbps modem, is faster downstream than upstream. Although downstream rates can reach 36 Mbps, as already mentioned, upstream rates are considerably slower. Although 10 Mbps is possible, a maximum of about 2 Mbps is more likely.

Altogether, a working cable-based modem connection involves:

- A PC with an Ethernet card and a cable modem connected to it

- A connection from the cable modem to the cable outlet in the wall

- A drop cable (in the house) that leads to a neighborhood feeder cable that, in turn, connects to a larger trunk cable

- A headend controller at the cable company that sends signals out over the cable and also regulates transmissions sent from the cable modem

Cable television is a broadband, broadcast technology, so how does a cable modem work with the same medium and equipment that show you the news and Monday night football? The technology is based on cable television, which operates in the frequency range between 40 MHz and 550 MHz and is divided into 6 MHz bands, each of which can be used for one television channel. These channels, however, can also be used to carry modem transmissions—as long as they're not being used for a television broadcast, of course.

In a downstream transmission, the headend controller modulates the signal and loads it onto an unused 6 MHz band. Various modulation schemes are in use, but the most common are quadrature phase shift keying (QPSK), which allows transmissions at up to 10 Mbps, and the faster but more noise-sensitive 64QAM—quadrature amplitude modulation with 64 constellation points—which allows transmissions at up to about 36 Mbps. However it is modulated, the transmission then travels over the trunk, feeder, and drop cables until it reaches the cable modem, which demodulates the signal and passes the transmission on to the PC through its 10BaseT Ethernet connection. In reverse, during an upstream transmission, the cable modem takes orders from the headend controller, which tells it when and how long it can transmit and what frequency band to use.

ISDN modems

ISDN, which stands for *Integrated Services Digital Network*, is a digital communications technology described in more detail later (the "ISDN" section later in this chapter). However, in this section, where modems are the order of the day, ISDN deserves at least quick mention because of the adapter—often misleadingly called an ISDN modem—that connects a PC to an ISDN communications line and provides bandwidth of up to about 2 Mbps.

The ISDN adapter, more correctly known as a *terminal adapter*, or *TA*, isn't a modem at all, even though it does serve to send and receive transmissions and, if it is an external unit, does act somewhat like a modem in the sense of interacting with the computer's communications software. Rather than modulating and demodulating transmissions as a modem does, however, an ISDN adapter serves as the device that adapts the signals—which are transmitted in several separate channels—to the communications standards understood by the computer. An ISDN adapter can be installed either internally, as a plug-in card, or externally, as a separate unit connected to the computer's serial or parallel port.

DSL modems

Like ISDN, *DSL* (*Digital Subscriber Line*) is a digital communications technology described in more detail in the "xDSL" section later in this chapter. Also, like ISDN, DSL is fast (with a possible downstream transfer rate of more than 7 Mbps), and it requires a type of modem in order to work. In fact, DSL requires two modems—one connected to the computer accessing the Internet or other network, and another (managed by the phone company) installed at the other end of the copper-based wiring that runs from a subscriber's home or office to the phone company.

DSL modems are cards installed inside a computer, and they are similar to typical telephone-based modems in that they connect the computer to a standard telephone wall outlet. Because DSL transmissions are completely digital, however, DSL modems do not have to convert transmissions from digital to analog and vice versa. Furthermore, DSL modems can be equipped with a chip called a splitter that literally splits the phone line into voice and data lines, so that modem communications do not interfere with regular voice calls.

Transmission Types

Although modems and modem-like devices are at the heart of computer-to-computer communications, they do not simply exchange streams of data willy-nilly. One modem does not call up another and transmit the computer equivalent of "psst, here it comes." Nor does the other sit quietly when contacted and soak up whatever the sender happens to transmit.

No; like people, modems must operate in ways that both understand, and they must exchange data in a form that both can recognize and handle. The rules of the game—as dictated by standards and protocols, of course—become quite complex when actual bits and bytes are involved, but on the broadest of levels, modem transmissions are easily divided into two basic types: asynchronous and synchronous. (Rather a neat parallel to the two basic ways people communicate.)

Of the two, asynchronous transmissions are the more common, so they provide a good starting point.

Asynchronous communications

Asynchronous means not synchronous, not governed by timing. In computer communications, this means that sending and receiving computers relying on *asynchronous communications* do not have to synchronize timing before a transmission can take place. The sender can transmit when it is ready, stop, and transmit after an indeterminate period of time, and the receiving computer will be able to determine where, in the flow of transmitted bits, any particular byte—representing one character—begins and ends.

This business of bits and bytes and beginnings and endings might sound a little impenetrable, but in actuality, it's one of the easier aspects of computer communications to understand. To start with, take a look at what a string of bits in a transmission might look like (these are the binary equivalents of the letters *h* and *i*—"hi":

```
    h         i
0110 1000 0110 1001
```

These 1s and 0s, in different combinations, are used, usually in groups of eight, to make up the larger units called bytes. And, as you probably know, a single byte commonly represents one character: a letter, such as a, b, or c; a number, such as 1, 2, or 3; a punctuation mark or special symbol, such as ?, !, and %; or any of a number of nonprinting characters, such as those that cause the computer to beep, recognize the Esc key, and so on.

These 1s and 0s are not, of course, actual numbers. In communications, they might be represented by frequency changes, amplitude changes, phase changes, or a combination, as is the case with quadrature amplitude modulation. Inside a computer, these same "atoms" of digital information are represented by small changes in voltage. Regardless, because all information boils down to strings made up of only two binary digits, there is nothing in any particular string of 1s and 0s to indicate where a particular byte begins and ends.

How, then, does a sending computer indicate to the receiving computer where a particular character starts and stops, if it is transmitting asynchronously and therefore can't use timing to separate one character from another? The answer is what are called *start bits* and *stop bits*. These are bits—actually, signals—that frame the bits making up one character. The start bit indicates the start of the character, and the stop bit or bits (there can be 1, 1.5, or 2 of them) mark the end of the character. Between the start and stop bits are the bits representing the character itself and, optionally, an additional bit known as the *parity bit* that is used for error checking. A byte transmitted asynchronously could thus be diagrammed as shown below. (The dark boxes are the start and stop bits, the gray boxes are the bits making up the actual character, and the white box is the optional parity bit.)

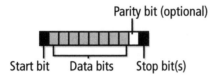

Parity bit (optional)

Start bit   Data bits   Stop bit(s)

Getting back to communications…

Modems typically rely on serial, asynchronous transmission, which works well over telephone lines. (The "serial" part of this description simply means that they transmit and receive bits serially, one after the other.) RS-232, described earlier, enters into the picture here as well, because it is the standard for serial asynchronous communications. RS-232 defines the electrical lines, pins, and signal characteristics used in this type of transmission and, to that extent, defines the "how" that modems use to make asynchronous communications happen.

Synchronous communications

Whereas asynchronous transmission is the norm for modem-to-modem communications, digital systems and networks rely more on *synchronous communications*. This method results in faster transmissions, but it is also more complex and more expensive.

Unlike asynchronous transmissions, in which the building blocks (so to speak) are bytes delineated by start and stop bits, synchronous transmissions are based on *frames*—blocks of bits separated by equal time intervals. In order to communicate synchronously, the sending and receiving computers must coordinate closely, relying on timing based on their internal clocks. Before and during transmission, the two computers use special synchronizing characters both to initiate communication and to carry out periodic checks on the accuracy of the timing.

Synchronous transmissions are dependent on protocols that govern the format of the frames as well as specify control and error-detection information included in each transmitted frame. Among the synchronous protocols often encountered are the following, all of which operate at the data link layer:

■ **Synchronous data link control (SDLC).** This is a protocol developed by IBM for use in its Systems Network Architecture (SNA)—its networking design for enabling IBM equipment of different types to communicate. SDLC is a *bit-oriented protocol*, meaning that information is transmitted as a stream of bits rather than as a stream of characters based on a particular character-encoding scheme, such as *ASCII (American Standard Code for Information Interchange)*. Because the bits have no point of reference in terms of a character set, SDLC, like other bit-oriented protocols, includes special bit sequences that take the place of control characters. An SDLC frame is organized as shown in the following illustration. (The gray boxes are 1-byte fields called flags that mark the beginning and end of the frame.)

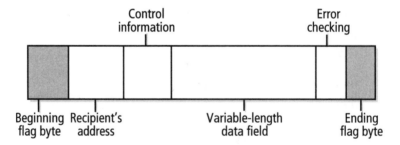

SDLC is based on the concepts of primary nodes, which control transmissions on the network, and secondary nodes, which are allowed to transmit only if given permission by the primary node.

This protocol can be used both in situations in which mainframes communicate with multiple terminals or workstations and in point-to-point (direct) connections between sender and receiver. It is widely used in closed networks, such as corporate WANs, based on mainframe computers.

■ **High-level data link control (HDLC).** HDLC is an outgrowth of SDLC that has been blessed by the ISO. Like SDLC, HDLC is a bit-oriented protocol. Unlike its precursor, however, it is widely used in public, rather than closed, private networks. HDLC comes in several sub-sets, or versions, one of which, known as HDLC NRM (Normal Response Mode), corresponds to SDLC in that it supports the same master-slave type of relationship between nodes. More commonly, however, when people refer to HDLC, they are referring to a subset known as *LAPB* (*Link Access Procedure, Balanced*), which supports full-duplex, peer-to-peer communications in which neither the sender nor the receiver has control of the other. HDLC (LAPB version) is used on the X.25 packet-switching public networks described in the next chapter. An HDLC frame is similar to an SDLC frame.

■ **Binary synchronous communications protocol (Bisync).** Bisync, which was replaced by SDLC, can be considered the original IBM data-link networking contender. Unlike its SDLC and HDLC descendants, Bisync is a *byte-oriented protocol* in which characters are encoded in either ASCII or IBM's *EBCDIC* (*Extended Binary Coded Decimal Interchange Code*), a well-known, mainframe-based coding scheme in which 8 bits are used to numerically encode 256 possible characters. Bisync messages are variable in length, but they always begin and end with synchronizing characters. The beginning of the message text is preceded by a control character called STX, and the end of the message is followed by another control character, ETX, followed by a set of characters included to ensure accuracy of transmission. The following illustration shows the structure of a bisync frame (synchronizing characters are light gray, and the message text is dark gray):

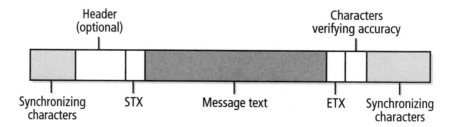

And now, having covered the messenger (the modem) and the method (transmission type), it's but a short step to the lines that deliver all good things, from e-mail to music and video to important documents in the wide networking world.

Communications Carriers

In terms of WANs and communications, practically everything eventually boils down to telecommunications carriers. Whether a modem connects via telephone or microwave, a telecommunications provider is involved. Whether a connection is made over an ISDN line or a T1 line, a telecommunications provider is involved. About the only reasonably widespread means of connecting to a network—in this case, the Internet—that does not involve a telephony-based provider occurs with cable modems. Because cable connections were described earlier, the following sections all deal with various communications connections that, in one way or another, rely on telecommunications companies, which these days provide both analog (telephone-based) and digital communications.

POTS

Analog communication via a modem is generally synonymous with POTS, the Plain Old Telephone Service provided by the phone company. Originally intended for voice communications, POTS has, in the past decade or so, become invaluable to telecommuters needing remote access to corporate networks. And, of course, POTS is now as basic as bread for home users who can't get enough of Web surfing, e-mail, chat rooms, bulletin boards and, increasingly, shopping on line.

POTS is a service provided by the *Public Switched Telephone Network* (*PSTN*). For networking, it can be used in either of two forms: dial-up or leased lines.

Dial-up

Dial-up networking is what people do when they call in to the office or access the Internet via modem. The call makes a temporary connection between the caller and the remote computer, and the connection is terminated as soon as the caller hangs up. Dial-up networking works well for individuals needing remote access to a company network, and it can be suitable for intermittently connecting two LANs, although the length of the connection and the amount of data transferred can be a deterrent, both in terms of cost and in terms of time.

In general, dial-up connections are considered slow and, under some conditions (such as noisy lines), unreliable. They are, however, easily made, easily ended, and inexpensive compared to other faster and more reliable options.

Leased lines

Leased lines are a step up from dial-up networking. When a customer leases a line from the phone company, that line is dedicated, full-time, to the customer's own use. The quality of a leased line and the speed at which data can be transferred are higher than they are on dial-up lines. Data transfer rates, for example, can range from 56 Kbps to many megabits per second. Of course, the cost is higher, too.

Often, leased lines are described as direct connections that aren't routed through the phone company's switching system. Although this can be true, long-distance connections are usually routed through switched circuits, even though the result appears to be a dedicated connection.

Leased lines are generally thought of as permanent versions of dial-up lines, but digital communications lines, such as ISDN and T1, are also leased lines in the sense of being reserved for use by a single customer.

Digital

Digital communications are "where it's at" these days. Why? In one word: speed.

Thanks to the Internet explosion, everyone wants faster connections, faster download times and, if possible, faster upload times. As people become more involved with the World Wide Web, they become increasingly disenchanted with even 56 Kbps modems and the sardonically renamed World Wide Wait. *Internet Service Providers*, or *ISPs*, now routinely tout their T1 lines to potential subscribers. And as businesses—especially large, national or international enterprises—rely more and more on networking, their needs for speed, security, and reliability also increase. These are the areas in which digital communications come into play, and there are several options to choose from.

DDS

DDS (*digital data service*) lines are dedicated, point-to-point connections that use synchronous communications to provide data transfer rates up to 56 Kbps. Like the T1 lines described later, DDS lines rely on a two-part device called a *Channel Service Unit*, or *CSU*, and a *Data Service Unit*, or *DSU*, to connect two networks. The device, usually referred to as the CSU/DSU, takes the place of a modem and performs the following tasks:

- The CSU part of the device mediates between the DSU and the actual telecommunications line at each end of the connection. Its job is to process the signals being sent over the digital line and to isolate the line from network equipment problems.

- The DSU part of the device mediates between the network—actually, the bridge or router that forwards packets from the network—and the CSU. Its job is to convert the data from its network-oriented, computer-based format to the form needed for synchronous transmission. The DSU also controls the flow of data to the CSU.

Figure 7-3 shows how the pieces of a DDS connection fit together.

ISDN

ISDN stands for *Integrated Services Digital Network*. Although it has been around for some time (since 1984), only during the past few years has it become a relatively easy-to-come-by digital communications option, at least in the United States. ISDN was developed as a means of providing end-to-end digital service over the telephone network. It is currently used

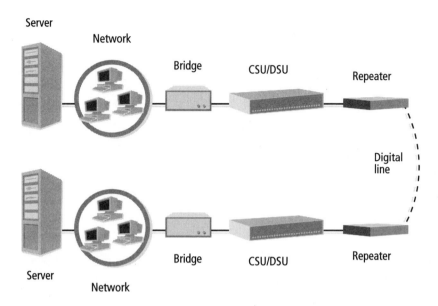

Figure 7-3. *A DDS connection relies on a CSU/DSU unit at each end to mediate between the network and the digital line.*

by businesses and by individual (home) subscribers, where it is available. ISDN is designed to deliver voice, data, and images including video at a speed of 64 Kbps.

Available in two different forms known as *BRI* (*Basic Rate Interface*) and *PRI* (*Primary Rate Interface*), ISDN is characterized by the way its band-width is divided into multiple channels. In the BRI form of ISDN, there are two *B* (*bearer*) channels that carry data at the rate of 64 Kbps and one *D* (*data* or *delta*) channel that carries signaling and other control information at the rate of 16 Kbps. BRI is the type of ISDN typical in home use.

64 Kbps B channel

64 Kbps B channel

16 Kbps D channel

BRI bandwidth

In the PRI form of ISDN, the line is divided into many more channels, with the exact number depending on where in the world the service is provided. In North America and Japan, PRI includes 23 B channels and 1 D channel, all operating at 64 Kbps. In other parts of the world, including Europe, PRI consists of 30 B channels and 1 D channel. The PRI form of ISDN is generally used to connect a business's PBX to the local or long-distance phone company.

Although, as explained earlier, ISDN does not require a modem, it does require a terminal adapter. This adapter converts ISDN signals to a standard form, such as RS-232, needed by equipment such as computers. To complicate matters a bit, the adapter actually sits between an ISDN unit known as an NT1 (network termination 1) device and non-ISDN equipment, such as the computer. Although the details are rather...well...detailed, basically the NT1 takes the ISDN signal that travels from the phone company's central office over two wires (known as the U interface) and converts it for use by four wires (known as the S/T interface), which, in turn, carry the signal from the wall jack to the ISDN adapter. Whew.

The important things to remember about ISDN:

- It is digital.

- It is divided into either 2 B channels and 1 D channel (BRI) or into 23 or 30 B channels and 1 D channel (PRI).

- It carries voice, data, and video.

- It is used by both individual subscribers and businesses.

- It costs less than the next option: T1 service.

T1/T3

T1, sometimes referred to as *T-1 carrier*, was developed by Bell Laboratories and introduced as long ago as the 1960s as a means of enabling telephone wires to carry more than one conversation at a time. Today, T1 is one of the most widely used—and one of the most expensive—technologies in digital communications. Much faster than ISDN, T1 lines carry information at the rate of 1.544 Mbps.

T1 was originally designed for full-duplex transmission over four twisted-pair copper wires, two used for sending and two used for receiving. These days, however, T1 lines can also be fiberoptic cable, coaxial cable, and microwave.

In order to attain such a high transmission speed, T1 multiplexes 24 separate 64 Kbps channels into a single digital data stream. Each of the 24 channels is sampled 8000 times per second, and the sample is transmitted as a 192-bit frame separated from the next frame by 1 bit. (Fun project: Multiply 192 times 8000 and add another 8000 for the extra bits in the transmission. The result is T1's 1.544 Mbps transmission rate.)

When you encounter T1 details, you often see 64 Kbps—the speed of a single T1 channel—referred to as *DS-0*, for *Digital Services* (or *Digital Signal*) level 0. The higher 1.544 Mbps speed is known as *DS-1*. The DS-1 rate, in turn, can be multiplexed further to provide even higher transmission rates, including the following:

- DS-2, which is the basis for T2 lines, incorporates four T1 channels and transmits at 6.312 Mbps.

- DS-3, which is the basis for T3 lines, incorporates 28 T1 channels and transmits at 44.736 Mbps.

- DS-4, which is the basis for T4 lines, incorporates 168 T1 channels and transmits at a blistering 274.176 Mbps.

Of these, T1 and T2 can be used on copper wire. T3 and T4 require fiberoptic cable or microwave.

To save on the potentially considerable expense of leasing a T1 line, businesses can opt for an alternative known as *fractional T1*, in which they lease part rather than all of the T1 bandwidth. At the other end of the scale, they can choose to use T3 lines in place of multiple T1 lines.

OTE T1 is available in North America, Japan, and Australia; equivalent technology known as E1 is available in Europe, Mexico, and South America. E1 transmits at the rate of 2.048 Mbps.

---

xDSL

xDSL (*Digital Subscriber Line*) stands for a new and promising group of digital communications technologies that can provide high-speed network access over the standard copper wires run into homes and offices by the telephone company. The x in DSL stands for any of several letters, described below, that represent different versions of basic DSL communications.

To start with, however...DSL has raised a great deal of interest *because* it operates over ordinary telephone wires. To achieve high data rates—ranging from 8 Mbps to as much as 52 Mbps—DSL relies on modulation and on the fact that digital signals do not have to be converted to analog form. Although the actual speed attained depends on several factors, including the distance the transmission must travel over copper wire and the quality of the wire itself, DSL speeds are fast enough to allow for smooth delivery of 3-D and high-quality sound and video. As an added benefit, DSL technologies allow for a connection to be split into data and voice components, so that networking does not interfere with ordinary voice telephone calls.

At present, at least in its most prevalent ADSL form (more about that below), DSL is being considered primarily in terms of fast access for telecommuters, small businesses, and individual phone subscribers using the Internet. As mentioned earlier, however, DSL comes in different forms and quite possibly will prove useful in larger networking contexts as well. The technology itself is still quite new as of 1999, and it is not yet available to many people. The following list describes DSL technologies that either currently exist or are under development:

- *ADSL*, or *Asymmetric Digital Subscriber Line*, is called Asymmetric because most of the ADSL bandwidth is devoted to downstream transmissions, on the assumption that more downloading than uploading takes place over the Internet and intranet connections ADSL is most likely to be used for. Depending in large part on distance from the phone company, ADSL can deliver information downstream at speeds up to 8 Mbps, and upstream at a maximum of 640 Kbps. (The closer to the phone company and the better the wire, the faster the transmission.) ADSL generally requires installation of a DSL modem containing a splitter to separate voice and data channels.

- *DSL Lite* is a variation of ADSL that is currently under development. In DSL Lite, splitting takes place at the phone company, rather than at the recipient's end. DSL Lite is less complex and less expensive to install than ADSL, but the tradeoff is that its maximum transmission rate is reduced to 1.544 Mbps.

- *HDSL*, or *High bit-rate Digital Subscriber Line*, is unlike ADSL in being symmetric—providing the same amount of downstream and upstream bandwidth and, hence, the same speed in both directions. Older and more established than ADSL, though less often mentioned as an Internet solution for end-user subscribers, HDSL provides the same rate of speed, 1.544 Mbps, as a T1 line (E1 in Europe and elsewhere). HDSL has a maximum range of 15,000 feet without repeaters that strengthen and pass the signal along.

- *SDSL*, or *Single-line Digital Subscriber Line*, is the same as HDSL but uses one pair of wires, rather than HDSL's two pairs, and it has a shorter transmission distance—10,000 feet as opposed to HDSL's 15,000 feet. Like HDSL, however, it transfers information at T1 (or E1) speeds.

- *RADSL*, or *Rate Adaptive Digital Subscriber Line*, is similar to ADSL but uses software to adjust the rate of transmission according to the quality of the line and the distance the transmission must travel. RADSL transmissions travel at up to 2.2 Mbps downstream and up to 1.088 Mbps upstream.

- *VDSL*, or *Very high rate Digital Subscriber Line*, is a developing form of DSL with the fastest possible transmission speed: up to 52 Mbps downstream and up to 2.3 Mbps upstream. Although VDSL transmission rates rank as spectacular, the downside to this technology is that it operates only over short distances of no more than 4500 feet.

Now, on to some fascinating topics related to WAN routing and transmission, as well as some advanced (new) WAN technologies.

WAN Technologies

WANs are all about exchanging information across wide geographic areas. They are also, as you can probably gather from reading about the Internet, about scalability—the ability to grow to accommodate the number of users on the network, as well as to accommodate the demands those users place on network facilities. Although the nature of a WAN—a network reliant on communications for covering sometimes vast distances—generally dictates slower throughput, longer delays, and a greater number of errors than typically occur on a LAN, a WAN is also the fastest, most effective means of transferring computer-based information currently available.

The Way of a WAN

To at least some extent, WANs are defined by their methods of transmitting data packets. True, the means of communication must be in place. True, too, the networks making up the WAN must be up and running. And the administrators of the network must be able to monitor traffic, plan for growth, and alleviate bottlenecks. But in the end, part of what makes a WAN a WAN is its ability to ship packets of data from one place to another, over whatever infrastructure is in place. It is up to the WAN to move those packets quickly and without error, delivering them and the data they contain in exactly the same condition they left the sender, even if they must pass through numerous intervening networks to reach their destination.

Picture, for a moment, a large network with many *subnetworks*, each of which has many individual users. To the users, this large network is (or should be) *transparent*—so smoothly functioning that it is invisible. After all, they neither know nor care whether the information they need is on server A or server B, whether the person with whom they want to communicate is in city X or city Y, or whether the underlying network runs this protocol or that one. They know only that they want the network to work, and that they want their information needs satisfied accurately, efficiently, and as quickly as possible.

Now picture the same situation from the network's point of view. It "sees" hundreds, thousands, and possibly even tens of thousands of network computers or terminals and myriad servers of all kinds—print, file, mail, and even servers offering Internet access—not to mention different types of computers, gateways, routers, and communications devices. In theory, any one of these devices could communicate with, or transmit information through, any other device. Any PC, for instance, could decide to access any of the servers on the network, no matter whether that server is in the same building or in an office in another country. To complicate matters even more, two PCs might try to access the same server, and even the same resource, at the same time. And of course, the chance that only one node anywhere on the network is active at any given time is minuscule, even in the coldest, darkest hours of the night.

So, in both theory and practice, this widespread network ends up interconnecting thousands or hundreds of thousands of individual network "dots," connecting them temporarily but on demand. How can it go about the business of shuffling data ranging from quick e-mails to large (in terms of bytes) documents and even larger graphic images, sound files, and so on, when the possible interconnections between and among nodes would make a bowl of spaghetti look well organized by comparison? The solution is in the routing, which involves several different switching technologies.

Switching of any type involves moving something through a series of intermediate steps, or segments, rather than moving it directly from start point to end point. Trains, for example, can be switched from track to track, rather than run on a single, uninterrupted piece of track, and still reach their intended destination. Switching in networks works in somewhat the same way: Instead of relying on a permanent connection between source and destination, network switching relies on series of temporary connections that relay messages from station to station. Switching serves the same purpose as the direct connection, but it uses transmission resources more efficiently.

WANs (and LANs, including Ethernet and Token Ring) rely primarily on packet switching, but they also make use of circuit switching, message switching, and the relatively recent, high-speed packet-switching technology known as *cell relay*.

Circuit Switching

Circuit switching involves creating a direct physical connection between sender and receiver, a connection that lasts as long as the two parties need to communicate. In order for this to happen, of course, the connection must be set up before any communication can occur. Once the connection is made, however, the sender and receiver can count on "owning" the bandwidth allotted to them for as long as they remain connected.

Although both the sender and receiver must abide by the same data transfer speed, circuit switching does allow for a fixed (and rapid) rate of transmission. The primary drawback to circuit switching is the fact that any unused bandwidth remains exactly that: unused. Because the connection is reserved only for the two communicating parties, that unused bandwidth cannot be "borrowed" for any other transmission.

The most common form of circuit switching happens in that most familiar of networks, the telephone system, but circuit switching is also used in some networks. Currently available ISDN lines, also known as *narrowband ISDN*, and the form of T1 known as *switched T1* are both examples of circuit-switched communications technologies.

Message Switching

Unlike circuit switching, message switching does not involve a direct physical connection between sender and receiver. When a network relies on message switching, the sender can fire off a transmission—after addressing it appropriately—whenever it wants. That message is then routed through intermediate stations or, possibly, to a central network computer. Along the way, each intermediary accepts the entire message, scrutinizes the address, and then forwards the message to the next party, which can be another intermediary or the destination node.

What's especially notable about message-switching networks, and indeed happens to be one of their defining features, is that the intermediaries aren't required to forward messages immediately. Instead, they can hold messages before sending them on to their next destination. This is one of the advantages of message switching. Because the intermediate stations can wait for an opportunity to transmit, the network can avoid, or at least reduce, heavy traffic periods, and it has some control over the efficient use of communication lines.

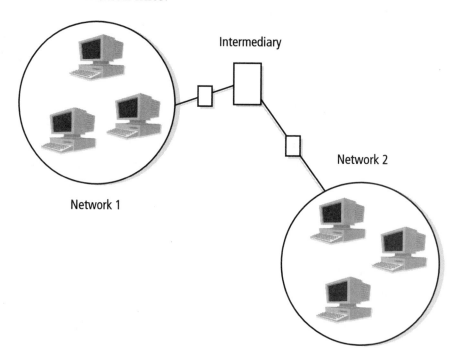

Packet Switching

Packet switching, although it is also involved in routing data within and between LANs such as Ethernet and Token Ring, is also the backbone of WAN routing. It's not the highway on which the data packets travel, but it *is* the dispatching system and to some extent the cargo containers that carry the data from place to place. In a sense, packet switching is the Federal Express or United Parcel Service of a WAN.

In packet switching, all transmissions are broken into units called packets, each of which contains addressing information that identifies both the source and destination nodes. These packets are then routed through various intermediaries, known as *Packet Switching Exchanges* (*PSEs*), until they reach their destination. At each stop along the way, the intermediary inspects the packet's destination address, consults a routing table, and forwards the packet at the highest possible speed to the next link in the chain leading to the recipient.

As they travel from link to link, packets are often carried on what are known as *virtual circuits*—temporary allocations of bandwidth over which the sending and receiving stations communicate after agreeing on certain "ground rules," including packet size, flow control, and error control. Thus, unlike circuit switching, packet switching typically does not tie up a line indefinitely for the benefit of sender and receiver. Transmissions require only the bandwidth needed for forwarding any given packet, and because packet switching is also based on multiplexing messages, many transmissions can be interleaved on the same networking medium at the same time.

Connectionless and Connection-Oriented Services

So packet-switched networks transfer data over variable routes in little bundles called packets. But how do these networks actually make the connection between the sender and the recipient? The sender can't just assume that a transmitted packet will eventually find its way to the correct destination. There has to be some kind of connection—some kind of link between the sender and the recipient. That link can be based on either *connectionless* or *connection-oriented* services, depending on the type of packet-switching network involved.

■ In a (so to speak) connectionless "connection," an actual communications link isn't established between sender and recipient before packets can be transmitted. Each transmitted packet is considered an independent unit, unrelated to any other. As a result, the packets making up a complete message can be routed over different paths to reach their destination.

■ In a connection-oriented service, the communications link is made before any packets are transmitted. Because the link is established before transmission begins, the packets comprising a message all follow the same route to their destination. In establishing the link between sender and recipient, a connection-oriented service can make use of either *switched virtual circuits* (*SVCs*) or *permanent virtual circuits* (*PVCs*):

■ Using a switched virtual circuit is comparable to calling someone on the telephone. The caller connects to the called computer, they exchange information, and then they terminate the connection.

■ Using a permanent virtual circuit, on the other hand, is more like relying on a leased line. The line remains available for use at all times, even when no transmissions are passing through it.

Types of Packet-Switching Networks

As you've seen, packet-based data transfer is what defines a packet-switching network. But—to confuse the issue a bit—referring to a packet-switching network is a little like referring to tail-wagging canines as dogs. Sure, they're dogs. But any given dog can also be a collie or a German shepherd or a poodle. Similarly, a packet-switching network might be, for example, an X.25 network, a frame relay network, an ATM (Asynchronous Transfer Mode) network, an SMDS (Switched Multimegabit Data Service), and so on.

X.25 packet-switching networks

Originating in the 1970s, X.25 is a connection-oriented, packet-switching protocol, originally based on the use of ordinary analog telephone lines, that has remained a standard in networking for about twenty years. Computers on an X.25 network carry on full-duplex communication, which begins when one computer contacts the other and the called computer responds by accepting the call.

Although X.25 is a packet-switching protocol, its concern is not with the way packets are routed from switch to switch between networks, but with defining the means by which sending and receiving computers (known as DTEs) interface with the communications devices (DCEs) through which the transmissions actually flow. X.25 has no control over the actual path taken by the packets making up any particular transmission, and as a result the packets exchanged between X.25 networks are often shown as entering a cloud at the beginning of the route and exiting the cloud at the end.

Network 1

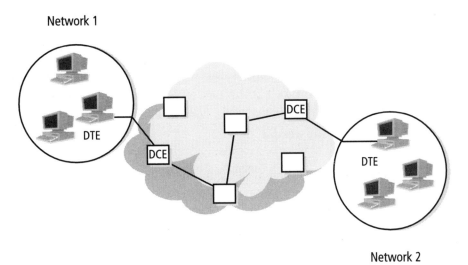

Network 2

A recommendation of the ITU (formerly the CCITT), X.25 relates to the lowest three network layers—physical, data link, and network— in the ISO reference model:

- At the lowest (physical) layer, X.25 specifies the means—electrical, mechanical, and so on—by which communication takes place over the physical media. At this level, X.25 covers standards such as RS-232, the ITU's V.24 specification for international connections, and the ITU's V.35 recommendation for high-speed modem signaling over multiple telephone circuits.

- At the next (data link) level, X.25 covers the link access protocol, known as LAPB (Link Access Protocol, Balanced), that defines how packets are framed. The LAPB ensures that two communicating devices can establish an error-free connection.

■ At the highest level (in terms of X.25), the network layer, the X.25 protocol covers packet formats and the routing and multiplexing of transmissions between the communicating devices.

On an X.25 network, transmissions are typically broken into 128-byte packets. They can, however, be as small as 64 bytes or as large as 4096 bytes.

DTEs and DCEs   As already mentioned, the sending and receiving computers on an X.25 network are not known as computers, hosts, gateways, or nodes. They are DTEs. In X.25 parlance, DTEs are devices that pass packets to DCEs, for forwarding through the links that make up a WAN. DTEs thus sit at the two ends of a network connection; in contrast, DCEs sit at the two ends of a communications circuit, as shown in the following illustration.

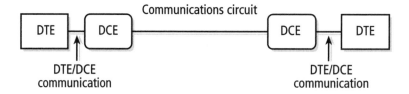

PADs   So far so good. But since packets are as important to a packet-switching network as atoms are to matter, what about the devices that create and reassemble the packets themselves? In some cases, such as an X.25 gateway computer (the DTE) that sits between a LAN and the WAN, the gateway takes care of packetizing. In other cases, as with an ordinary PC (another type of DTE), the job is handled by a device known as a *packet assembler and disassembler*, or *PAD*. In this case, the PAD sits between the computer and the network, packetizing data before transmission and, when all packets have been received, reconstituting the original message by putting the packets back together in the correct order.

Is this work difficult? Well, to a human it might be, because packets are sent along the best possible route available at the time they are forwarded. Thus, it's quite possible for the packets representing a single message to travel over different links and to arrive at their destination out of order. Considering the amount of traffic flowing over a WAN, and considering the possible number of transmitting and receiving nodes, it would seem that the job of reconstructing any given message represents a Herculean task. Well, to people, it probably does. To a PAD, it does not. Putting Humpty Dumpty back together again is all in a day's work for the PAD. It does such work over and over again.

Frame relay

Frame relay is a newer, faster, and less cumbersome form of packet switching than X.25. Often referred to as a *fast packet switching* technology, frame relay transfers variable-length packets up to 4 KB in size at 56 Kbps or T1 (1.544 or 2 Mbps) speeds over permanent virtual circuits.

Operating only at the data link layer, frame relay outpaces the X.25 protocol by stripping away much of the "accounting" overhead, such as error correction and network flow control, that is needed in an X.25 environment. Why is this? Because frame relay, unlike X.25 with its early reliance on often unreliable telephone connections, was designed to take advantage of newer digital transmission capabilities, such as fiberoptic cable and ISDN. These offer reliability and lowered error rates and thus make the types of checking and monitoring mechanisms in X.25 unnecessary.

For example, frame relay does include a means of detecting corrupted transmissions through a cyclic redundancy check, or CRC, which can detect whether any bits in the transmission have changed between the source and destination. But it does not include any facilities for error correction. Similarly, because it can depend on other, higher-layer protocols to worry about ensuring that the sender does not overwhelm the recipient with too much data too soon, frame relay is content to simply include a means of responding to "too much traffic right now" messages from the network.

In addition, because frame relay operates over permanent virtual circuits (PVCs), transmissions follow a known path and there is no need for the transmitting devices to figure out which route is best to use at a particular time. They don't really have a choice, because the routes used in frame relay are based on PVCs known as *Data Link Connection Identifiers*, or

DLCIs. Although a frame relay network can include a number of DLCIs, each must be associated permanently with a particular route to a particular destination.

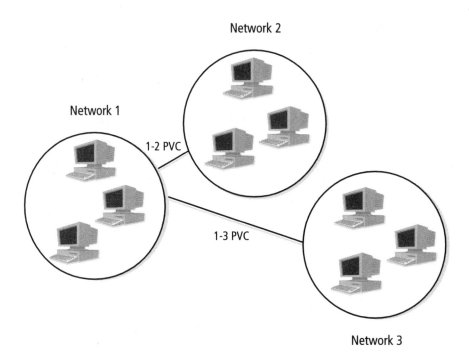

Also adding to the speed equation is the fact that the devices on a frame relay network do not have to worry about the possibility of having to re-package and/or reassemble frames as they travel. In essence, frame relay provides end-to-end service over a known—and fast—digital communications route, and it relies heavily on the reliability afforded by the digital technologies on which it depends. Like X.25, however, frame relay is based on the transmission of variable length packets, and it defines the interface between DTEs and DCEs. It is also based on multiplexing a number of (virtual) circuits on a single communications line.

So how, exactly, does frame relay work? Like X.25, frame relay switches rely on addressing information in each frame header to determine where packets are to be sent. The network transfers these packets at a predetermined rate that it assumes allows for free flow of information during normal operations.

Although frame relay networks do not themselves take on the task of controlling the flow of frames through the network, they do rely on special bits in the frame headers that enable them to address congestion. The first response to congestion is to request the sending application to "cool it" a little and slow its transmission speed; the second involves discarding frames flagged as lower-priority deliveries, and thus essentially reducing congestion by throwing away some of the cargo.

Frame relay networks connecting LANs to a WAN rely, of course, on routers and switching equipment capable of providing appropriate frame-relay interfaces.

ATM

You're focused on networks when ATM no longer translates as "Automated Teller Machine" but instead makes you immediately think "Asynchronous Transfer Mode." All right. So what is Asynchronous Transfer Mode, and what is it good for?

To begin with, ATM is a transport method capable of delivering not only data but also voice and video simultaneously, and over the same communications lines. Generally considered the wave of the immediate future in terms of increasing both LAN and WAN capabilities, ATM is a connection-oriented networking technology, closely tied to the ITU's recommendation on *broadband ISDN* (*BISDN*) released in 1988.

What ATM is good for is high-speed LAN and WAN networking over a range of media types from the traditional coaxial cable, twisted pair, and fiberoptic to communications services of the future, including Fiber Channel, FDDI, and SONET (described in later sections of this chapter).

Although ATM sounds like a dream, it's not. It's here, at least in large part.

Cell relay   ATM, like X.25 and frame relay, is based on packet switching. Unlike both X.25 and frame relay, however, ATM relies on cell relay, a high-speed transmission method based on fixed-size units (tiny ones only 53 bytes long) that are known as *cells* and that are multiplexed onto the carrier.

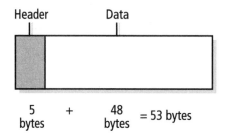

Header   Data

    5   +   48   = 53 bytes
 bytes   bytes

Because uniformly sized cells travel faster and can be routed faster than variable-length packets, they are one reason—though certainly not the only one—that ATM is so fast. Transmission speeds are commonly 56 Kbps to 1.544 Mbps, but the ITU has also defined ATM speeds as high as 622 Mbps (over fiberoptic cable).

How it works   Imagine a "universal" machine—one that can take in any materials, whether they are delivered sporadically or in a constant stream, and turn those materials into lookalike packages. That's basically how ATM works at the intake end. It takes in streams of data, voice, video…whatever…and packages the contents in uniform 53-byte cells. At the output end, ATM sends its cells out onto a WAN in a steady stream for delivery, as shown in Figure 8-1.

That all seems simple enough, but now take a look at the "magic" of ATM in a little more technical detail.

To begin with, remember that ATM is designed to satisfy the need to deliver multimedia. Well, multimedia covers a number of different types of information that have different characteristics and are handled differently, both by the devices that work with them and by higher-level networking protocols. Yet, in order to make use of ATM, something must interface with the different devices and must package their different types of data in

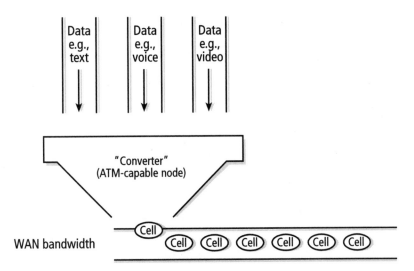

Figure 8-1   *ATM breaks data streams into fixed-size cells and delivers them over a WAN. (The "converter" here is not a real ATM switch—it's meant to suggest a hopper or funnel into which the various data streams flow...just an attempt to lighten things up, but the concept is accurate.)*

ATM cells for transport. That something is an ATM-capable node that handles the conversions specified in the three-layer ATM model shown in the following illustration:

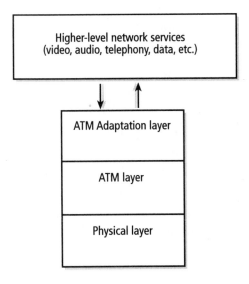

These are the layers and what they do:

- The topmost layer, the *ATM Adaptation Layer (AAL)*, sits between what you might consider "ATM proper" and the higher-level network devices and protocols that send and receive the different types of information over the ATM network. AAL, as the *adaptation* in its name suggests, mediates between the ATM layer and higher-level protocols, remodeling the services of one so that they fit the services of the other. It's a fascinating "place," in that AAL takes in all the different forms of data (audio, video, data frames) and hands the data over to comparable AAL services (audio, video, data frames) that repackage the information into 48-byte payloads before passing them along to the ATM layer for further grooming.

- The ATM layer attaches headers to the ATM payloads. That might seem simple enough, but the header does not simply say, "this is a cell." Part of the header includes information that identifies the paths and circuits over which those cells will travel and so enables ATM switches and routers to deliver the cells accurately to their intended destinations. The ATM layer also multiplexes the cells for transmission before passing them to the physical layer. This layer, as you can see, has a big job to do. It's somewhat reminiscent of a busy airport, railroad station...or maybe a large department store during the holiday season.

- The physical layer, the lowest layer, corresponds to the physical layer in the ISO/OSI Reference Model. As in the OSI model, it is concerned with moving information—in this case, the 53-byte ATM cells—into the communications medium. As already mentioned, this medium can be any of a number of different physical transports, including the fiberoptics-based SONET (Synchronous Optical NETwork), a T1 or E1 line, or even a modem. The medium and the message in this case are clearly separable because ATM is a transport *method* and is independent of the transmissions medium over which the messages travel.

So what happens after ATM filters information down through the AAL, ATM, and physical layers? Once the physical layer sends the cells on their way, they travel to their destinations over connections that might switch them from one circuit to another. Along the way, the switches and routers work to maintain connections that provide the network with at least the minimum bandwidth necessary to provide users with the *quality of service (QOS)* guaranteed them.

When the cells arrive at their destinations, they go through the reverse of the sending process. The ATM layer forwards the cells to the appropriate services (voice, data, video, and so on) in the AAL, where the cell contents are converted back to their original form, everything is checked to be sure it arrived correctly, and the "reconstituted" information is delivered to the receiving device.

Availability   So ATM is a wonderful means of transmitting all kinds of information at high speed. It is reliable, flexible, scalable, and fast because it relies on higher-level protocols for error checking and correction. It can interface with both narrowband and broadband networks, and it is especially suitable for use in a network backbone.

Is there a downside? Well, yes. To begin with, ATM networks must be made up of ATM-compatible devices, and they are both expensive and not yet widely available. In addition, there is a chicken-or-egg dilemma facing serious ATM deployment: businesses are not likely to incur the expense of investing in ATM-capable equipment if ATM services are not readily available through communications carriers over a wide area, yet carriers are reluctant to invest in ATM networking solutions if there is not enough demand for the service.

Eventually, no doubt, ATM will win over both carriers and users, and the world will be treated to extremely fast, reliable ATM delivery. Until then, ATM continues to mature, especially with the help of an organization known as the ATM Forum—a group of vendors and other interested parties working together to develop standards, provide information, and generally encourage the development of ATM-related technology. As time passes, ATM is expected to build up a complete head of steam and begin to fulfill its promise. Certainly, with increasing reliance on networking and growing demand for faster and more sophisticated methods of delivering multimedia, there's a place for this technology.

And that, in a nutshell, is ATM. However, before leaving the subject, it's worth taking a quick look at broadband ISDN, another immature but promising technology, and the one for which the ATM layers were defined.

BISDN   BISDN is next-generation ISDN, a technology that can deliver all kinds of information over the network. In BISDN terms, this information is divided into two basic categories, *interactive services* and *distributed (or distribution) services.*

- Interactive services include you-*and*-me types of transactions, such as videoconferencing, messaging, and information retrieval.

- Distributed services include you-*to*-me types of information that are either delivered or broadcast to the recipient. These services are further divided into those that the recipient controls (for example, e-mail, video telephony, and telex) and those that the recipient cannot control other than by refusing to "tune in" (for example, audio and television broadcasts).

But, you might think, current narrowband ISDN is also capable of delivering data, voice, video, and sound, so what's the difference? The difference is in the method of delivery. Narrowband ISDN transmissions are based on time division multiplexing (TDM), which uses timing as the key to interleaving multiple transmissions onto a single signal. In contrast, BISDN uses ATM, with its packet switching and its little 53-byte cells, for delivery.

Thus, ATM defines BISDN, or at least the part of it concerned with delivering the goods. In a sense, BISDN is comparable to a catalog shopping service that delivers everything from food to clothing, and ATM is like the boxes in which those products are packaged and delivered.

Developing Technologies

ATM is but one example of an advanced technology. ATM is here, though not yet widely available. So is it the only one to choose from? No, there are others. One, FDDI, is well known and used in both LANs and WANs. Two others are SONET, another developing technology, and SMDS, which is available through some carriers. All three—FDDI, SONET, and SMDS—tie in with ATM, at least in the sense of being high-speed networking technologies that are recommended by the ATM Forum as interfaces for ATM networks.

All three of the networks described in the following sections are, of course, designed for speed, speed, and more speed. Along with reliability, of course....

FDDI

FDDI, variously pronounced either "fiddy" or "eff-dee-dee-eye," is short for *Fiber Distributed Data Interface*. As you've no doubt guessed, it's based on fiberoptic transmission. It's also based on a ring topology and token passing. It's advanced technology, yes, in the form of token ring over fiber.

FDDI was developed for two primary reasons: to support and help extend the capabilities of older LANs, such as Ethernet and Token Ring, and to provide a reliable infrastructure for businesses moving even *mission-critical* applications to networks. Based on a standard produced by an ANSI committee known as X3T9.5, the FDDI specification was released in 1986—a relatively long time ago in networking terms.

Although FDDI isn't really a WAN technology (its rings are limited to a maximum length of 100 kilometers, or 62 miles), the ground it can cover does make it suitable for use as a backbone connecting a number of smaller LANs, and it can provide the core of a network as large as a Metropolitan Area Network (MAN). In that sense, FDDI is more than LAN but less than WAN. In addition, because FDDI transfers information extremely quickly (100 Mbps), it is often used to connect high-end devices, such as mainframes, minicomputers, and peripherals, or to connect high-performance devices within a LAN. Engineering or video/graphics workstations, for instance, benefit from FDDI because they need considerable bandwidth in order to transfer large amounts of data at satisfactorily high speeds.

As its name indicates, FDDI was developed around the idea of using optical cable. This is, in fact, the type of cable used, especially when high-speed transmission is needed over relatively long distances (2000 to 10,000 meters, or roughly 1 to 6 miles). However, over shorter distances (about 100 meters, or 330 feet), FDDI can also be implemented on less expensive copper cable. In all, FDDI supports four different types of cable:

- **Multimode fiberoptic cable.** This type of cable can be used over a maximum of 2000 meters and uses LEDs as a light source.

- **Single mode fiberoptic cable.** This can be used over a maximum of 10,000 meters and uses lasers as a light source. Single mode cable is thinner at the core than multimode, but it provides greater bandwidth because of the way the light impulse travels through the cable.

- **Category 5 Unshielded Twisted Pair copper wiring.** This cable contains eight wires and, like the next category, can be used over distances up to 30 meters.

- **IBM Type 1 Shielded Twisted Pair copper wiring.** This is a shielded cable that contains two pairs of twisted wires, with each pair also shielded.

FDDI topology and fault tolerance

FDDI topology and operation are similar to Token Ring, *except* (there's always an exception, is there not?) that FDDI is primarily based on optical transmission. In addition, FDDI is characterized by two *counter-rotating* rings (known as a *dual-ring topology*).

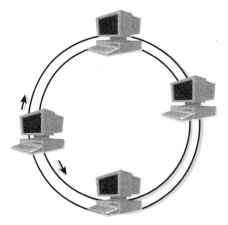

Why two rings? The second one is there mostly for insurance. Normally in a FDDI network, one ring (known as the primary ring) actually carries the tokens and data, and the secondary ring remains idle and is used as a backup for fault tolerance—insurance. Because the secondary ring is available if needed, whenever a nonfunctioning node causes a break in the primary ring, traffic can "wrap" around the problem node and continue carrying data, only in the opposite direction and on the secondary ring. That way, even if a node goes down, the network continues to function.

Of course, it is also possible for two nodes to fail. When this happens, the wrap at both locations effectively segments the one ring into two separate, noncommunicating rings. To avoid this potentially serious problem, FDDI networks can rely on bypass devices known as concentrators. These concentrators resemble hubs or MAUs in that multiple nodes plug into them. They are also able to isolate any failed nodes, while keeping the network traffic flowing.

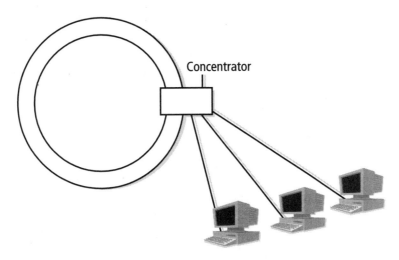

Sometimes, however, both rings are used for data. In this case, the data travels in one direction (clockwise) on one ring, and in the other direction (counterclockwise) on the other ring. Using both rings to carry data means that twice as many frames can circulate at the same time and, therefore, the speed of the network can double—from 100 Mbps to 200 Mbps.

FDDI token passing
Token passing on a FDDI network works much the way it does on a Token Ring network. That is, nodes pass a token around the ring, and only the

node with the token is allowed to transmit a frame. There is a twist to this, however, that's related to FDDI's fault tolerance. When a node on the ring detects a problem, it doesn't simply sit around and say, "gee, I can't pass the token along, I guess I'll just hang onto it." Instead, it generates a frame known as a *beacon* and sends it on to the network. As neighboring nodes detect the beacon, they too begin to transmit beacons, and so it goes around the ring. When the node that started the process eventually receives its own beacon back—usually after the network has switched to the secondary ring—it then assumes that the problem has been isolated or resolved, generates a new token, and starts the ball rolling once again.

Structure of a FDDI network

A FDDI network, as already mentioned, cannot include rings longer than 100 kilometers apiece. Another restriction on a FDDI network is that it cannot support more than 500 nodes per ring. Although the overall network topology must conform to a logical ring, the network doesn't actually have to look like a circle. It can include stars connected to hubs or concentrators, and it can even include trees—collections of hubs connected in a hierarchy. As long as the stars and trees connect in a logical ring, the FDDI network is happy.

In terms of the nodes that connect to the network, they come in two varieties, depending on how they are attached to the FDDI ring. One variety, called a *single attachment station*, or *SAS*, connects to a concentrator and, through it, to the primary ring. Because an SAS connects to a concentrator, the latter device can isolate the node from the rest of the ring if it happens to fail.

The second type of node, called a *dual attachment station*, or *DAS*, has two connections to the network. These can link it either to another node and a concentrator or—if their operation is critical to the network—to two concentrators, one of which serves as a backup in case the other fails. This type of two-concentrator connection for a single resource, such as a mission-critical server, is known as *dual homing* and is used to provide the most fail-safe backup mechanism possible.

In sum: FDDI is a high-speed, high-bandwidth network based on optical transmissions. It is relatively expensive to implement, although the cost can be held down by the mixing of fiberoptic with copper cabling. Because it has been around for a few years, however, it has been fine-tuned to a high level of stability. It is most often used as a network backbone, for connecting high-end computers (mainframes, minicomputers, and peripherals), and for LANs connecting high-performance engineering, graphics, and other workstations that demand rapid transfer of large amounts of data.

SONET

SONET, or *Synchronous Optical NETwork*, is an ANSI standard for the transmission of different types of information—data, voice, video—over the optical (fiberoptic) cables widely used by long-distance carriers. Designed to provide communications carriers with a standard interface for connecting optical networks, SONET was formulated by an organization known as the Exchange Carriers Standards Assocation (ECSA) and later incorporated into an ITU recommendation known as *Synchronous Digital Hierarchy*, or *SDH*.

Today, apart from relatively small differences, SONET and SDH are equivalent—SONET in North America and Japan, and SDH in Europe. Together, they represent a global standard for digital networks that enables transmission systems around the world to connect through optical media. SONET is comparable to a standard that ensures that train tracks, regardless of manufacturer, follow the same design specifications and therefore can interconnect to allow trains to pass over them freely and without problem.

Originally designed in the mid-1980s, SONET works at the physical layer and is concerned with the details related to framing, multiplexing, managing, and transmitting information synchronously over optical media. In essence, SONET specifies a standard means for multiplexing a number of slower signals onto a larger, faster one for transmission.

In relation to this multiplexing capability, two signal definitions lie at the heart of the SONET standard:

- Optical carrier (OC) levels, which are used by fiberoptic media and which translate roughly to speed and carrying capacity

- Synchronous transfer signals (STS), which are the electrical equivalents of OC levels and are used by non-fiber media

So what does that mean? Well, let's back up a little. SONET is an optical transport, true. But remember that it is a long-distance transport. Although transmissions flow through the SONET system in optical form, they do not begin and end that way. Transmissions are multiplexed onto the SONET optical medium, but they come from—and go to—other, electrically based, types of digital transport such as T1. In this, it helps to think of SONET as something like the Mississippi River, and of the channels it connects to as tributaries that flow into and out of it. (In SONET terminology, those channels actually *are* called tributaries, so the analogy is reasonably accurate.) The following illustration shows basically what happens during a SONET transmission:

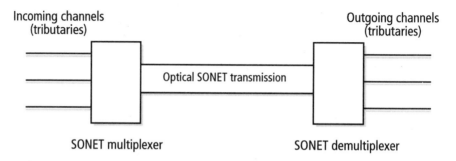

Because SONET is a synchronous transport, the signals it works with are tied to timing, and the various transmission speeds it handles are based on multiples of a single base signal rate known as STS-1 (Synchronous Transport Signal level-1) and the equivalent, optical, OC-1. This base rate operates at 51.84 Mbps. That sounds really fast, and it begins to show why SONET is seen as a desirable transport method, but remember—51.84 Mbps is *base* signal. SONET rates get even better. Higher-level SONET rates really fly. The next step up, for instance, is STS-3 (equivalent to OC-3), which multiplexes three STS-1 signals onto a single stream and operates at three times the base signal rate—155.520 Mbps. And there's more. STS-12 (OC-12) operates at 12 times the base signal, which works out to 622.08 Mbps. And at the top end, there's STS-48 (OC-48), with a defined transmission speed of 2.488 Gbps (that's *gigabits* per second).

How it works

As you can see from the preceding illustration, SONET converts electrical (STS) signals to optical (OC) levels for transport. It also "unconverts" them (OC to STS) at the point where the transmissions leave the SONET media for further travel on whatever carrier takes them the rest of the way to their destination. How this all happens is both impressive and intriguing.

To start off with, SONET is not a single, very long piece of optical fiber. (Of course not—that would mean one piece of cable stretching around the world....) Along the way from source to destination, a transmission can pass through more than one intermediate multiplexer, as well as through switches, routers, and repeaters for boosting the signal. Different parts of this route are given different SONET names:

- A *section* is a single length of fiberoptic cable.

- A *line* is any segment of the path that runs between two multiplexers.

- A *path* is the complete route between the source multiplexer (where signals from tributaries are combined) and the destination multiplexer (where the signals are demultiplexed so they can be sent on their way).

The transmissions themselves are made up of 810-byte frames that are sent out at the rate of 8000 per second. These frames contain not only data but also a number of bytes related to overhead—monitoring, management, and so on. To an interested bystander, there are two especially remarkable aspects to the way these frames are managed:

- First, they pour out in a steady stream, whether or not they contain any information. In other words, they are like freight cars on an endless train. If some data happens to arrive at the time SONET is putting a frame together, that data gets popped into the frame—the freight car is loaded. If no data arrives, the frame leaves the "station" empty.

- Second, because SONET is a synchronous transport, each frame contains a device called a pointer that indicates where the actual data in the frame begins. This pointer is necessary because timing is such an important part of SONET transmission, but the network itself cannot assume that the arriving data streams are synchronized to the same clock. (That would, in fact, be impossible.) Instead, SONET allows for a certain amount of variation in timing and uses a pointer to ensure that the beginning of the data payload is clearly marked for retrieval at its destination.

Protocol layers in the SONET standard

In doing all of the work of organizing, multiplexing, transmitting, and routing frames, SONET relies on four protocol layers, each of which handles one aspect of the entire transmission. These layers and what they do are:

- **The photonic layer,** which converts signals between electrical and optical form

- **The section layer,** which creates the frames and takes care of monitoring for errors in transmission

- **The line layer,** which is in charge of multiplexing, synchronizing, and demultiplexing

- **The path layer,** which is concerned with getting the frame from source to destination

There are many more technical details involved in the definition of a SONET network, but these are the basics, and they should help you understand at least roughly how SONET works. Perhaps the most important lesson to carry away from this is the realization that SONET represents a fast, reliable transport for developing or future WAN technologies, including BISDN (and, by extension, ATM).

SMDS

And finally, you come to *SMDS*, more lengthily known as *Switched Multimegabit Data Service*. SMDS is a broadband public networking service offered by communications carriers as a means for businesses to connect LANs in separate locations. It is a connectionless, packet-switched technology designed to provide business with a less expensive means of linking networks than through the use of dedicated leased lines. Besides reducing cost, SMDS is notable for being well-suited to the type of "bursty" traffic characteristic of LAN (or LAN-to-LAN) communications. In other words, it does the job when it's needed.

Because SMDS is connectionless, it is available when and as needed, rather than being "on" at all times. It is also a fast technology, transmitting at speeds of 1 Mbps to (in the United States) 45 Mbps. The basis of an SMDS connection is a network address designed as a telephone number that includes country code and area code, as well as the local number. This address is assigned by the carrier and is used to connect LAN with LAN. A group address can also be used to broadcast information to a number of different LANs at the same time.

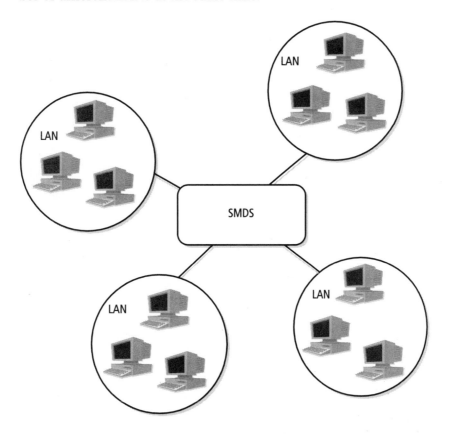

Users who need to transfer information to one or more LANs simply select the appropriate addresses in order to indicate where the information is to be delivered. SMDS takes it from there and makes a "best effort" to deliver the packets to their destinations. It does not check for errors in transmission, nor does it make an attempt at flow control. Those tasks are left to the communicating LANs.

The packets transferred through SMDS are simple, variable-length affairs containing the source and destination addresses and up to 9188 bytes of data. These packets are routed individually and can contain data in whatever form the sending LAN works with—Ethernet packet, Token Ring packet, and so on. SMDS essentially just passes the information from one place to the other and doesn't deal with the form or format of the data. In other words, SMDS acts somewhat like a courier service—it picks up and delivers but does not concern itself with the contents of its packages.

9

The Internet and the Web

And now, having traveled the road from small peer-to-peer networks to clients and servers, LANs, extended LANs, and WAN technologies, you come to the biggest, "baddest" network of them all: the Internet, the offspring in large part of Vinton Cerf, who is often called the "father of the Internet" for his work in developing the now ubiquitous TCP/IP networking protocol.

But why discuss the Internet—or more specifically, the World Wide Web—in a book about networking? Well, why not? Even though many people see the Internet as something of an entertainment and shopping medium, that same Internet has fueled the explosion of interest in "Net" technologies ranging from Web browsing, cross-platform software development, intelligent agents, and push-and-pull information retrieval to e-commerce and the very business-oriented development of intranets and (to a lesser extent as yet) of extranets. The Internet has even caught the attention of governments around the world. Although the world has yet to find out whether government interest is a good thing, the question is certainly vigorously debated by technical and nontechnical people alike.

But this digresses.

Structure of the Internet

As mentioned early in the book, the Internet (capital I) is an internetwork (lowercase i), a global conglomeration of smaller networks able to communicate and transfer information among themselves. These days—since the early to mid 1990s—it is also the highest flying, most widely publicized aspect of high technology since...well, since what? Perhaps since the Apple II and the IBM PC took center stage and started the process of convincing the entire world that computing was within the grasp of ordinary nontechnical mortals.

To most people, the Internet is something you connect to through a modem and a telephone line or, if you're lucky, through a much faster ISDN or xDSL line or a cable modem. But even though this single connection is all that's needed to access the Internet, the network itself is a complex creation. If you were able to see the structure of the Internet, say from a vantage point in space, you would see it as a global mesh of different networks and network levels, as shown in Figure 9-1:

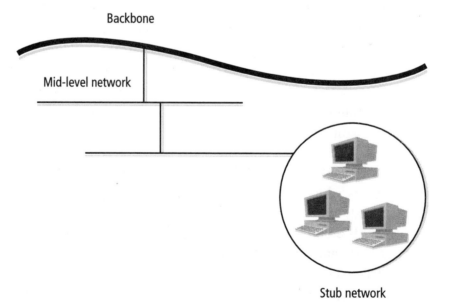

Figure 9-1.   *The Internet is a hierarchy made up of stub networks, mid-level networks, and Internet backbones.*

And if you could look even closer, you would see that this intricate web (no pun intended) consists of servers, gateways, routers, and the numerous communications lines connecting them. *That* is the Internet, the ever-growing networking phenomenon that has exploded in the mid and late 90s...the phenomenon with the potential to be bigger than television and which is even now far more engaging in terms of user participation. The Internet—created for academia and the military, but now maintained to serve the information needs of dial-up clients everywhere.

Regional and Other Networks

Of course the world is a big place, and so geography also plays a large role in determining the structure of the Internet. In the United States, for example, the Internet is made up of a number of regional networks serving the northeast, midwest, west, east, southeast, northwest, and central California. There is also one regional network—appropriately named CERFnet—for international and western United States traffic. To join up with the larger Internet, these regional networks connect to a national backbone through one of four major locations known as *network access points* or *NAPs* located near large cities: San Francisco, Washington, D.C., Chicago, and New York.

Internet Providers

So now comes the question of how everyone connects to this universal marketplace of ideas and products. The answer: through an *Internet Service Provider* (*ISP*) or an online service provider, such as the Microsoft Network (MSN) or America Online (AOL). Both ISPs and online service providers are the vendors, so to speak, that provide a pipeline to the Internet—usually through a connection to a regional network and, through that connection, to the Internet backbone. As a group, these providers are businesses with the equipment and technology needed to provide high-speed access to the Internet over communications lines such as T1. Some of these providers are national or international companies, such as MCI and AOL. Others are small organizations that provide access to individual cities or relatively small geographic regions.

Internet and Web Commonalities

Although the Internet is text-based and the World Wide Web is graphical, the Web is, as most everyone knows, part of the Internet. It just happens to be the popularized part inhabited by small businesses, multinational corporations, Hollywood, television, the news media, and even providers of hardware and software for accessing the Internet. The Web is also the part of the Internet characterized by pretty pictures, sound, video, and animated banner ads that visually scream "click me" as they scroll, bounce, jump, fly, or slither across the screen.

NOTE Although the Web is sometimes referred to as an "Internet service," that description seems a little disingenuous in light of its size and the impact it has had on the pre-millennium mid to late 90s. Somehow, the description seems about as appropriate as calling brain surgery a "BAND-AID® service." (No disrespect to BAND-AIDs intended—it's a question of magnitude.)

At any rate, since the Web is actually the collection of hyperlinked documents that forms part of the global Internet, there must be at least a few things the two have in common. And so there are, starting with the way Internet and Web sites are organized and named.

Domains

In addition to its physical structure and organization, the Internet is built upon the concept of *domains*. These domains and the conventions used in creating and managing them were devised as a means for:

- maintaining order in what might otherwise become a chaotic virtual world

- allowing for orderly, continued growth of the Internet

The domain name system

Somewhat like the names used in classifying plants and animals (for example, mammal/big cat/lion), Internet domains contribute to a classification system—the *Domain Name System*, or *DNS*—that uniquely identifies sites based on a tree-like hierarchy that includes a *top-level domain*, a *second-level domain* and, often, one or more *subdomains*.

So what does all this mean to you? Well, first of all, a DNS site name looks like the following:

microsoft.com

where:

- **com** represents the top-level domain

- **microsoft** represents the second-level domain—in this case, the name of a rather familiar business

- **a period** (pronounced "dot") separates the top-level and second-level domain names

But that's just the beginning. Because the DNS is based on a treelike hierarchy, domains at one level can be "parents" to multiple domains on the next (lower) level like this:

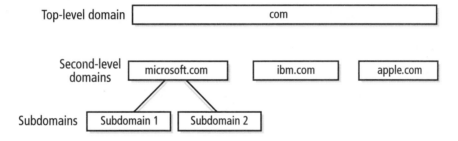

So, for example, a domain name like the preceding one can be extended further to include multiple subdomains within the site and, possibly, the names of host computers within the subdomains. Using an imaginary example, here are two names representing different subdomains and hosts within a business:

lion.bigcat.msftcats.com
tabby.smallcat.msftcats.com

where:

- **msftcats.com** represents the second-level and top-level domain names

- **bigcat** and **smallcat** represent different subdomains within the site

- **lion** and **tabby** represent different hosts within the subdomains

Notice, by the way, that even though your eye probably reads domain names from left to right, the name is *resolved* from right to left, with the highest-level domain at the far right.

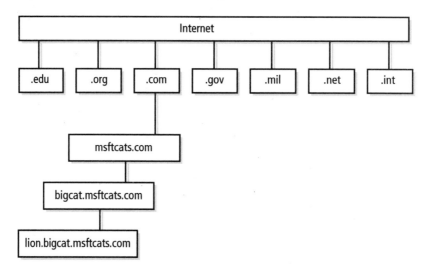

Top-level Internet domains

The word *domain* itself brings to mind such synonyms as *kingdom* and *realm*, and Internet domains are, indeed, something like virtual "kingdoms," though not in the sense of being ruled by different leaders, but rather in the sense of being united by something that all members have in common. For the top-level domains, that "something" is either geography or type of organization.

The geographic domains group sites by country, with each country assigned a two-letter abbreviation. Some examples:

- **.fr** for France
- **.de** for Germany
- **.ca** for Canada
- **.es** for Spain
- **.ar** for Argentina
- **.jp** for Japan

- **.za** for South Africa
- **.us** for the United States

The domains that group sites by type use the three-letter abbreviations so familiar to Internet users:

- **.com** for commercial sites
- **.org** for noncommercial organizations
- **.gov** for the U.S. government
- **.net** for network-related groups
- **.edu** for educational institutions
- **.mil** for the U.S. military
- **.int** for international organizations

And within all these domains is the vast array of Internet sites—comparable to stalls in the world's biggest bazaar—that are created, owned, and maintained by various individuals and organizations wanting to announce themselves, their products, their interests, and even their philosophies to anyone who cares to seek out and visit them. (Some sites are selective enough to require visitors to subscribe and possibly pay for their services, but most are free.)

DNS Databases and IP Addresses

The preceding sections have described the DNS in terms of naming Internet sites, because those names are the ones you see in ads ("come visit our Web site at *www.microsoft.com*"), and they are the ones you type in the address bar of your Web browser whenever you want to visit a particular site.

It's very important to note, however, that DNS *also* refers to databases distributed among a number of *DNS name servers*. To understand why this is important, start by thinking about how computers contact each other on the Internet. When you type *www.microsoft.com* to visit the Microsoft Web site, does your computer send out that particular stream of characters and hope that another computer named *www.microsoft.com* answers? Not at all.

What your computer does is use the microsoft.com site's *IP* (*Internet Protocol*) *address* in communicating. This address is totally numeric, although it does use dots just like the friendly text-based DNS names do, and it looks something like this: 207.46.130.149. This address is very strictly defined, byte-by-byte, and is technically known as dotted octet format. It is also the only "name" computers use to recognize one another on the Internet.

However, not many people would be able to remember such strings of numbers, crucial though they are, and so DNS and its databases come to the rescue. Through its databases, DNS matches friendly names to IP addresses, rather like a phone book matches people names to telephone numbers. In so doing, the DNS databases ensure that humans can use human-friendly words and computers can use computer-friendly numbers, while also guaranteeing that the site you request and the site your computer contacts are always one and the same.

Root servers

As you can see, the job performed by the DNS name servers is critical, since they, and they alone, can turn a typed address into its corresponding numeric IP address. However…DNS name servers are not monolithic machines that sit somewhere "out there," surveying the entire Internet, matching clients (visiting computers) and servers (Internet sites) like some digital dating service.

The Internet hierarchy, remember, is composed of different domain levels. DNS name servers do their matchmaking at different levels, too, and the DNS name server at any given level is considered the name/address *authority* for that level.

At the very highest level, for example, the one that corresponds to the top-level domains (com, org, net, and so on), the DNS authority for top-level domain names is known as a *root server*. This server contains the information needed to locate the server for, say, microsoft.com. But that's all it does. The root server does not concern itself with any lower levels—subdomains—within microsoft.com. That job belongs to lower-level servers that contain information about subdomains, sub-subdomains, and so on. In a sense, you can think of the process of passing authority from one level down to the next as a computer equivalent of trickle-down economics.

Making connections

So, given the existence of top-level domains, subdomains, DNS name servers, and address resolution from site name to IP address, how exactly does computer A go about contacting site B (say, *bigcat.msftcats.com*), when both are total strangers? This is what happens:

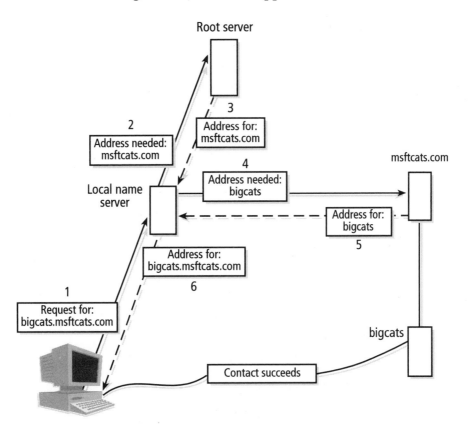

1. First, computer A contacts its local DNS name server, saying "I want to get in touch with site B."

2. If the local name server already knows how to do this, it responds by sending A the address for site B. If the local name server does *not* know the address, it sends the request on to a root server. How does

it know what root server to contact? That information is already part of its "knowledge base."

3. The root server, although it cannot resolve the entire address for site B, does give the local name server the information it needs to contact msftcats.com.

4. Armed with this information, the local name server then contacts msftcats.com, which is then able to provide the complete address for bigcat.msftcats.com.

This whole process of name resolution is known as an iterative query because the request is sent repeatedly (iteratively) through name servers in the domain hierarchy until the complete address—or a "no such site exists" response—is produced.

Although the process sounds tedious and time-consuming, there are two ways in which the DNS system speeds things along. First, the top-level database is replicated (reproduced) on many root servers located throughout the world, so the task of resolving addresses at the highest level does not need to be handled by one or two overworked machines. Second, servers at all levels cache the addresses they've already resolved. When a request for a particular location arrives, these servers consult their cache first. So, if they find the needed address, they can send an immediate response to the requesting computer. Only if they cannot find the address in their cache do they then have to go through the iterative string of queries needed to resolve the name.

NSI, IANA, ICANN, and the Future

As you've probably guessed, the Domain Name System involves some heavy-duty tracking and record keeping to ensure that site names are not duplicated, that site names and IP addresses are correctly maintained, and that new sites and their corresponding IP addresses are added to the appropriate databases. So who does all this?

Within an organization, it's the responsibility of the organization itself to keep track of its subdomains, hosts, and various subgroups (called zones) that are defined by either administrative or authoritative responsibilities.

For the top-level domains, the responsibility for registering names for com, net, and org has until recently been in the hands of a for-profit organization called Network Solutions, Inc. (NSI). The responsibility for assigning IP addresses has been handled by a group known as IANA (Internet Assigned Numbers Authority) located at the University of Southern California. Both groups operated under exclusive contracts with the United States government.

In 1998, however, the U.S. Department of Commerce, after considerable review and sometimes contentious debate, approved an agreement to privatize these responsibilities and hand them over to a new corporation known as *ICANN* (*Internet Corporation for Assigned Names and Numbers*). As of the beginning of 1999, ICANN is in the process of developing its organization under the supervision of a 19-member board of directors.

Organizations and Standards Groups

In addition to IANA (and now ICANN), there are numerous organizations involved in various aspects of the Internet. Some are highly technical organizations concerned with developing and maintaining Internet standards. Others are concerned with Internet-related issues such as security, privacy, and—in the case of the Electronic Frontier Foundation (EFF)—the preservation of civil liberties and free speech for Internet users. The following list briefly describes some globally recognized and technically oriented organizations frequently mentioned in terms of the Internet and its continued growth and evolution:

■ The *Internet Society*, or *ISOC*, is a nonprofit membership organization based in Reston, Virginia, with members from around the world. Its focus is, as described on its home page (*www.isoc.org*), on "standards, education, and policy issues" that affect the Internet.

■ The *Internet Architecture Board*, or *IAB*, is an ISOC technical advisory group involved in several aspects of the Internet. As part of its function, it advises the Internet Society on technical and other matters. This group also oversees the architecture for Internet protocols and procedures, supervises standards processes, and represents the

Internet Society in dealing with other organizations concerned with Internet standards and other issues.

- The *Internet Engineering Task Force*, or *IETF*, is an organization of individuals interested in the evolution and operation of the Internet. The work of the IETF is handled by various working groups that deal with issues such as routing, operations and management, user services, and security. The IETF is open to new members worldwide and is overseen by the Internet Engineering Steering Group (IESG), a supervisory arm of the Internet Society.

- The *Internet Research Task Force*, or *IRTF*, is a group of volunteers, complementary to the IETF, that focuses on long-term projects related to the Internet—for example, the issue of privacy as it relates to e-mail. The IRTF is supervised by the Internet Research Steering Group (IRSG) and, like the IETF, is part of the Internet Society.

- The *World Wide Web Consortium*, or *W3C*, is (as the name clearly indicates) concerned solely with the World Wide Web—specifically, with standards and protocols designed to promote both the growth and interoperability of the Web. The W3C is often in the technical news as the standards body to which developing technologies are submitted for consideration and possible approval. The organization is young—dating only from 1994—but it boasts an international membership and an influential voice in Web development and standards.

Well, that's the "scoop," more or less, on the Internet as a whole and the way it is organized and maintained. Now, move in for a closer look at how it operates and (the fun part) what it offers.

Internet Connections

Despite its mammoth size and scope and the speed of the backbones, routers, and other elements of its infrastructure, the Internet is at heart—at least for now—a dial-up network in that end users don't normally connect through ISDN lines, cable modems, or other high-speed technologies. They use plain old telephone service.

Where the Internet is concerned, however, this voice-based telephone service is required to carry serial transmissions and enable computer-to-computer connections. And the computers themselves must be able to establish and terminate sessions as well as agree on framing, error control, and other communications niceties that occur at the data link layer. The solution used during most sessions happens to be one of three IP protocols, known as PPP, SLIP, and CSLIP (a compressed version of SLIP).

PPP

Of the three protocols used by most ISPs, *PPP*, the *Point–to-Point Protocol*, is the newest and fastest. It is also an Internet standard. A flexible means of enabling computers to communicate, PPP supports multiple protocols, including the Internet's TCP/IP (of course), as well as IPX, AppleTalk, and others. PPP is based upon two main elements:

■ A *Link Control Protocol* (*LCP*), which is used to set up, test, negotiate, and end a computer-to-computer link

■ A *Network Control Protocol* (*NCP*), which is used to negotiate and establish the details related to the protocols to be used during the transmission

Essentially, this is how the pieces fit together in a PPP connection to the Internet:

1. First, a PC uses its modem to call the user's ISP.

2. Then, LCP comes into play. During this phase of the connection, LCP establishes a link with the ISP's equipment, tests the link, and negotiates options, such as frame type and packet size, to be used for communication.

3. Next, the NCP is used to configure protocol-specific characteristics for use during the session. For example, it is at this point in many connections that the calling computer, through the NCP, is dynamically assigned a temporary IP address, which is needed in order for the computer to use the TCP/IP protocol stack. (As a side note, because PPP supports the dynamic allocation of IP addresses, matters

are greatly simplified for the end user, who would otherwise have to provide a valid address himself or herself—not a very friendly option for nontechnical individuals.)

4. Now that the groundwork is complete, data transmission begins.

5. When it's time to end the session, NCP swings into action again to dismantle the network layer connection.

6. And finally, the LCP takes responsibility for terminating the connection gracefully.

In addition to all this, PPP supports two methods of authenticating users, PAP (Password Authentication Protocol) and CHAP (Challenge-Handshake Authentication Protocol). Both provide a measure of security in that the communicating computers can verify that they are, indeed, who they say they are.

SLIP

SLIP is short for *Serial Line Internet Protocol.* A simpler, older means of enabling computers to communicate over a serial transmission line, SLIP has been widely used for Internet connections. Unlike PPP, SLIP supports TCP/IP only, but that is not a particular disadvantage, since the Internet itself is based on TCP/IP. SLIP, however, does suffer from some restrictions that make it less desirable than PPP for Internet connections:

■ SLIP does not include any means of error detection or correction.

■ SLIP does not support dynamic allocation of IP addresses, so the caller must know and be able to provide not only his or her own IP address, but the one assigned to the remote computer as well. If an ISP assigns IP addresses dynamically, the caller's software must be able to "catch" and use the assigned address, or else the caller must provide that information manually.

■ SLIP is not an Internet standard and so exists in a number of different, incompatible versions.

■ SLIP does not authenticate users, so there is no means of verifying the identities of the calling and called computers.

Despite these disadvantages, however, SLIP is still in wide use. That situation is likely to change over time, as support for PPP continues to grow.

CSLIP

CSLIP, as the initials in its name indicate, is a variation of SLIP. The *C* stands for *Compressed*, so CSLIP's complete name works out as *Compressed Serial Line Internet Protocol.*

Like SLIP, CSLIP is designed for serial traffic and supports TCP/IP. Where it differs from SLIP is in the packet header, which is compressed from the 24 bytes used in SLIP packets to a mere 5 bytes in CSLIP. In order to compress the packet headers, CSLIP takes advantage of the fact that certain header fields are repeated in packet after packet. CSLIP eliminates the fields that succeeding packets have in common with those that have already been transmitted, and thus it includes only those that differ in each packet. Although shrinking the header without also shrinking the data portion of a packet would not seem to be that much of an advantage, in actuality it does optimize SLIP, especially when long documents are transmitted.

Internet and Web Protocols and Services

There's a lot more to learn about the Internet, as you would imagine—not only more technologies, but more details about the technologies described here: bits and bytes per header field, frame construction, communication signals ("yes, I got it," "garbled—please resend," and so on), and many details about how software manages to allow remote connections, automatic logons, password verification, and on and on. And this recitation doesn't even begin to take into account the technologies currently under development, those awaiting approval from some standards body, or—significantly—the dreams firing the imaginations of the current and next generation of Internet pioneers who will take the world to the high-speed Internet2 and beyond.

Until these visionaries perform their miracles, there is still the current global network. Slow though it can sometimes be, especially where the Web is concerned, it is still a technological marvel. After all, how else can anyone, anywhere, access such a wealth of information so inexpensively (typically about $20 per month) through a simple telephone call?

And that brings you to the fun part of this chapter, a survey of some of the services and protocols that make the Internet and the Web what they are today.

Search Engines and Services

Given the massive number of sites and the even more massive number of documents available on the Internet, a beginner's first question is likely to be, "How do I find what I'm looking for?" Well, obviously, there are several ways:

- Seeing the address of an Internet (usually a Web) site on television, in a newspaper, on a business card, and so on

- Being told where to go by someone else ("Hey, you've gotta go check out the *www.amazon.com* Web site!")

- Finding it yourself

And that last approach brings you to *search engines* and information services, of which there are many.

Web search engines

Search engines generally relate to Web searches. They are, in fact, a fact of life on the Web. With them, you can find sites related to just about any conceivable topic. Without them, finding sites on the Web would be comparable to exploring the rain forests of the Amazon with blinders on. They are, in other words, necessary. And there are many well-known ones to choose from:

- AltaVista

- Infoseek

- MSN Web Search

- Yahoo

- Lycos

- Excite

Although some search engines, such as AltaVista, simply return lists of sites, others, such as Yahoo and Infoseek, categorize their search results for ease of use and may even rate the results for you. Despite such differences, however, all search engines have a few features in common: They use *keywords* to index documents, and they rely on databases of stored information to retrieve Web sites relevant to a search.

Most search engines also provide the user with the means of performing either a simple search based on one or more keywords or a more elaborate search that allows the use of logical (Boolean) operators, such as AND, OR, and NOT.

In developing their stores of keywords and Web sites, some search engines rely on human indexers, some rely on existing indexes, and some rely on fascinating software tools—often called *spiders* or *robots*—that literally roam the Web to find and bring "home" new lists of sites and documents.

Services

Although search engines and the Web make finding information a snap, there are also other ways—older, Internet-based ways—to find and retrieve information. One of the most widely used is the *File Transfer Protocol*, or *FTP*, which makes downloading both text and binary files extremely fast and easy. FTP is assisted by a service named *Archie* that helps in searches. Another frequently used search service is named *Gopher*. Like the less entertainingly named FTP, Gopher also has a search assistant—actually, two of them, named *Veronica* and *Jughead*. In addition, information seekers can turn to a UNIX-based search service named *WAIS* (for *Wide Area Information Service*).

Brief descriptions of these services follow.

FTP and Archie

FTP is a longtime staple of the Internet. A protocol in the TCP/IP suite, FTP runs at the application layer and provides access to huge numbers of files that have been publicly posted and made available for downloading. These files are maintained on numerous FTP servers, which people access as "anonymous" or guest users after providing their e-mail address as a password. To find information stored on FTP servers, users can turn to Archie, a search service that can help locate files either by name or through a descriptive keyword.

Gopher, Jughead, and Veronica

Gopher takes its name from the slang term "go-fer," for someone (or something) required to run back and forth, fetching this and that for someone else. Unlike FTP, which accesses different documents stored on different servers, Gopher links information servers through indexes into a single, searchable "place" known as *Gopherspace.*

Within Gopherspace, documents and other information are organized hierarchically, and visitors use a menu-driven system to work through increasingly specific levels until they reach the information they seek. At that point, they can also rely on Gopher to deliver the information to their computers.

To help with searches in Gopherspace, users can rely on one of two search services: Veronica and Jughead:

- Veronica, the Gopher counterpart of Archie, searches the menus on all Gopher servers for information that matches the user's search. To help in narrowing a search, Veronica allows for the use of substrings and Boolean operators. Although the name Veronica is generally understood to be a reference to a friend of the comic-strip character Archie, the name is also considered an acronym for the rather convoluted *Very Easy Rodent-Oriented Netwide Index to Computerized Archives.* (Someone had to work hard on *that* one.)

- Jughead is a service provided by special Jughead servers that indexes the highest-level Gopher menus by keyword. With Jughead, a user can limit a search to specific Gopher servers rather than all of Gopherspace. Like the name Veronica, the name is a two-edged reference. Here, it refers to a friend of both Archie and Veronica, and it is also an acronym for *Jonzy's Universal Gopher Hierarchy Excavation and Display.*

E-mail

Although businesses and corporations implement their own e-mail services within their own networks, everyone who uses the Internet knows that e-mail is not limited to such private services. One of the most popular uses of the Internet is, in fact, e-mail. This global message service is available through numerous software applications, all of which enable Internet users to communicate with family, friends, strangers, and even Internet sites—with anyone, in fact, who can be addressed by the familiar:

username@location

where:

- **username** is the recipient's e-mail name (sometimes all or part of the person's real name, other times an identifying "handle")
- **@** is the "at" sign, which is always included in the address
- **location** is the place—the electronic post office—where the recipient's mail is delivered and stored

Internet mail transport and delivery standards are supported by the *Simple Mail Transfer Protocol*, or *SMTP*, which runs at the application layer. SMTP is part of the TCP/IP protocol suite and provides, as the name suggests, a simple e-mail service.

News

News on the Internet has two different meanings. First, there is news of the sort defined by television anchors, newspapers, and various special-focus magazines and journals. This type of news is widely available on the Web. Some of it is subscription-based, but much news is provided free— for example:

- MSNBC News on MSN
- CNN and CNN Finance
- *The New York Times*
- *Fortune* magazine
- *Slate* magazine

And then there is the news that ordinary people like to exchange through online posts to discussion groups and real-time chats. This type of information most likely won't make the ten o'clock news programs, but it's usually of great interest to the people involved (and to those who *lurk* in the background, reading but not contributing to the general discussion).

This type of news is handled on the Internet by services based on the *Network News Transfer Protocol* (*NNTP*), a de facto standard that is used to distribute collections of articles called *newsfeeds* to a bewildering array of interest-based *newsgroups*.

Since this is a book about networks, take a quick look at NNTP itself before going on to the news services and how they operate.

NNTP is a reliable, fast protocol that provides for downloads, just like FTP, but it also offers much more in terms of interactivity and selectivity. On the interactive front, NNTP supports communication between two news servers and also between clients and servers. Because of this interactivity, NNTP enables clients to download newsfeeds and newsgroups selectively, omitting those that are of no interest. In addition, NNTP supports the ability to query servers and to post news articles.

One of the most popular, widely used, and well known news services implementing NNTP is known as USENET. USENET is a huge, 24-hour-a-day, every-day-of-the-year service that includes bulletin boards and chat rooms in addition to supporting thousands of newsgroups dedicated to topics of all sorts.

In order to access USENET, users subscribe (that's the term, though there's no charge) to the service, download a viewing program called a newsreader, and then subscribe to the newsgroups whose contents interest them. Once subscribed, users can then download some or all articles from a newsfeed and, if they choose, join in the fray by posting their own opinions or their responses to other opinions expressed in a particular *thread* (series of posts on the same topic).

Telnet

Telnet is a TCP/IP protocol that runs on the application layer and exists for one purpose: to allow a computer to log in to a remote computer and pretend it is a terminal attached directly to the host. The remote computer can be anywhere, thanks to the Internet's geographic scope. As long as the connecting computer is provided with *terminal emulation* capabilities (available, for example, in Windows NT and Windows 95/98), it can use the resources and programs installed on the remote machine.

MUDs, Chats, and Other Forms of Play

And, finally, what about some of the really fun things people get involved in on the Internet? There are some, though to a great extent, your definition of "fun" determines which services interest you most. Some newsgroups, for example, are fun—or at least entertaining. Others are serious, a fair number are highly technical, and sadly, some are downright disgusting.

However, for those with a more traditional idea of fun, two resources stand out as places to go when time allows: MUDs for those who like games, and chat rooms for those who prefer real-time conversations.

*MUD*s, or *mult*iuser *d*ungeons, are an outgrowth of the popular dungeons-and-dragons type of interactive, multiplayer role-playing games (RPGs). On the Internet, a MUD provides participants with a virtual game environment where each can play the part of a different character and all can interact in real time. A MUD is sometimes referred to instead as a MUSE (multiuser simulation environment). Along the same lines, for those who prefer high-tech to fantasy, there are similar real-time environments known as *MOO*s (*M*UD, *o*bject *o*riented) where individuals can, again, interact but tend to concentrate on matters of the mind—programming, for example.

And what about chats? Many people, from children to senior citizens, relish these services. Available both on the Internet and on the World Wide Web, chats provide participants with a means of carrying on real-time conversations. On the Internet, chats are supported not only by news services, such as USENET, but also by other services that allow two or more people to chat in real time. One such service, known as Talk, allows two people to connect and carry on a conversation. Another, known as *IRC* (*Internet Relay Chat*) allows multiple participants to chat with one another. IRC generally dedicates channels to different topics and broadcasts comments to the entire group.

And that pretty much is that, as far as overviews of the Internet and the Web in general are concerned. The next stop—and the last chapter in this book—moves on to look specifically at the Web.

The Basic Web

The World Wide Web certainly has come a long way from Tim Berners-Lee's original vision back at the CERN particle physics laboratory in Switzerland. Though it is still thoroughly grounded in the use of hyperlinks for navigating from document to document, the Web is a much bigger, more colorful, and—frankly—far noisier place than it once was.

Today, it has also grown beyond its academic bounds to become a considerable force in both personal and business computing. It now represents not only a vast electronic library of information but also a new electronic marketplace that growing numbers of businesses see as a critically important, rapidly evolving arena for selling, marketing, advertising, buying, and even financing purchases.

It's a little difficult to tell: was it the explosion of new users that encouraged businesses to venture onto the Web, or was it the presence of well-known businesses that attracted tens of millions of new "surfers" to this virtual universe? In the end, resolving this chicken-or-egg question doesn't really matter. Today, the Web is a fact of computing life and, in little more than a few years, it has become an everyday source of information, entertainment, and shopping. Web technologies and protocols have standardized business computing to the point that *intranets* have become integral to many corporations, *extranets* are becoming increasingly useful tools for businesses to interact with customers and partners, and *e-commerce* is projected to grow by the billions of dollars in the next few years.

To paraphrase a recent American presidential campaign, "it's the Web, stupid." And since the Web also happens to be the ultimate in networks, it's a more than fitting "place" to end a survey of networks and networking.

The Internet and the World Wide Web

Everyone these days seems to use *Internet* and *World Wide Web* more or less interchangeably. But as you already know, they are not the same thing. The Internet is the vast, interconnected collection of servers and networks attached to backbones around the world. The Web is but a portion of the Internet, even though many, if not most, end users think of it as "the Internet."

So what makes the Web the Web, and how do people find their way around it? If you've used the Web, of course you know the answer already. But take a quick look behind the scenes, so to speak, at what's involved when you open a browser window, type a site name in the address bar, and press Enter.

Web Sites

Although people talk about surfing the Web as if it were some geographic locality with well-defined borders, it is not. It is not even a place. It is a collection of documents. These documents are known as *pages*, and collectively these pages make up the millions of *sites* that anyone with Internet access can visit at will.

These pages and sites together present information in the colorful, sometimes eye-searing format that includes not only text but graphics, sound, animation, video, and the omnipresent *links* that require nothing more than a mouse to enable a visitor to navigate from page to page and from site to site. With recent (in the past few years) advances in Web technology, pages even can contain small programs—*scripts*, *applets*, *ActiveX controls*—that add interactive capabilities that allow the user to do things beyond merely viewing the page.

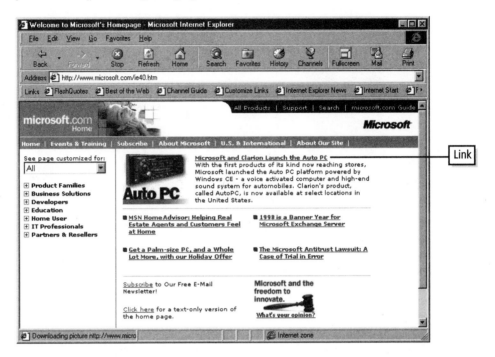

There are literally uncounted millions of pages out there on the Web. But do they just float around like leaves in the autumn breeze? Snicker...obviously not. They are organized hierarchically within individual Web sites. Some of these sites are one-stop, single-page affairs. More often, however, they are collections of related pages arranged somewhat like chapters in a book. Depending on the site, these chapters can consist of a relatively few pages, as the one at the top of the next page does.

Illustration courtesy of Little Bit Therapeutic Riding Center and Current Image[SM] graphic art and Web site design.

Or they can consist of hundreds or even thousands of related pages, like those in the Microsoft Web site illustrated earlier.

But no matter the size of the site, any or all of these pages can contain links to other pages, either in the same or in related sites, and a visitor can work through the site's hierarchy by starting at the main, or *home,* page. This *home page* provides access to the various subcollections of pages that make up the site. In the case of Microsoft's Web site, for example, the home page guides visitors to subsets of pages on products, support, events, and so on. To see the pages in a particular subset, the visitor points and clicks on the desired topic and, when that topic's main page appears, points and clicks again to view specific pages, as shown at the top of the next page.

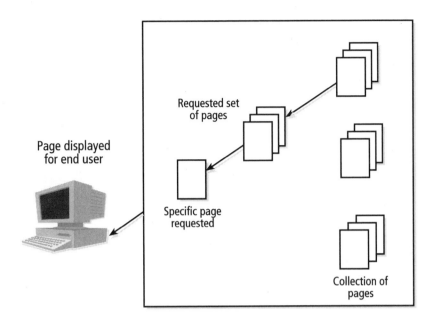

Page displayed
for end user

Requested set
of pages

Specific page
requested

Collection of
pages

Web site

Web Addresses and URLs

But how does someone tell a computer—a nonthinking piece of machinery—how to find a particular site and page? By its address. Each site is a collection of documents put together and maintained by a single individual or organization—a collection stored on one or more servers—and these documents are accessed, in the case of the Web, by an address known as a *Uniform Resource Locator*, or *URL*.

URLs look a lot like path/filename combinations and, like them, they are used to specify the exact location and name of a resource on the Web. Although URLs differ as much as any street addresses, they all take the following form:

Protocol://[www.]servername/path

where:

■ **Protocol** specifies the protocol needed to access the resource. For the Web, this is usually the protocol named HTTP (Hypertext Transfer Protocol), which is described in more detail a little later.

- **www** specifies a site on the World Wide Web. This part of the URL is shown in brackets here because some, but not all, browser applications automatically insert the letters for the user.

- **Servername** is the name of the computer on which the resource is stored. This is the part of the URL most people think of as the actual Web site—for example, microsoft.com or whitehouse.gov. The site isn't, however, an actual place, so to avoid confusion it's good to think of it, at least now and then, as a computer rather than as a storefront or library or whatever physical building comes to mind when you think of a Web site.

- **Path** is the route to the actual resource, including the name and type of the document to be displayed.

So, for example, the following URL:

http://www.microsoft.com/ie40.htm

tells you (actually the *browser* software that sends the request and displays the result) to use the HTTP protocol to connect to the World Wide Web (www) server named microsoft.com and display the document named ie40.htm. (The htm is a filename extension that identifies the document as an HTML—Web—document.)

This URL is what people type into the address bar of a browser window or, sometimes, click in an e-mail message or a document if they are running a Web-enabled application, such as Microsoft Word or Microsoft Outlook. It is also the path—unseen by the user—that browser software follows whenever a link is clicked on a Web page.

Web Browsers

So far, so good. Open a browser window and type the URL you want, or point, click, and follow a link to view a Web page. But just how does that page, often consisting of many different kinds of information, manage to be displayed on screen? For that matter, how is it that someone can click a link and immediately—or sometimes not so immediately—be transported to an entirely different page or Web site? What makes a link a link, and how does it differ from the remaining text and other objects on the page (besides usually being displayed in a different color)?

The key to all this is the Web browser, the software that finds Web sites and then translates the codes that describe the page in order to produce the display that appears on screen. Whether built as a standalone application (as is Netscape Navigator) that runs on top of an operating system or as part of an operating system (as is Internet Explorer), browser software is designed to understand Web technologies and to display pages correctly.

Just as a word processor or a spreadsheet program must understand the hidden codes and commands that determine how a letter, a chart, or a budget must be displayed, browser software must understand the codes and commands embedded in a Web page that determine how, where, and in what fonts and colors the elements on the page must be displayed within the browser window. Those codes and commands are part of the Web markup language known as *HTML*, or *Hypertext Markup Language*.

HTML: The Language of the Web

HTML is the universal language of Web page creation. To the uninitiated, it is as cryptic as a foreign language and as enlightening as mud. To the initiated and to browser software, however, HTML describes a Web page and everything on it with crystalline clarity (most of the time, anyway).

To understand a little bit of what HTML is all about, start by examining its name:

- **Hypertext** refers to the fact that HTML is designed to describe hypertext, that is, Web documents. (In actuality, Web documents are better described as *hypermedia* because they contain more than plain text. However, hypertext is at the root of the Web, so continuing use of the word is, if nothing else, a nice tribute to the Web's origins.)

- **Markup** refers to the fact that HTML is used to mark up documents. That is, it describes elements on a page in much the same way an editor (of the human variety) describes the way a printed page should look by marking up a manuscript with special codes and symbols for italics, boldface, indented paragraphs, and so on.

■ **Language** refers to the fact that HTML, like any other language, is based on certain codes and conventions that enable anyone familiar with them to read and understand "sentences" written in HTML.

Entire books have been and are being written about HTML and how to use it. Unless you plan to specialize in Web page design and creation, there's no need to know the intricacies of HTML in any great detail, other than to satisfy curiosity. However, it doesn't hurt to understand at least a little about how it works, so here goes.

HTML is based on the concept of embedded *tags* that define certain properties of a document. What kinds of properties? There are lots of them, including such easy-to-understand ones as those that indicate where a new paragraph begins, where boldfacing begins and ends, and where an image should appear. Tags are enclosed in angle brackets, like this:

    <TAG>

and they sometimes appear in pairs, in which case they take the form:

    <TAG>...</TAG>

(Note the / preceding the ending tag.)

So, for example, a Web designer wanting to start a new paragraph would use a new paragraph tag to show where the paragraph begins, like so:

    <P>

and would enclose text to be boldfaced in begin-boldface and end-boldface tags like this:

    <B>This text is bold</B>

HTML includes a number of common tags, including one special one known as an *anchor*. This particular tag is used to indicate a link, a hypertext reference (HREF) to a specific URL. An anchor begins with the characters A HREF, followed by the URL and the "friendly" text (or image) that will be used to represent the URL in the document, and it ends with the characters /A. So, for example:

<A HREF="http://www.microsoft.com/">Microsoft</A>

shows that the highlighted or underlined word *Microsoft* on a Web page would be associated with the Microsoft home page described by the link *http://www.microsoft.com.*

In addition to tags in general, HTML is also characterized by the way it divides the coding of a document into complementary sections called the *head* and the *body*. The head section, marked off by the <HEAD> and </HEAD> tags, describes the document itself—for example, the document title. The body section, marked by the <BODY> and </BODY> tags, contains the actual document content—text, images, sound files, and so on—plus, of course, the tags that describe how the body of the document appears on screen.

So you can see how these and other HTML elements are actually used, the following illustration shows a small portion of the HTML coding for a real Web page:

```
<html><head>


<META NAME="MS.LOCALE" CONTENT="EN-US">
<meta http-equiv="PICS-Label" content='(PICS-1.1 "http://www.rsac.org/ratingsv01.html'
<TITLE>Microsoft CarPoint - Home Page</TITLE></head>
<BODY BGCOLOR=WHITE TOPMARGIN=0 LEFTMARGIN=0 marginwidth=0 marginheight=0 LINK="#0033(

<TABLE width=613 border=0 cellpadding=0 cellspacing=0>
                <TR><TD WIDTH=145 HEIGHT=60><A HREF="http://go.msn.com/npl/msnt.asp" t
                <TD VALIGN=TOP width=468 HEIGHT=60 align=left>
                <a href="http://ownership.carpoint.msn.com/ownership"><img src="/image
                <tr><TD width=145 height=40><img src="/images/chan/title2.gif" alt="Ca
                    <td width=468 height=40 align=right><STYLE TYPE="text/css"><!-- A.

<STYLE TYPE="text/css">
<!--
.Menu {border-right:1px solid white}
.nu {text-decoration:none}
//-->
</STYLE>
```

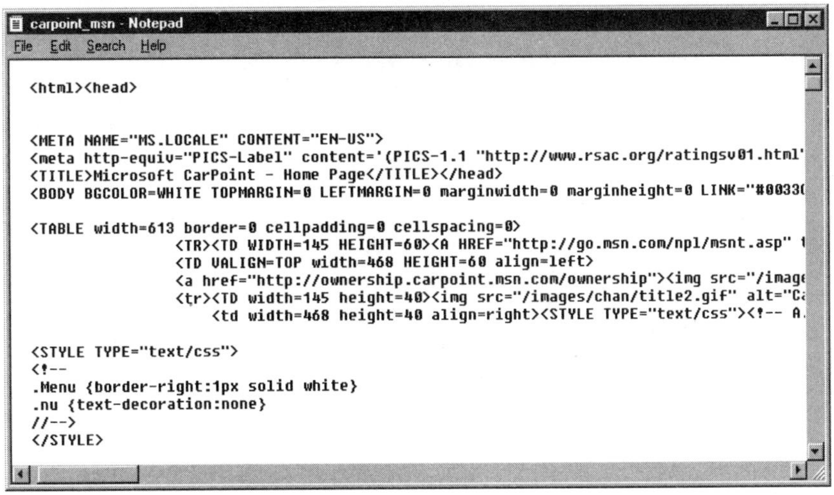

And this is the page that coding describes:

Some difference, but without the former, you would never see the latter.

HTTP: The Web Transport Service

HTML is what makes page display possible within a browser window. It does not, however, transport a page to the browser. That job belongs to the Web protocol identified by the near-ubiquitous letters *http*, which appear at the beginning of every URL clicked or typed to visit a Web site or to request a specific document within the site.

HTTP, the *Hypertext Transfer Protocol*, operates between two, and only two, types of entities, Web browsers and Web servers, and its function is equally clear-cut: it carries requests from browsers to servers, and it transports requested pages (if available) from servers back to browsers.

HTTP is an object-oriented protocol, which—in part—means that it relies on commands known as methods to work with Web pages (the objects). These HTTP methods include a number of commands whose meanings are relatively easy to interpret. For example:

- GET is a request to read a page.

- HEAD is a request to read the header of a page—for example, to determine when it was last modified.

- PUT is a request to store a page on a server.

- POST is a request to append, or add, information to a resource identified by an URL—for example, to post a response to a bulletin board.

A typical HTTP interaction between a browser and a Web server would thus be a relatively simple two-step process like this:

- The browser sends a request to a server by using an HTTP command, such as GET to request a particular Web page.

- The server finds the page, if it can, and sends it back to the browser. To let the browser know how its request fared, the server also sends back one of several numeric messages. If the server is able to carry out the request, for example, its return message would be the HTTP response signaling "success." If the request failed for some reason, the server would return a signal indicating the type of error—for example, the numeric response indicating "unable to carry out the request."

Although HTTP is widely used and has, in fact, deliberately been left open to improvement and evolution, it was not designed with high security in mind. However, HTTP has been extended to meet security concerns in a form known as *SHTTP* (*Secure HTTP*), a development that adds encryption and security features to HTTP. Also, and rather confusingly, there is another form of HTTP that is sometimes called Secure HTTP and sometimes called HTTP Secure. Abbreviated in URLs as *HTTPS*, it is a protocol developed by Netscape for encrypting pages and accessing Web servers through a secure port. HTTPS essentially allows HTTP to run on top of a Netscape-devised security layer known as SSL (briefly described later in this chapter). Both of these security-minded extensions of HTTP were designed to support privacy and commercial transactions on the Web.

N **OTE** Encryption and other approaches to ensuring security on the Internet and the World Wide Web are described in the "Security" section later in this chapter.

Businesses and the Web

Web technologies already play important parts in business networking and seem destined to become even more important as the Internet grows faster and more sophisticated. The Web's all-important hyperlinks, for instance, are now routinely embedded as "live" links within documents and e-mail, providing users with the ability to jump from information source to information source as randomly (and even illogically) as their needs or moods take them.

On a larger scale, Web technologies are also causing the line between the network "out there" and the network "within" to grow fainter all the time. Features that originated in browser software, for example, now contribute to functions as basic as file management and display, to provide a degree of consistency across applications. More importantly, these features also help end-user software erase the difference between local and remote files, so that users can now concentrate on what they want to see, rather than where they must look to find it.

On an even larger scale, in the past few years Internet and Web technologies have become deeply ingrained in business networking. Businesses in increasing numbers are establishing their presence on the Web, and in many cases they are providing Internet/Web access to employees who need, or at least can make use of, the many resources to be found on the global network. Internet technologies are also becoming basic to business communications and telecommuting.

Within the enterprise, large corporations are finding that intranets provide an easy-to-use, secure, and cost-effective means of distributing information of all types. In addition, some businesses are even opening up their intranets on a limited basis to trusted outsiders—vendors, partners, suppliers, and so on. And finally, there is e-commerce, the latest, greatest use of the Internet that, more than any before, has perked up the ears of corporations and governmental agencies alike because of its growing economic clout and mass-market appeal, even to computing "newbies."

Intranets and Extranets

Probably, the most significant application of Web-related technologies to corporate networks is the creation of intranets and extranets, both of which resemble miniature Internets—or, rather, miniature Webs. Both intranets and extranets rely on browser software as the key to accessing, viewing, and using the applications and documents they are based on. Intranets are internal to a corporation. Extranets take the concept of intranets a step further by opening up part of the intranet to access by trusted outside parties.

Both intranets and extranets rely on Internet protocols and technologies, including HTTP and TCP/IP for transport and HTML for describing documents. In widespread enterprises, they may also cover multiple LANs or spread across an entire WAN. Basically, you can think of intranets and extranets as being "applications" of a sort that overlie a corporate network to give it the "look and feel" of the World Wide Web.

Both intranets and extranets can also provide access to the "real" Internet outside the corporation. In this case, of course, securing the internal network from strangers on the Internet is a considerable concern. Typically, corporations protect their security by using a firewall to separate the internal network from the outside world and by providing access to the Internet through proxy servers that relay requests to and from internal computers and those on the Internet. (Proxies and firewalls are described in more detail in the "Security" section later in this chapter.)

Electronic Commerce

Electronic commerce, or *e-commerce*, is the latest rage to hit the Web. Droves of businesses both large and small are actively setting up shop on the Web. Most use the Web for retail merchandising, but service-oriented businesses are taking it seriously as well. Online ticketing, for example, is available for both airlines and concerts, travel sites offer electronic hotel reservations and car rentals, and even banks and brokerages are beginning to investigate the Web as a means of doing business.

Many businesses, ranging from Eddie Bauer clothing to Dell Computer and that prodigy of electronic retailing, amazon.com, maintain their own Web sites, of course. But many are also extending their visibility by entering into partnership with the owners of a few large and heavily used sites known as *portals*.

Portals

If you have followed news reports in the past year, you have probably read about portals. In everyday life, a portal is an entryway, or a gateway, to somewhere else—often, an exotic somewhere else. In the Internet world, a portal serves much the same purpose: It is a gateway to the Web, a site designed to provide visitors with all the comforts of a familiar home base. It is meant to be the place to which they go automatically whenever they access the Web, and the place from which they can easily romp off in numerous preselected directions—to bulletin boards, chat rooms, and e-mail services, as well as to sites devoted to sports, news, weather, entertainment, shopping, searching the Web, and so on.

One of the main goals of a portal—in terms of its visitors—is to provide access to certain sites and services, including electronic shopping "stores" and even "malls." Some of the sites and services offered are owned by the organization that maintains the portal, but many are supplied by partners that "rent" space on the portal screen much as merchants rent shops in a mall. Some portals are highly customizable, others are not. All, however, attempt to give their users a sense of order, often categorizing sites by type, to help people search and navigate the bewildering number of variety of sites on the Web. To use marketing-related language, a portal is a means of capturing hearts and "eyeballs," in the process also generating advertising-related revenue for the portal owner.

Portals are not directly related to networking as it has been covered in most of this book, but they are related to e-commerce, which, in turn, will probably become a fact of life for many network administrators. They are, after all, expected to continue growing in popularity, and that popularity will surely have an impact on e-commerce. In addition, portals have attracted the attention and finances of large and well-known corporations, and they are currently being created and maintained by equally well-known Web technology companies, including Microsoft (MSN) and Netscape/AOL (Netcenter), and search providers such as Excite, Yahoo, and Infoseek.

In short, economics and (Web) accessibility are the driving forces behind the development and expansion of the portal concept. And both of these factors influence corporate networks, if not directly then certainly in the way the networks are designed, managed, and secured.

Security

Network security, as mentioned earlier in the book, covers a range of different issues. There is the matter of ensuring uninterrupted power to servers. There is the matter of backing up disks, mirroring or striping valuable data, and otherwise ensuring that information is not lost. On the people front, there is the need for usernames and passwords that restrict network access to authorized users, and there is the need for access control that determines who can view and modify documents, databases, and other files in which company data is stored. In terms of the Web, there are additional issues that a network faces, including:

- Protecting the internal network from access by unauthorized individuals

- Protecting information as it is transported over the Internet

- Protecting the privacy and security of people's personal and financial information

Although proponents of the Internet's current openness are rightfully protective and proud of its accessibility, those qualities of accessibility and openness have both pluses and minuses. To help ensure that private communications and private information remain private without compromising the free spirit of the Internet, technology companies and standards bodies have developed (or are in the process of developing) a number of ways to provide security and peace of mind without unnecessarily hampering the individual.

 OTE The following sections do not cover such developments as the Clipper Chip and rating or filtering software designed to control youthful (or employee) access to unacceptable materials on the Internet. These concerns can no doubt be assisted by technological barriers to access, but in the end, parental guidance (for the young) and corporate policy (for the employed) are, or should be, more effective than censorship.

Authentication and encryption

There are various approaches to ensuring that people—and programs—are legitimate, and that communications cannot readily be hijacked by electronic eavesdroppers. Among these are software devices such as *digital signatures,* which can be used to authenticate the sender of the message; *encryption,* which is used to scramble transmissions and make them unreadable; and *virtual private networks*, which use a technique known as *tunneling* to turn the very public Internet into a secure communications medium. These approaches (most of which could easily merit an entire chapter, if not an entire book) are described briefly in the following sections.

Digital signatures and personal keys   If you use Microsoft Windows with Internet Explorer, you have probably seen a certificate-like window appear when you downloaded a piece of software from the Web. This window is the viewable portion of a Microsoft code-verification feature known as *Authenticode*. Authenticode is a means of assuring end users that the code they are downloading (a) has been created by the group or individual listed on the certificate and (b) that the code has not been changed since it was created. Although Authenticode cannot verify that the program to be downloaded is either bug-free or completely safe to use, it does verify that the code has not been tampered with after it was completed and signed by the creator.

At the heart of Authenticode is a security feature known as a *digital signature*, a form of *cryptography* that is used not only to authenticate the creator of a program but also—in circumstances such as transmission of sensitive e-mail—the sender of a small file or message. In order to work, a digital signature relies on a set of two *keys,* known as a *public key* and a *private key*, both of which must be acquired from a valid organization known as a *certification authority* (the equivalent of a locksmith). In essence, these public and private keys are comparable to the username and password that validate network users at logon. The public key, like the username, is one that can be given out to other people. The private key, like the password, is one that should be known by only one person, its owner.

When these keys are used to sign a program or file, the process involves the calculation of a value known as a hash number, which is based on the size of the file and on other information, including information about the sender. This hash number is then "signed"—turned into an encrypted string of bits—with the sender's private key to create (ideally) a value that can be matched only by the information used to create the hash number. In other words, the hash number fits the original file the way a fingerprint fits only one person, and thus it guarantees that if even a single character is changed, there will be a mismatch between the hash number and the file, and the recipient will be able to tell that the file has been changed or tampered with. On the receiving end, the hash number is recalculated and verified against the signature with the help of the sender's public key (which the recipient must, of course, already have been given).

Encryption   Although digital signatures are valuable in authenticating and validating programs and messages, an even higher level of security is provided in the encrypting of important files before transmission—essentially, turning the files into unreadable gibberish to all but the sender and receiver. Encryption can be used either in addition to or instead of a digital signature.

The process of encryption turns a readable message (known to cryptographers as plaintext) into a garbled version (known as ciphertext) for transmission. The coding itself relies on one of several encryption algorithms—roughly, sets of steps or instructions—that are based on the use of either a public key (asymmetric algorithm) or a private key (symmetric algorithm):

- When an asymmetric algorithm is used, the key is public and the transmission can be encrypted by anyone who possesses the key. However, the encrypted transmission can be decoded (decrypted) only by someone who has a corresponding private key.

- When an encrypted transmission is based on a symmetric algorithm, both the coding and decoding are performed by the same (presumably secret) key or by a decryption key that can be derived from the one used to encrypt the transmission.

The strength of encryption itself is dependent on the number of bits used for the key. This number varies, but certain lengths are currently standard:

- 40 bits, which would take about 1 trillion attempts to "crack" by brute force (meaning by trying every possible bit combination in sequence). Despite this seemingly daunting number, keys of this length have, in fact, proved to be breakable.

- 56 bits, which is known as the DES (Data Encryption Standard) and is currently the maximum length key allowed for U.S. export. DES keys are much harder to break than 40-bit keys, but they too have been cracked.

- 128 bits, which is considered unbreakable by current methods. Keys of this length are available for use within the United States, but software based on 128-bit keys cannot currently be exported to other countries.

Although encryption has been around as long as human beings have wanted to exchange coded messages, it has now entered the information age as a significant factor in Internet transmissions. It has grown beyond romantic spy stories and cereal-box secret decoder rings.

Securing the Internet

In addition to authentication and encryption, which concentrate on securing the message, there are technologies that extend this security to the Internet itself. One of these is an e-mail protocol known as *S/MIME* (*Secure/Multipurpose Internet Mail Extensions*). Two others, known as *SSL* (*Secure Sockets Layer*) and *PCT* (*Private Communication Technology*), are designed to provide privacy through client/server authentication. Yet another is based on a concept known as *VPN—virtual private network*.

S/MIME

To back up a bit...*MIME* (*Multipurpose Internet Mail Extensions*) is a well-known and widely used protocol for Internet e-mail. Developed by the IETF, MIME was designed to allow mail messages to include not only text but also sound, graphics, audio, and video. To do this, MIME uses the message header—the part of an e-mail message that describes the message for transmission—to define the content of the message itself. That is, if the message includes a sound file, the header says so. At the receiving end, software can use the information in the header to call on appropriate programs to display, play, or otherwise handle the different media types. Although MIME standardizes the transmission of multimedia documents, it does not provide much in the way of security. To handle this task, S/MIME was invented. S/MIME, in brief, is MIME with support for digital signatures and encryption.

SSL and PCT

SSL was developed by Netscape Communications; PCT was developed and submitted as an IETF draft by Microsoft. Both SSL and PCT have the same goal in mind: to ensure communications privacy through the use of authentication and encryption as transmissions pass between client and server. Although the two protocols differ in certain respects, both allow application-related protocols such as HTTP, FTP, and Telnet to run on top of them without problem. Both also begin a session with an initial *handshake* (exchange between client and server) during which the communicating computers agree on an encryption algorithm and key and verify that they are, indeed, the parties they appear to be. Once these formalities are over with, communications between the client and server are encrypted throughout the session.

VPNs

Virtual private networks—VPNs—are a relatively recent phenomenon, but they are rapidly gaining in popularity as a cost-effective means of using public telecommunications and the Internet to provide secure, private, computer-to-computer communications between LANs and between telecommuters and the corporate network.

In essence, a VPN uses the Internet as a corporation's private communications medium and thus bypasses the cost of supporting leased lines or other dedicated, private networking options. Security on a VPN involves encryption and, usually, a method of transmitting packets over the Internet through a connection known as a tunnel, which forms a private, though temporary, path between the two communicating computers.

Among the protocols that support VPNs is one known as *PPTP* (*Point to Point Tunneling Protocol*), which was developed by Microsoft and has gained significant support in the networking industry. An extension of the standard PPP (Point to Point Protocol) used to package datagrams and transmit them over a TCP/IP connection, PPTP encapsulates encrypted PPP packets in secure (and securely addressed) "wrappers" suitable for transmission over the Internet. It also sets up, maintains, and ends the connection forming the tunnel between the communicating computers.

Proxies and firewalls

Secure protocols, encryption, and digital signatures are essential for guarding the data that travels over the Internet, but although they can keep that information away from prying eyes, they cannot do much to physically keep outside intruders away from an internal network. That job is handled nicely by firewalls and, to a lesser extent, by agents known as proxies, or proxy servers.

A network firewall, like the firewall in a house, is a barrier designed to prevent something bad from happening. In the house, the firewall is meant to keep a fire from spreading out of control. On a network, a firewall is used primarily to keep intruders out, although it can, in a reversal of roles, also be used to block outgoing traffic to certain sites from the inside. Typically, a firewall is a barrier set up in a router, bridge, or gateway that sits between the network and the outside world. This firewall stands at the only "doorway" into or out of the network, and like a sentry at a gate, it watches over the traffic, examining each packet to determine whether to discard it (bad packet) or let it through (good packet).

In deciding whether to score a particular packet as a "pass" or as a "fail," a firewall typically relies on a mechanism called a packet filter and on a table that lists acceptable and unacceptable addresses. As packets pass through, the firewall examines source and destination addresses and/or the ports to which the packets are sent. If the address or port on a packet happens to be unacceptable, it blocks the packet. If the address or port is on the OK list, it sends the packet on through. In this way, the firewall can, say, block all packets addressed to a particular destination or those sent to the port associated with a particular service, such as Telnet.

On a higher level, firewalls can also act at the application level where, instead of examining addressing information, they examine the packets themselves, discarding those that fail certain criteria. Such firewalls can be used, for example, to filter e-mail based on content, size, or some other important feature.

Proxy servers, or proxies, are like firewalls in forming a barrier between the internal network and the outside world. In this case, however, the proxies serve the network by standing in for internal computers as they access the Internet. By presenting a single IP address to the world and thus hiding the identities (addresses) of the computers within the network, proxies defend against intrusive practices. One example of such practices is *spoofing*, in which an invader masquerades as a computer on the network, either to "attack from within" or to intercept information sent to the computer it pretends to be. Like firewalls, proxies can also be used to limit Internet access, for example to prevent employees from visiting undesirable sites or those that are not work-related.

Summing Up

Well, there you have it, an introduction to networking that started with peer-to-peer PC networks and ends with the guardians at the corporate gates. Is there more to know? Of course. Not only is there more to learn about networks in terms of both depth (detail) and breadth (topics not covered here), but networks themselves hardly intend to become static environments that never change.

Because this book began with a quick look back at networking in the past, let's end it with an equally quick look at networking to come. No one, of course, can predict the future, and there is always the possibility that some still-unknown visionary will come up with a new development that will radically change networking, the Internet, or computing in general. Still, here are some network-related developments that are either already here or looming on the not-too-distant horizon.

Network throughput is leaping from megabits per second to gigabits per second. Faster and more reliable hardware continues to evolve, and a myriad of new devices, from pagers to phones and so-called smart cards (chips on a card), are being readied for Internet access, e-mail, and other such network-related uses. New approaches to networking, such as ATM and FDDI, are either approaching or entering the mainstream.

Security, as you've seen, has taken on added—and critical—dimensions as networks have ventured beyond the corporate walls into the telecommunications network and the Internet. E-commerce is encouraging the development of electronic "money" and electronic wallets, as well as driving standards for ensuring financial and personal privacy. And work on the Internet itself is under way to provide the world with much-needed increased speed and bandwidth.

In the corporate world, the Web itself has worked its way into business networking in ways that will continue to blur the distinction between local and remote resources. Web technologies are now in many areas inseparable from networking technologies, and they too have no intention of standing still. Currently, for example, HTML is in the process of giving way to a newer markup language called *XML* (*Extensible Markup Language*). XML, while still evolving and not yet fully standardized, is being developed to enable Web site creators to describe not only the *look* of a Web page, but also the *content* on that page in a way that will add new levels of flexibility and interactivity to the Web.

And, although they are not strictly network-based, recent developments such as *Java* and so-called *open source* software are both finding their way into networks, networking, and the Internet. Java, developed by Sun Microsystems, is a programming language created to allow programs to run, unmodified, on multiple computer platforms. Right now, it is commonly used, as is Microsoft's *ActiveX* technology, for creating small programs (known as ActiveX objects or as Java applets, depending on the technology used) that can be embedded in Web pages in order to customize them or to make them more interactive and thus more responsive to the user. Open source, which refers to programs whose developers make their program code freely available, is closely tied to a free operating system known as *Linux* (roughly based on the UNIX operating system) that is widely touted by its admirers as a fast, stable environment for network servers. It also appears that open source software will, in some manner, play a role in the evolution of Java, too.

Such is the past, present, and immediate future of the networking world—an interesting place, as you've hopefully come to see. Although this book parts company with you now, it's to be hoped that it has helped you a little way down the road to understanding networks. From this point on, no matter how fast or how much farther you choose to travel, may your journey be a good one.

Glossary

100BaseVG A form of 100 Mbps Ethernet based on voice-grade twisted-pair wiring. Unlike other Ethernet networks, 100BaseVG, or 100BaseVG-AnyLAN, relies on an access method called demand priority, in which nodes send requests to hubs, which in turn give permission to transmit based on the priority levels included with the requests.

100BaseX Descriptor used for any of three forms of 100 Mbps Ethernet networks also called Fast Ethernet. 100BaseX networks are distinguished by the type of wiring used: four pairs of medium to high grade twisted pair (100BaseT4), two pairs of high-grade twisted pair (100BaseTX), or fiberoptic cable (100BaseFX).

10Base2 Also known as Thin Ethernet, a popular form of 10 Mbps Ethernet based on thin (3/16 inch) coaxial cable.

10Base5 Also known as Thick Ethernet, a form of 10 Mbps Ethernet based on thick (3/8 inch) coaxial cabling and usually used for network backbones.

10BaseFL A form of 10 Mbps Ethernet based on fiberoptic cable. 10BaseFL is capable of covering up to 2 kilometers (1.25 miles) and is useful in linking separate buildings.

10BaseT A popular form of 10 Mbps Ethernet based on twisted-pair wiring.

AAL See *ATM Adaptation Layer.*

access permission Authorization to use a network resource. Several levels of access can be given: read only, read and write (view and change), or read, write, and delete (basically, do whatever one wants—presumably responsibly).

access point In a wireless LAN, a transceiver connected to a wired network that links the two network types.

account The recordkeeping mechanism used by networks and multiuser operating systems for keeping track of authorized users. Network accounts are created by network administrators and are used both to validate users and to administer policies—for example, access permissions—related to each user.

acoustic coupler An archaic device once used in computer communications. The coupler was a cradle-like instrument into which the headset of a telephone was placed. Its function was somewhat similar to the job now done by modems.

active hub A type of hub used on ARCnet networks that both regenerates (boosts) signals and passes them along. Compare *passive hub, intelligent hub.*

ActiveX A technology developed by Microsoft based on reusable software components that can interact with one another, especially in a networked environment. ActiveX components can be written in any of a number of programming languages. The technology is the basis for creating the ActiveX controls often used to customize and add interactivity to Web pages.

ActiveX control A software component based on Microsoft's ActiveX technology that is used to add interactivity and more functionality, such as animation or a popup menu, to a Web page. An ActiveX control can be written in any of a number of languages, including Java, C++, and Visual Basic.

address As in everyday life, a reference to a location. In terms of networking, an address is the name or number that identifies a particular computer or a site on the Internet. Computing, however, is full of different types of addresses—for example, e-mail addresses identify mailboxes for specific individuals, and memory addresses identify specific locations in memory. In all cases, however, addresses are used to pinpoint something or someone.

ad-hoc network A temporary "network" formed by communicating stations in a wireless LAN.

ADSL Stands for Asymmetric Digital Subscriber Line, a form of DSL that transfers information at up to 8 Mbps downstream and up to 640 kbps upstream. See also *DSL*.

Advanced Program to Program Communication See *APPC*.

AE Stands for application entity, in the ISO/OSI Reference Model, one of the two software parties involved in a communications session.

algorithm A sequence of steps used to solve a problem or perform a task; essentially, a "recipe" for carrying out some action.

AM See *amplitude modulation*.

American National Standards Institute See *ANSI*.

American Standard Code for Information Interchange See *ASCII*.

amplitude modulation A means of loading information onto a carrier wave by modulating (altering) its height. Compare *frequency modulation*.

amplitude shift keying A form of amplitude modulation that uses two different wave heights to represent the binary values 1 and 0. See also *amplitude modulation*.

analog A reference to something, such as a sound wave, that is continuously variable rather than based on discrete units, such as the binary digits 1 and 0. A lighting dimmer switch is an analog device because it is not based on absolute settings. Compare *digital*.

anchor In HTML, a special tag associated with a hyperlink.

ANSI Stands for American National Standards Institute, an organization of business and industry groups concerned with fostering the development and adoption of standards in the United States. Among its many concerns, ANSI focuses on various networking technologies. It also represents the United States in the ISO.

APPC Stands for Advanced Program to Program Communications, a specification that extends IBM's SNA model to include minicomputers and microcomputers.

applet A small program that can be downloaded over the Internet. Applets are often written in the Java programming language and run within browser software, and they are typically used to customize or add interactive elements to a Web page.

AppleTalk The LAN hardware and software designed by Apple for Macintosh computers.

application entity See *AE*.

Archie A search program used to find files stored on FTP servers.

architecture In general, the design underlying computer hardware or software. In terms of networks, *architecture* covers the infrastructure, functionality, protocols, and standards implemented in a particular network design.

ARCnet Stands for Attached Resource Computer Network, a form of token bus network architecture for PC-based LANs developed by Datapoint Corporation. ARCnet relies on a bus or star topology and can support up to 255 nodes. Different versions run at speeds of 1.5 mbps, 20 Mbps (ARCnet Plus), and 100 Mbps.

ASCII Stands for American Standard Code for Information Interchange, a coding scheme that assigns numbers to 256 characters, including text, numbers, punctuation marks, and certain special characters. ASCII is divided into two sets: 128 characters (known as standard ASCII) and an additional 128 known as extended ASCII. Standard ASCII has for years been used as a near-universal "common language" in the microcomputer environment for enabling different programs to exchange information reliably. Compare *EBCDIC*.

ASK See *amplitude shift keying*.

Asymmetric Digital Subscriber Line See *ADSL*.

asynchronous A reference to something that is not dependent on timing—for example, asynchronous communications can start and stop at any time instead of having to match the timing governed by a clock.

asynchronous communications Computer-to-computer communications in which the sending and receiving computers do not rely on timing as a means of determining where transmissions begin and end. Compare *synchronous communications*.

asynchronous transfer mode See *ATM*.

ATM A high-speed networking technology designed to deliver transmissions consisting of many different kinds of information, including text, voice, audio, and video. By relying on small, fixed-length packets that it multiplexes onto the carrier, ATM achieves speeds as high as 622 Mbps (over fiberoptic cable). The basic unit of ATM transmission is known as a cell, a packet consisting of 5 bytes routing information and a 48-byte payload (data).

ATM Adaptation Layer The ATM layer that mediates between higher-level and lower-level services, converting different types of data (such as audio, video, and data frames) to the 48-byte payloads required by ATM.

Attached Resource Computer Network See *ARCnet*.

attachment unit interface See *AUI*.

attenuation The weakening of a transmitted signal as it travels farther from the source.

AUI Stands for attachment unit interface, a 15-pin (DB-15) connector commonly used to connect a network interface card to an Ethernet cable.

Authenticode A mechanism devised by Microsoft for identifying the source (author) of code to be downloaded and assuring users that the code has not been changed since it was created. Authenticode does not ensure bug-free or virus-free code, but it does authenticate programs before they are downloaded.

authority On the Internet and World Wide Web, a DNS name server responsible for resolving Internet names and IP addresses at a particular level of authority: top-level domain, second-level domain, or subdomain.

B channel See *ISDN*.

back end In terms of networking, roughly a reference to a server computer or the processing that takes place on it. Compare *front end*.

backbone The communications path that carries the majority of traffic within a network. A backbone is often a high-speed transmissions medium and can be used to link network segments, small networks, or (in the case of the Internet) multiple networks spread out over vast geographic distances.

BackOffice A suite of software components developed by Microsoft and designed to work with Windows NT to provide a network with services including e-mail (Exchange), intranet capabilities (Site Server), management (Systems Management Server), high-end database development (SQL Server), and so on.

backward learning A means of contributing to better performance or efficiency by relying on an information store to which new data are added as they become available.

bandwidth In the analog world, the range between the highest and lowest frequencies for a given segment of the electromagnetic spectrum, measured in Hertz (cycles per second)—for example, FM radio operates between 88 MHz and 108 MHz, for a bandwidth of 20 MHz. In the digital world, however, bandwidth refers to speed of transmission, measured in bits per second (bps).

Basic Rate Interface See *ISDN*.

Basic Service Set Communicating stations on a wireless LAN.

beacon On a FDDI network, a special frame generated and passed along when a node detects a problem.

bearer channel See *ISDN*.

binding The process by which protocols are associated with one another and the network adapter to provide a complete set of protocols needed for handling data from the application layer to the physical layer.

BISDN See *broadband ISDN*.

bit-oriented protocol A communications protocol in which information is transmitted as a stream of bits, rather than whole characters, and which relies on special bit sequences to represent control information. Compare *byte-oriented protocol*.

bits per second See *bps*.

BNC A type of connector used to join segments of coaxial cable. The letters BNC are commonly, though not always, considered an abbreviation for British Naval Connector.

body In general, the main portion of something, for example, the text of a document or the segment of a data packet containing the actual data. In HTML, the body is the section of a Web document that contains the content of the document, along with tags describing the content—for example, text format and color and the positioning of elements on the screen.

boost To strengthen a network signal before it is transmitted further.

bps Stands for bits per second, the measure of transmission speed used in relation to networks and communication lines. Although bps represents the basic unit of measure, networks and communications devices, such as modems, are so fast that speeds are usually given in multiples of bps—Kbps (kilobits, or thousands of bits, per second), Mbps (megabits, or millions of bits, per second), and Gbps (gigabits, or billions of bits, per second).

BRI See *ISDN*.

bridge A network device used to connect two LANs and allow messages to flow between them.

broadband ISDN Next-generation ISDN based on Asynchronous Transfer Mode technology. Broadband ISDN divides information into two categories: interactive services, which are controlled by the user, and distributed (or distribution) services that can be broadcast to the user.

browser Software that functions either in addition to (as with Netscape Navigator) or as part of (as with Internet Explorer) an operating system to enable use of the Internet, the World Wide Web, and Web technologies implemented in other software, such as word processors and online Help systems.

BSS See *Basic Service Set*.

buffer A portion of computer memory set aside as a temporary holding area for data being transferred from one place (or device) to another.

bus A data pathway that connects the different parts of a computer—memory, processor,

disk drives, and so on. The bus consists of multiple conducting wires (lines) running in parallel. Different lines are used to carry different types of information, including memory locations, data, and control signals.

bus topology A network configuration based on a single main communications line (trunk) to which nodes are attached; also known as linear bus.

byte-oriented protocol A communications protocol in which information is transmitted as a stream of encoded bytes (characters). Compare *bit-oriented protocol*.

cable modem The device used to connect a PC to a cable television outlet. Cable modems do not operate at the same rate upstream (when sending information) and downstream (when receiving information). Upstream rates vary from about 2 Mbps to 10 Mbps, downstream rates from about 10 Mbps to 36 Mbps.

callback A security feature used to authenticate users calling in to a network. During callback, the network validates the caller's username and password, hangs up, and then returns the call, either to a number requested during the initial call or to a predetermined number.

carrier sense multiple access with collision detection See *CSMA/CD*.

cascaded star topology A star-wired network in which nodes connect to hubs and hubs connect to other hubs in a hierarchical (cascaded) parent/child relationship. This topology is characteristic of 100BaseVG networks.

CCITT Stands for Comité Consultatif International Télégraphique et Téléphonique, a standards organization now part of the International

Telecommunication Union, standardization sector (ITU-T). Before becoming part of the ITU, CCITT was instrumental in defining numerous communications-related standards, among them the CCITT V series specifications for modems and related technologies and the CCITT X series specifications for networking equipment and protocols.

cell A fixed-length packet, the basic transmission unit on high-speed networks, such as ATM. See also *ATM*.

cell relay A form of packet switching in which information is multiplexed onto a carrier and transferred in fixed-length packets (cells).

centralized network A network in which nodes connect to and use resources on a single central computer, typically a mainframe.

certification authority An organization that assigns encryption keys.

CGI Stands for Common Gateway Interface, a specification that allows Web developers to customize or add interactivity to Web pages. CGI provides a means for passing data to and from a Web user and a Web server through applications commonly known as scripts. When a Web server receives information from the user (through the browser), it relies on a CGI application to process the information and provide whatever return data the server needs to send back to the user.

Channel Service Unit See *DDS*.

circuit switching A means of connecting two communicating parties that relies on the creation of a physical link between the two. Circuit switching is characteristic of telephone connections. Unlike other methods of transmission, such as packet switching, it requires the link to be established before any communication can take place. Compare *packet switching*.

client/server network A LAN built around the division of nodes into client machines (users) and server computers that function as providers of services and resources. Servers on a client/server network commonly perform some of the processing work (called back-end processing) for client machines—for example, sorting through a database before delivering only the record(s) requested by the client. Compare *peer-to-peer network*.

clustering The grouping of multiple servers in a way that allows them to appear to be a single unit to client computers. Clustering is a means of increasing network capacity and improving data security.

coaxial cable A round, flexible cable consisting of—from the center outwards—a copper wire, a layer of protective insulation, a braided metal mesh sleeve, and an outer shield, or jacket of PVC or fire-resistant material. Coaxial cable is widely used in networks. It is the same type of wiring as that used for cable television. Compare *twisted-pair wiring, fiberoptic cable*.

Common Gateway Interface See *CGI*.

Compressed Serial Line Internet Protocol See *SLIP*.

computer Any device capable of processing information to produce a desired result. No matter how large or small they are, computers typically perform their work in three well-defined steps: (1) accepting input, (2) processing the input according to predefined rules (programs), and (3) producing output.

connection A link between two communicating computers.

connectionless Transmission over a flexible path that can include multiple routes between source and destination. Compare *connection-oriented*.

connection-oriented Transmission over a set path between sender and receiver. Compare *connectionless*.

connector A piece of hardware used to join devices and cables. Connectors are usually male—plugs with pins—or female—sockets or jacks designed to accept male connectors.

content The "meat" of a document, as opposed to its format, or appearance.

contention A competitive form of gaining network access, in which the first node to seize control of the carrier earns the right to transmit at that time.

crack To gain unauthorized access to a network by breaching its security. Also, to decipher encrypted information.

CRC A form of error checking used in network transmissions in which a value based on the information in the packet is calculated and included in the packet by the sending computer. The receiving computer recalculates the value. If there is no difference, the transmission is assumed to have arrived without error.

crosstalk In communications, interference caused by signal transference from one wire to another.

cryptography The encoding of information so that it is unreadable by anyone other than the person(s) holding the key to the code. See also *key*.

CSLIP See *SLIP*.

CSMA/CA Stands for Carrier Sense Multiple Access with Collision Avoidance, a method of controlling network access similar to CSMA/CD, in that nodes listen to the network and transmit only when it is free. But in CSMA/CA, nodes avoid data collisions by signaling their intention with a brief request to send (RTS) signal and then waiting for acknowledgment before actually transmitting.

CSMA/CD Stands for Carrier Sense Multiple Access with Collision Detection. A form of network access in which nodes listen to the line and attempt to transmit only when they sense that the carrier signal is free (not in use). If two nodes attempt to transmit at the same time, thus causing a collision, both nodes back off for random periods before attempting to transmit again.

CSU See *DDS*.

cut-through switch A network switch that routes packets immediately to the port associated with the packet's recipient.

cyclical redundancy check See *CRC*.

D channel See *ISDN*.

DAS See *dual attachment station*.

data channel. See *ISDN*.

Data Communications Equipment See *DCE*.

Data Link Connection Identifier A virtual circuit on frame relay networks that permanently identifies the path to a particular destination.

Data Link Control See *DLC*.

Data Service Unit See *DDS*.

Data Terminal Equipment See *DTE*.

datagram A packet of data with addressing information, sent through a packet-switching network.

DB-15 See *AUI*.

DCE Stands for Data Communications Equipment, the term used in RS-232 and X.25 specifications for a device, such as a modem, that provides another device (known as the DTE) with access to a communications line. Compare *DTE*.

DDS Stands for digital data service, a dedicated communications line that provides transmission at speeds up to 56 Kbps. DDS lines use a device known as a CSU/DSU rather than a modem for connecting two networks. The CSU, or Channel Service Unit, connects the network to the transmission line; the DSU, or Data Service Unit, converts data for transmission by the CSU and controls data flow.

DECnet The hardware, software, and protocol stack designed by Digital Equipment Corporation for its Digital Network Architecture (DNA).

dedicated connection A permanent, private communications link between two parties. A dedicated connection is leased from the telephone company and is always available for use.

dedicated server A computer—usually quite powerful—that is used solely as a network server. Compare *nondedicated server*.

deferral time The length of time that nodes on a CSMA/CD network wait before trying to retransmit after a collision.

delta channel See *ISDN*.

demand priority A network access method in which hubs control network access; a feature of 100BaseVG Ethernet networks. With demand priority, nodes send requests to hubs, and the hubs give permission to transmit based on priority levels assigned to the requests by the nodes.

demodulation The process by which a receiving modem unloads information from a modulated carrier wave and converts the information to the digital form required by the computer to which it is attached. Compare *modulation*.

dial-up networking Connection to a remote network through use of a modem; typically used in reference to telecommuting, although the term is equally applicable to connecting to the Internet.

dielectric Insulating material, such as rubber or plastic, that does not conduct electricity.

differential phase shift keying A form of phase shift keying in which each phase change is relative to the preceding state of the wave.

digital A reference to something based on digits (numbers) or their representation. PCs are digital computers because they deal with information of all types as different combinations of the binary digits 0 and 1. Compare *analog*.

digital data service See *DDS*.

Digital Services See *DS*.

Digital Signal See *DS*.

digital signature A security mechanism used on the Internet that relies on two keys, one public and one private, that are used to encrypt messages before transmission and to decrypt them on receipt.

Digital Subscriber Line See *DSL*.

DIP switch Stands for Dual Inline Package switch, one of a set of small (sometimes very small) toggle switches on a circuit board that are used for configuring the device.

directory Roughly, a list, index, or catalog of items. On a network, directories contain names and pertinent information related to authorized users and network resources. On a computer, a directory (or folder) is a device used to organize related files.

directory services A network service, installed on server computers, that handles the information databases (directories) required to identify the users and resources on the network.

distributed (distribution) services See *BISDN*.

distributed system A non-centralized network consisting of numerous computers that can communicate with one another and that appear to users as parts of a single, large, accessible "storehouse" of shared hardware, software, and data. A distributed system is conceptually the opposite of a centralized, or monolithic, system in which clients connect to a single central computer, such as a mainframe.

DIX Stands for Digital Intel Xerox, the companies that developed the AUI connector for thicknet Ethernet cable. See also *AUI*.

DLC Stands for Data Link Control, a protocol supported by Microsoft's Windows NT designed to provide access to IBM mainframe computers and to Hewlett-Packard printers connected to the network.

DLCI See *Data Link Connection Identifier*.

DNS Stands for Domain Name System, the hierarchical system used in naming sites on the Internet. DNS names consist of a top-level domain (such as .com, .org, and .net), a second-level domain (the site name of a business, organization, or individual), and possibly one or more subdomains (servers within a second-level domain).

DNS name server A server computer holding one of the DNS databases through which friendly names are matched to the corresponding IP addresses that computers use in contacting one another on the Internet.

domain In general, a group of some sort that is characterized by a particular attribute or set of features. In reference to the Internet, a domain is a unit in which one or more computers are organized in a particular hierarchy. At the highest level (top-level domain), the computers are grouped by type (commercial, educational, organization, and so on) or by country (France, England, Germany, United States, and so on). At the next level (second-level domain), computers are grouped by site (Microsoft.com, amazon.com, and so on). At optional lower levels (subdomains within a site), computers are grouped by site administrators into whatever units best suit the needs of the organization.

domain controller In Windows NT, the master server that holds the directory services database that identifies all network users and resources.

Domain Name System See *DNS*.

downstream Delivery of information from a (Web) server to a client. Compare *upstream*.

DPSK See *differential phase shift keying*.

driver A device-specific program that enables a computer to work with a particular piece of hardware, such as a printer, disk drive, or network adapter. Because the driver handles device-specific features, the operating system is freed from the burden of having to understand—and support—the needs of individual hardware devices.

drop cable A cable, also known as a transceiver cable, that is used to connect a network interface card to a Thick Ethernet network.

DS Stands for Digital Services or Digital Signal, a category used in referencing the speed, number of channels, and transmission characteristics of T1, T2, T3, and T4 communications lines. The basic DS unit, or level, is known as DS-0, which corresponds to the 64 Kbps speed of a single T1 channel. Higher levels are made up of multiple DS-0 levels. DS-1 represents a single T1 line that transmits at 1.544 Mbps. For higher rates, T1 lines are multiplexed to create DS-2 (a T2 line consisting of four T1 channels that transmits at 6.312 Mbps), DS-3 (a T3 line consisting of 28 T1 channels that transmits at 44.736 Mbps), and DS-4 (a T4 line consisting of 168 T1 channels that transmits at 274.176 Mbps).

DSL Stands for Digital Subscriber Line, a recently developed (late 1990s) digital communications technology that can provide high-speed transmissions over standard copper telephone wiring. DSL is often referred to as xDSL, where the x stands for one or two characters that define variations of the basic DSL technology. Currently, ADSL (Asymmetric DSL) is the form most likely to be provided, but even it is, as yet, available only to limited groups of subscribers. See also *ADSL, DSL Lite, HDSL, SDSL, RADSL, VDSL*.

DSL Lite Stands for Digital Subscriber Line Lite, a variation of ADSL currently under development that simplifies installation but transmits more slowly, at 1.544 Mbps. See also *DSL*.

DSU See *DDS*.

DTE Stands for Data Terminal Equipment, the term used in RS-232 and X.25 specifications for a device, such as a PC, that transfers information to a mediating device (known as the DCE) for communication. Compare *DCE*.

dual attachment station A FDDI node with two connections to the network—either through a node and a concentrator or through two concentrators. Compare *single attachment station*.

dual homing A form of fault tolerance used with critical network devices on FDDI networks, in which such devices are attached to both the primary and secondary (backup) rings through two concentrators to provide the maximum possible security in case the primary ring fails.

Dual Inline Package switch See *DIP switch*.

dual-ring topology A token-passing ring topology implemented in FDDI networks that consists of two rings in which information travels in opposite directions. One ring, the primary ring, carries information; the second ring is used for backup.

dumb terminal See *terminal*.

duplex See *half duplex, full duplex*.

EBCDIC Stands for Extended Binary Coded Decimal Interchange Code, a coding scheme developed by IBM that assigns 256 numeric values to text, numbers, punctuation marks, and transmission-control characters.

Although EBCDIC, like ASCII, is used to represent 256 different characters, the characters represented in the two sets are different. EBCDIC is used primarily with mainframes and minicomputers, ASCII with microcomputers. Compare *ASCII*.

e-commerce The use of the Internet, especially the World Wide Web, as a commercial sales and marketing medium.

EIA Stands for Electronics Industries Association, a standards organization based in the United States that focuses on the development of hardware-related industry standards. EIA is the source of the widely used RS-232 standard that defines the structure of connectors used in serial transmissions.

electronic commerce See *e-commerce*.

Electronics Industries Assocation See *EIA*.

encrypt To encode (scramble) information in such a way that it is unreadable to all but those individuals possessing the key to the code.

encryption Scrambling of information so that it is unreadable by anyone other than those possessing the keys, or codes, required to return the information to readable form.

end-to-end delivery Communications in which packets are delivered and then acknowledged by the receiving system.

enterprise computing A vague term used generally to refer to networks and other computing needs implemented throughout a large, often widely dispersed corporation. Microsoft and IBM, for example, are enterprises; a small business is not.

Ethernet A widely used network that formed the basis for the IEEE 802.3 standard for bus

networks that rely on CSMA/CD to control network transmissions. Ethernet is available in various forms, including those known as Thin Ethernet, Thick Ethernet, 10BaseX Ethernet, and 100BaseX Ethernet. Essentially, it is a 10 Mbps or 100 Mbps baseband network, although there is also a recently developed Gigabit Ethernet that operates at 10 times 100 Mbps speed.

Extended Binary Coded Decimal Interchange Code See *EBCDIC*.

Extensible Markup Language See *XML*.

extranet A semiprivate network based on Internet technologies; essentially, an intranet that has been extended to allow access to certain authorized outsiders, such as vendors and business partners.

Fast Ethernet See *100BaseX*.

fast packet switching Term used in reference to high-speed packet-switching networks, such as frame relay and ATM, that perform little or no error checking. The term is often, however, restricted to high-speed networking technologies, such as ATM, that transmit fixed-length cells rather than including those, such as frame relay, that transmit variable-length packets.

fault tolerance In terms of computers and network operating systems, refers to the ability to withstand severe problems that can bring a network to a standstill, damage hardware, or cause loss of data. Although all computers and operating systems should be as fault-tolerant as possible, network hardware and operating systems must strive to be paragons of virtue in this regard.

FDDI Stands for Fiber Distributed Data Interface, a high-speed (100 Mbps) networking technology based on fiberoptic cable, token passing, and a ring topology.

female connector See *connector.*

Fiber Distributed Data Interface See *FDDI.*

fiberoptic cable A form of network cabling that transmits signals optically, rather than electrically as do coaxial and twisted-pair cable. The light-conducting heart of a fiberoptic cable is a fine glass or plastic fiber called the core. This core is surrounded by a refractive layer called the cladding that effectively traps the light and keeps it bouncing along the central fiber. Outside both the core and the cladding is a final layer of plastic or plastic-like material called the coat, or jacket. Fiberoptic cable can transmit clean signals at speeds as high as 2 Gbps. Because it transmits light, not electricity, it is also immune to eavesdropping.

file sharing The act of making files on one computer accessible to others on a network.

File Transfer Protocol See *FTP.*

firewall A protective mechanism, usually a combination of hardware and software, designed to act as a barrier, keeping external networks, such as the Internet, completely separate from an internal network. Firewalls forbid access to anyone but individuals authorized to use the network.

fractional T1 A form of T1 service in which part, rather than all, of a T1 line can be leased.

frame Often, a term used to refer to data packets at lower networking layers. Also, a single unit of information in a synchronous transmission.

frame relay A digital packet switching technology that transmits variable-length data packets at speeds up to 2 Mbps over

predetermined, set paths known as permanent virtual circuits, or PVCs.

frequency modulation A means of loading information onto a carrier wave by modulating (altering) its timing. Compare *amplitude modulation.*

frequency shift keying A form of frequency modulation that uses two different frequencies to represent the binary values 1 and 0. See also *frequency modulation.*

front end In terms of networking, roughly a reference to a client computer or the processing that takes place on it. Compare *back end.*

FSK See *frequency shift keying.*

FTP Stands for File Transfer Protocol, a fast, application-level TCP/IP protocol widely used for transferring both text-based and binary files to and from remote systems, especially over the Internet.

full duplex Modem operation in which transmission can occur in both directions at the same time. Compare *half duplex, simplex.*

gateway On a network, a device—often a specialized computer—that enables communication between networks based on different architectures and using different protocols. A gateway converts information being transmitted to a form in which it can be understood by the receiving network.

gender changer A type of connector used to enable male-to-male or female-to-female connections.

Gigabit Ethernet A recently developed form of Ethernet that operates at 1000 Mbps (1 gigabit per second). Gigabit Ethernet is expected to be used primarily as a high-speed LAN backbone.

Gopher A search program used to find documents on the Internet. Gopher searches all available Gopher servers, a virtual library known as Gopherspace, and it presents the user with menus and submenus with which to narrow a search and, eventually, choose desired documents. Gopher is assisted by two programs: Veronica, which narrows searches by combing the menus on all Gopher servers for information matching search criteria entered by the user, and Jughead, which searches for keywords on the top-level menus on specific Gopher servers.

Gopherspace See *Gopher.*

groupware A relatively vague term used to describe various types of software applications that enable network users to interact or work together. Groupware typically includes such applications as e-mail and scheduling software.

half duplex Modem operation in which transmission occurs in both directions, but not at the same time. Compare *full duplex, simplex.*

handshake A transmission that occurs at the beginning of a session between communicating computers. The handshake ensures that the two computers agree on how the transmission will proceed.

Hayes command set The set of transmission signals—commands—used originally by Hayes modems for exchanging status information, such as readiness to send or receive. The command set now represents a de facto standard for modem-to-modem communications.

HDSL Stands for High bit-rate Digital Subscriber Line, a form of DSL that transmits at 1.544 Mbps in both directions. See also *DSL.*

head In relation to software or documents, the top or beginning of something. In HTML, the head is the section of coding that precedes the body of a document and is used to describe the document itself (title, author, and so on) rather than the elements within the document. In terms of hardware, of course, *head* typically refers to the read/write device that transfers information to and from storage. Compare *body.*

High bit-rate Digital Subscriber Line See *HDSL.*

home page On the World Wide Web, the starting page for a Web site.

hop One leg of the journey taken by a packet from router to router in order to reach its destination.

host The main computer in a mainframe or minicomputer environment, that is, the computer to which terminals are connected. In PC-based networks, a host is a computer that provides access to other computers.

HTML Stands for HyperText Markup Language, the coding scheme used to tag the elements of Web documents (text format, font, color, image identifier, and so on) so that browser software can display the documents correctly on screen.

HTTP Stands for HyperText Transfer Protocol, the protocol used to carry requests from a browser to a Web server and to transport pages from Web servers back to the requesting browser. Although HTTP is almost universally used on the Web, it is not an especially secure protocol. One variation of HTTP known as SHTTP (Secure HTTP) adds encryption and other security features. Another, known as HTTPS (HTTP Secure) provides for encryption and transmission through a secure port. HTTPS was devised by Netscape and allows HTTP to run over a security technology known as SSL (Secure Sockets Layer). See also *SSL*.

HTTPS See *HTTP*.

hub A hardware device to which nodes connect on star-wired networks. Hubs can be passive, active, or intelligent, depending on how they operate. A passive hub simply acts as a connection point; an active hub both acts as a connection point and has the ability to regenerate signals; an intelligent hub is one with additional capabilities, such as the ability to configure the network.

hyperlink A connection that enables a user to jump from one element in an HTML document to another document or Web site. A hyperlink is associated with a normally invisible tag, coded in a markup language such as HTML, that enables a Web browser to find and display the linked document. See also *HTML*.

hypermedia The combination of text, video, graphic images, sound, hyperlinks, and other elements in the form typical of Web documents. Essentially, hypermedia is the modern extension of hypertext, the hyperlinked, text-based documents of the original Internet.

HyperText Markup Language See *HTML*.

HyperText Transfer Protocol See *HTTP*.

IAB See *Internet Architecture Board*.

ICANN Stands for Internet Corporation for Assigned Names and Numbers, the organization approved in 1998 as the successor to NSI and IANA as the controlling body responsible for domain names and IP addresses.

IEEE Stands for Institute of Electrical and Electronics Engineers, a society of technical professionals based in the United States but boasting membership from numerous other countries. The IEEE (pronounced "eye triple ee") focuses on electrical, electronics, computer engineering, and science-related matters. In the networking world, it is especially well known for its development of the IEEE 802.x specifications dealing with networking standards.

IEEE 802.x A series of specifications developed by the IEEE that defines numerous networking standards. The x following 802 is a placeholder for individual specifications, including 802.3 (Ethernet), 802.4 (Token Bus), and 802.5 (Token Ring).

IETF Stands for Internet Engineering Task Force, a worldwide organization of individuals interested in networking and the Internet. The work of the IETF is carried out by various Working Groups that concentrate on specific topics, such as routing and security. The IETF is the publisher of the specifications that led to the TCP/IP protocol standard.

Institute of Electrical and Electronics Engineers See *IEEE*.

Integrated Services Digital Network See *ISDN*.

Integrated Services LAN See *isochronous network*.

intelligent hub A type of hub that, in addition to transmitting signals, has built-in capability for other network chores, such as monitoring or reporting on network status.

Intelligent hubs are used in different types of networks, including ARCnet and 10BaseT Ethernet.

interactive services See *BISDN.*

interface The connection between two elements that enables them to work together or exchange information. A user interface, for example, is the connecting point between a computer user and the computer's software.

International Organization for Standardization A federation of standards bodies representing 130 countries throughout the world. Although the ISO is concerned with numerous standards unrelated to computing, it is justly famed in networking references as the originator of the seven-layer ISO/OSI Reference Model. See also *ISO/OSI Reference Model.*

International Telecommunication Union See *ITU.*

Internet Architecture Board The advisory arm of the Internet Society focused on technical matters.

Internet Corporation for Assigned Names and Numbers See *ICANN.*

Internet Engineering Task Force See *IETF.*

Internet Protocol See *IP.*

Internet Protocol address See *IP address.*

Internet Reference Model See *TCP/IP Reference Model.*

Internet Relay Chat See *IRC.*

Internet Research Task Force An arm of the Internet Society focused on long-term, Internet-related research projects.

Internet Service Provider See *ISP.*

Internet Society A nonprofit organization based in Reston, Virginia, with a worldwide membership of individuals concerned with Internet standards, education, and policy. See also *Internet Architecture Board, Internet Engineering Task Force, Internet Research Task Force.*

internetwork A network made up of smaller, interconnected networks.

Internetwork Packet Exchange/Sequenced Packet Exchange See *IPX/SPX.*

interrupt A signal from a device to a computer's processor requesting the processor's attention. Interrupts are generated for many reasons, including software errors and the signaling of the presence of data to be processed.

intranet A private network based on Internet technologies but confined to use within an organization, such as a corporation. Compare *extranet.*

IP Stands for Internet Protocol, the TCP/IP protocol responsible for routing packets. IP runs at the internetwork layer in the TCP/IP model—equivalent to the network layer in the ISO/OSI Reference Model.

IP address The 32-bit numeric address that identifies an Internet host to other computers on the Internet.

IPX/SPX Stands for Internetwork Packet Exchange/Sequenced Packet Exchange, a set of two protocols designed by Novell for NetWare networks. IPX is a connectionless protocol that handles addressing and routing of packets. SPX, which runs above IPX, ensures correct delivery. IPX/SPX is comparable to the TCP and IP protocols in the TCP/IP suite.

IRC Stands for Internet Relay Chat, an Internet service that enables participants to chat in real time.

IRTF See *Internet Research Task Force.*

ISDN Stands for Integrated Services Digital Network, a high-speed communications network developed to provide all-digital service over the existing telephone network. ISDN was designed to carry not only voice but data, images, and video. ISDN is available in two forms, known as BRI (Basic Rate Interface) and PRI (Primary Rate Interface). BRI consists of two B (bearer) channels that carry data at 64 Kbps and one D (data) channel that carries control and signal information at 16 Kbps. In North America and Japan, PRI consists of 23 B channels and 1 D channel, all operating at 64 Kbps; elsewhere in the world, PRI consists of 30 B channels and 1 D channel.

ISLAN See *isochronous network.*

ISO See *International Organization for Standardization.*

ISO/OSI Reference Model A well-known standard that defines networks in terms of seven protocol layers, each concerned with a different level of service that contributes to preparing data for transmission over a network. The ISO/OSI Reference Model covers all aspects of a network, from the physical medium to the ways in which applications access the network. It is a fundamental blueprint designed to help guide the creation of networking hardware and software.

ISOC See *Internet Society.*

isochronous network Also known as Integrated Services LAN, or ISLAN, a type of network defined in the IEEE 802.9 specification that combines ISDN and LAN technologies to enable networks to carry multimedia.

ISP A business that provides Internet access to individuals and businesses.

ITU Stands for International Telecommunication Union, an international organization based in Geneva, Switzerland. The ITU focuses on telecommunications and is divided into three sectors dealing with radiocommunications, standardization, and development. The standardization sector is the new (and current) home of the organization formerly known as the CCITT. See also *CCITT.*

Java An object-oriented programming language developed by Sun Microsystems and designed around the idea that a program, once written, can run without modification on more than one computing platform, such as Windows and Macintosh. Unlike programs created in other languages, such as C++, Java programs are compiled (translated for execution) into a form known as bytecode. This bytecode, which is not refined to the point of relying on platform-specific instructions, runs on a computer in a special software environment known as a virtual machine. Java is difficult for non-programmers to understand, so don't be appalled if it doesn't make much sense to you. Its primary impact on end users is its use in creating Web applets and, increasingly, distributed network applications.

Jughead See *Gopher.*

key In encryption and digital signatures, a string of bits used for encrypting and decrypting information to be transmitted. Encryption commonly relies on two different types of keys, a public key known to more than one person (say, both the sender and the receiver) and a private key known only to one person (typically, the sender).

keyword In search programs, a word or phrase used as the key for searching databases to locate information.

LAN See *local area network.*

LANtastic A network operating system from Artisoft designed to support both peer-to-peer and client/server networks.

layered architecture The division of a network model into multiple discrete layers, or levels, through which messages pass as they are prepared for transmission. In a layered architecture, protocols at each layer provide specific services or functions and rely on protocols in the layers above and below them for other needed services.

LCP See *Point-to-Point Protocol.*

line A segment in a SONET network that runs between two multiplexers. See also *path, section.*

linear bus See *bus topology.*

link See *hyperlink.*

Link Control Protocol See *Point-to-Point Protocol.*

Linux A UNIX-like operating system developed by Linus Torvalds and numerous programmers throughout the world. Linux is distributed free, and its source code is open to modification by anyone who chooses to work on it. It is often used as an operating system for network servers.

LLC Stands for Logical Link Control. In the IEEE 802.x specifications, the higher of two sublayers that make up the ISO/OSI data link layer. The LLC is responsible for

managing communications links and handling frame traffic. See also *MAC.*

local area network A network that is relatively limited in scope—for example, one that connects computers in a single department or building.

local loop The (end) portion of a telephone connection running between the subscriber and the local telephone exchange.

log on To gain access to a network by identifying oneself with a username and a password.

logical Conceptually true to a particular design or idea—for example, transmissions travel in a circle around a logical ring, even though the ring shape itself is not physically apparent. Compare *physical.*

Logical Link Control See *LCC.*

LU Stands for Logical Unit, an entity that enables applications and devices to communicate on an SNA network.

MAC Stands for Media Access Control. In the IEEE 802.x specifications, the lower of two sublayers that make up the ISO/OSI data link layer. The MAC manages access to the physical network, delimits frames, and handles error control. See also *LLC.*

male connector See *connector.*

MAU Stands for Multistation Access Unit, a hub to which nodes connect on a Token Ring network.

maximum transmission unit See *MTU.*

Media Access Control See *MAC.*

microcomputer A computer based on a microprocessor. Essentially, in today's terms, a desktop PC.

MIME Stands for Multipurpose Internet Mail Exensions, a protocol widely used on the Internet for enabling e-mail to include multiple types of information, including text, graphics, sound, and video. MIME uses the message header for describing media types included in the document. This information is then used by software on the destination machine to determine whether the particular data types can be "replayed," and if so, by what programs.

mirroring A means of protecting data on a network by duplicating it, in its entirety, on a second disk. Mirroring is one strategy implemented in RAID security. See also *RAID*.

modem The device that enables computer-to-computer communication over a telephone line. Modems work by modulating and demodulating computer signals. When transmitting, the modem transforms (modulates) signals from the digital form required by the computer to the analog form required by the phone line. When receiving, the modem reverses the action, demodulating the signal from analog back to digital form.

modulation The process of modifying a carrier wave in such a way that the modification(s) to the wave represent information. Transmitting modems use modulation to load information onto a telephone signal (carrier). Compare *demodulation*.

MOO Stands for MUD, object oriented, a type of virtual environment on the Internet, similar to a game-oriented MUD but based on an object-oriented language and generally focused more on programming than on games.

MTU Stands for maximum transmission unit, the largest packet size that can be supported by a particular network implementation.

MUD Stands for multiuser dungeon, an interactive environment on the Internet where users can get together to play multiuser role-playing, dungeons and dragons types of games.

multiplexing The process of weaving multiple signals onto a single channel or communications line. In multiplexing, segments of information from each signal are interleaved and generally separated by time, frequency, or space.

multiport repeater See *active hub*.

multiprogramming A form of processing in which a computer holds more than one program in memory and works on them in round-robin fashion—that is, by sharing out the processor's time so that each program receives some attention some of the time. This way of working is in contrast to using the processor to run one program at a time.

Multipurpose Internet Mail Extensions See *MIME*.

Multistation Access Unit See *MAU*.

multitasking A form of processing supported by most current operating systems in which a computer works on multiple tasks—roughly, separate "pieces" of work—seemingly at the same time by parceling out the processor's time among the different tasks. Multitasking can be either cooperative or preemptive. In the former, the operating system relies on the task to voluntarily cede control to another task; in the latter, the operating system decides which task receives priority.

NAP See *network access point.*

narrowband ISDN Name used to distinguish current ISDN lines from the developing broadband ISDN technology.

NC See *network computer.*

NCP See *Point-to-Point Protocol.*

NDIS Stands for Network Device Interface Specification, a software-interface specification developed by Microsoft and 3Com that mediates between network adapters and higher-level protocols to enable the adapter to support multiple protocol stacks.

NetBEUI Stands for NetBIOS Extended User Interface, a transport-layer protocol provided with Microsoft networking products. NetBEUI is capable of rapid data transfer but is limited to LANs because it is a nonroutable protocol (meaning it does not support routing, which relies on network addresses to move transmissions from one network to another).

NetBIOS Extended User Interface See *NetBEUI.*

NetWare A network operating system from Novell, developed in both peer-to-peer and client server versions, the latter available for both servers and workstations.

network access point Also called national attachment point, one of the four locations in the United States through which Internet Service Providers connect to the Internet backbone.

network computer A computer designed for use on a network in which programs and storage are provided by servers. Network computers, unlike dumb terminals, have their own processing power, but their

design does not include local storage, and they depend on network servers for applications.

Network Control Protocol See *Point-to-Point Protocol.*

Network Device Interface Specification See *NDIS.*

network interface card The circuit board needed to provide network access to a computer or other device, such as a printer. Network interface cards, or NICs, mediate between the computer and the physical media, such as cabling, over which transmissions travel.

Network News Transfer Protocol See *NNTP.*

network operating system An operating system specifically designed to support networking. A server-based network operating system, or NOS, provides networking support for multiple simultaneous users as well as administrative, security, and management functions. On the desktop, a network-aware operating system provides users with the ability to access network resources.

newsfeed A collection of news articles delivered through the NNTP protocol by news servers on the Internet.

newsgroup A group of individuals on the Internet with a common interest in a particular subject or set of related subjects. Newsgroups receive and post articles and discussions bearing on their area of interest.

NIC See *network interface card.*

NNTP Stands for Network News Transfer Protocol, a de facto protocol standard on the Internet used to distribute news articles and query news servers.

node A device on a network—for example, a client computer, a server, or a shared printer.

noise Electromagnetic interference that distorts or degrades a communications signal.

nondedicated server A computer on a network that can function as both a client and a server; typically, a desktop machine on a peer-to-peer network. Compare *dedicated server.*

ODI Stands for Open Data-Link Interface, a software-interface specification developed by Novell and Apple for providing a common boundary between network adapters and higher-level protocols so that the adapters can support more than one protocol stack.

Open Data-Link Interface See *ODI.*

open source A movement in the programming community for making source code (program instructions) free and freely available to anyone interested in using or working with it.

Open Systems Interconnection Reference Model See *ISO/OSI Reference Model.*

optical fiber See *fiberoptic cable.*

OS Stands for operating system, the foundation software that interacts with the computer, runs applications, provides needed services to software and attached devices, and presents the user with a keyboard-based or mouse-based user interface for controlling the computer.

OSI protocol stack The set of protocols based on—and corresponding to—the ISO/OSI Reference Model.

OSI Reference Model See *ISO/OSI Reference Model.*

packet The fundamental message unit transmitted over a network. A packet consists of a header that contains addressing information, a block of data (the largest portion of the packet), and a trailer that often contains error-checking information. Packet size and makeup vary with the network and protocols in use.

packet assembler and disassembler See *PAD.*

packet header The portion of a data packet that precedes the body (data). The header contains data, such as source and destination addresses and control and timing information, that is needed for successful transmission.

packet switching A transmission method by which information is broken into same-sized units called packets that are addressed and routed over a network from source to destination. Although the packets forming a single transmission can be sent over different routes and can arrive at their destination at different times, the receiving computer reassembles them in the correct order. Packet switching does not require a physical link between communicating parties, nor does it require that a connection be made before transmission can occur. Compare *circuit switching.*

Packet Switching Exchange An intermediary switching station in a packet-switching network.

packet trailer The portion of a data packet that follows the body (data). The trailer typically contains information related to error checking and correction.

PAD Stands for packet assembler/disassembler, a device on a packet-switching network that assembles packets for transmission and reassembles packets in the correct order on receipt.

page On the World Wide Web, a document called up by, and viewed through, browser software. A Web page can be a multimedia document containing text, graphics, sound, and video. It is also characterized by the inclusion of hyperlinks that enable users to move directly from one document (page) to another.

parallel transmission A form of transmission in which groups of bits—typically the 8 bits forming 1 byte—are sent at the same time over multiple wires. Compare *serial transmission.*

parity bit A bit in asynchronous communications used to indicate the type of error checking used in a transmission.

passive hub A type of hub used on ARCnet networks that passes signals along but has no additional capability. Compare *active hub, intelligent hub.*

passive node A network node that "listens" for transmissions but is not actively involved in passing them along the network; typical of a node on a bus network.

password The private string of characters entered by a user to verify his or her identity to the network. Ideally a password is a combination of text, numbers, and punctuation or other characters that cannot be guessed at or easily cracked by intruders.

path The complete route from source to destination multiplexer on a SONET network. See also *line, section.*

PCT Stands for Private Communication Technology, a protocol standard drafted by Microsoft and submitted to the IETF for consideration. PCT, like the Netscape-designed SSL (Secure Sockets Layer), supports authentication and encryption for securing privacy in Internet communications.

peer-to-peer network A network in which computers function as equals, with each one being able to function as a client, a server, or both, depending on the resources being used and/or shared out. In LANs, typically a small network of desktop PCs. Compare *client/server network.*

permanent virtual circuit A connection established by a connection-oriented service in which a permanent link exists between the communicating parties.

phase shift keying A means of loading information onto a carrier wave by modulating (altering) the phase of the wave.

physical Of or relating to something real, visible, or tangible—for example, a physical ring would be one that forms a visible circle. Compare *logical.*

physical address In networking, a unique numeric address (value) assigned to a network interface card.

Plain Old Telephone Service See *POTS.*

platform In general, a reference to a particular type of computer or operating system—for example, the Windows platform or the Macintosh platform. More specifically, a platform refers to the technology—the details—that differentiate one computer or operating system from another.

plug See *connector.*

Point to Point Tunneling Protocol See *PPTP.*

Point-to-Point Protocol See *PPP.*

point-to-point tunneling A means of setting up secure communications over an open, public network such as the Internet. See *PPTP*.

port A channel, or conduit, through which information flows to or from a computer and attached input or output devices.

portal A site designed to act as an entryway to the World Wide Web.

post office The server and associated storage and mail handling services that provide the centralized location for collection and distribution of e-mail over a network.

POTS Stands for Plain Old Telephone Service, that is, the network of telephone lines and switching facilities that forms the basis of everyday telephone service.

PPP Stands for Point-to-Point Protocol, a widely used Internet protocol for transmitting TCP/IP packets. PPP supports dynamic allocation of IP addresses and so is easier to use than the older SLIP. The PPP protocol itself is based on a Link Control Protocol (LCP) responsible for setting up a computer-to-computer link over telephone lines and a Network Control Protocol (NCP) responsible for negotiating network-layer details related to the transmission. See also *PPTP*.

PPTP Stands for Point to Point Tunneling Protocol, an extension of the Point-to-Point Protocol used for communications on the Internet. PPTP was developed by Microsoft to support virtual private networks (VPNs), which allow individuals and organizations to use the Internet as a secure means of communication. PPTP supports encapsulation of encrypted packets in secure wrappers that can be transmitted over a TCP/IP connection.

PRI See *ISDN*.

Primary Rate Interface See *ISDN*.

Private Communication Technology See *PCT*.

private key See *key*.

Project 802 The IEEE project to define networking standards that resulted in the 802.x specifications. See also *IEEE, IEEE 802.x*.

promiscuous mode On a network, a method of operation in which a device monitors all network traffic.

protocol A set of rules governing the way in which computers communicate, either with one another or with attached devices. Networking is filled with a bewildering variety and number of protocols, many of which perform the same, or similar, services. All, however, are designed to enable reliable communication.

protocol stack A complete set of protocols that work together to enable communication on a network. Compare *protocol suite*.

protocol suite A set of protocols designed, usually by one vendor, as complementary parts of a protocol stack. Compare *protocol stack*.

proxy A computer (or the software that runs on it) that acts as a barrier between a network and the Internet by presenting only a single network address to external sites. By acting as a go-between representing all internal computers, the proxy protects network identities while still providing access to the Internet.

PSE See *Packet Switching Exchange*.

PSK See *phase shift keying*.

PSTN See *Public Switched Telephone Network.*

public key See *key.*

Public Switched Telephone Network The public telephone system.

push A technology developed in relation to the World Wide Web, designed to provide end users with personalized Web access by having a site actively "push" requested information to the user's desktop, either automatically or at specified intervals. Push was developed as a means of relieving users from having to actively retrieve ("pull") information from the Web. It is not, as yet, especially popular.

PVC See *permanent virtual circuit.*

QAM See *quadrature amplitude modulation.*

QOS Stands for quality of service, a term used generally to refer to performance at or above a certain standard. More specifically, QOS refers to the maximum amount of delay and data loss considered acceptable for transmissions on an ATM network.

quadrature amplitude modulation A means of loading information onto a carrier wave by modulating both its phase and amplitude. Quadrature amplitude modulation creates a constellation of points that allow a single signal change to represent multiple bits of information.

quality of service See *QOS.*

RADSL Stands for Rate Adaptive Digital Subscriber Line, a form of DSL that adjusts transmissions based on line quality and distance traveled. RADSL operates at 2.2 Mbps downstream and up to 1.088 Mbps upstream.

RAID Stands for Redundant Array of Inexpensive Disks, a means of improving network performance and ensuring data integrity and security by storing information on multiple disk drives. Different levels of RAID security can be implemented, depending on the levels of reliability and performance desired.

Rate Adaptive Digital Subscriber Line See *RADSL.*

real time Occurring in the same time frame experienced by people.

redirector Software on a client computer that intercepts requests for information and, when appropriate, directs them to the network. Redirectors can either be built into the client operating system or be part of an added networking package.

Reduced Instruction Set Computing See *RISC.*

repeater A network device that cleans and boosts a signal before sending it on its way.

resource sharing The act of making files, printers, and other network resources available for use by others.

ring topology A network configuration in which nodes are attached to the main communications line in a logical or physical ring shape.

RISC Pronounced "risk." An acronym for Reduced Instruction Set Computing, a description applied to microprocessors optimized for carrying out a relatively small number of instructions extremely quickly. In terms of the simple instructions most often carried out by computers, RISC chips are faster than the general-purpose CISC (Complex Instruction Set Computing) chips typical of many desktop computers. For complex instructions that must be broken down into numerous simpler ones, RISC chips are slower than their CISC brethren.

RJ-45 A type of connector used with twisted-pair wiring; similar to, but larger than, a telephone jack.

robot See *spider.*

root server A DNS name server that is the authority for resolving Internet names and IP addresses at the highest domain level, the top-level domain.

routable protocol A network protocol that can be used to route packets from one network to another.

router A network device that transmits message packets, routing them over the best route available at the time. Routers are used to connect multiple network segments, including those based on differing architectures and protocols.

routing table A table of network addresses used by routers and bridges in determining where to forward transmissions. Although both routers and bridges use routing tables, the tables are not the same for both devices. Tables for routers, for example, include information about different paths between other routers, whereas tables for bridges include network addresses only.

S/MIME Stands for Secure/Multipurpose Internet Mail Extensions, a security-oriented protocol that adds encryption and support for digital signatures to the widely used MIME e-mail protocol.

SAS See *single attachment station.*

scalability In relation to network hardware and software, the ability to support larger or smaller numbers of computers as needs and

circumstances dictate. Essentially, the ability to grow or shrink gracefully.

script A program that interacts with an application or a utility program. On the World Wide Web, scripts are commonly used to customize or add interactivity to Web pages.

SDH See *Synchronous Digital Hierarchy.*

SDSL Stands for Single-line Digital Subscriber Line, a variation of HDSL that uses one pair rather than two pairs of wires and transmits at 1.544 Mbps.

search engine On the Internet, a document-finding program used to find and retrieve information based on keywords indexed in databases.

second-level domain The level immediately beneath the top-level domain in the Internet's DNS hierarchy.

section A length of fiberoptic cable in a SONET network. See also *line, path.*

Secure HTTP See *HTTP.*

Secure Sockets Layer See *SSL.*

Secure/Multipurpose Internet Mail Extensions See *S/MIME.*

Serial Line Internet Protocol See *SLIP.*

serial transmission A form of transmission in which bits are sent sequentially, one at a time, over a single line. Compare *parallel transmission.*

service Specialized, software-based functionality provided by network servers—for example, directory services that provide the network equivalent of "phone books" needed for locating users and resources.

session The time during which two computers are communicating.

shared medium The communications medium shared by network nodes; essentially, the network bandwidth.

shielded twisted-pair wiring See *twisted-pair wiring.*

SHTTP See *HTTP.*

Simple Mail Transfer Protocol See *SMTP.*

Simple Network Management Protocol See *SNMP.*

simplex Modem operation in which transmission occurs in one direction only. Compare *full duplex, half duplex.*

single attachment station A FDDI node that connects to the primary ring through a concentrator. Compare *dual attachment station.*

Single-line Digital Subscriber Line See *SDSL.*

site On the World Wide Web, a collection of documents (pages), as well as files and databases, belonging to a particular individual or organization.

SLIP Stands for Serial Line Internet Protocol, a protocol used for Internet connections. SLIP enables computers to transmit TCP/IP packets over serial lines. It is an older, less secure protocol than the PPP (Point-to-Point Protocol) and does not support dynamic allocation of IP addresses. A newer form of SLIP, known as CSLIP (Compressed SLIP), optimizes transmission of long documents by compressing header information. See also *PPP.*

SMDS Stands for Switched Multimegabit Data Service, a connectionless, packet-switched

technology used by businesses to connect LANs in different locations.

SMP See *symmetric multiprocessing.*

SMS See *Systems Management Server.*

SMTP Stands for Simple Mail Transfer Protocol, a protocol in the TCP/IP suite used to transfer e-mail over the Internet.

SNA Stands for Systems Network Architecture, a network model devised by IBM to enable IBM products, including mainframes, terminals, and peripherals, to communicate and exchange data. SNA started out as a five-layer model and was later extended with two additional layers to correspond more closely to the ISO/OSI Reference Model. More recently, the SNA model was modified to include minicomputers and microcomputers in a specification known as APPC (Advanced Program to Program Communications). See also *APPC.* Compare *ISO/OSI Reference Model.*

snail mail Semi-sarcastic jargon used by e-mail fans to refer to non-electronic (paper-based) mail sent and delivered through traditional postal services.

SNMP Stands for Simple Network Management Protocol, a protocol in the TCP/IP suite used for network monitoring and management.

socket In networking, a means of enabling client and server applications to communicate over a network. A socket is essentially an end point in a communications session. In reference to hardware, a socket is a receptacle, a female connector. See also *connector.*

SONET Stands for Synchronous Optical NETwork, a high-speed network that provides a standard interface for communications carriers to connect networks based on fiberoptic cable. SONET is designed to handle multiple data types (voice, video, and so on). It transmits at a base rate of 51.84 Mbps, but multiples of this base rate go as high as 2.488 Gbps (gigabits per second).

spider A program that roams the World Wide Web, seeking documents to be indexed in a database that can then be examined for matches by search engines. Also called a crawler, robot, or bot.

spoofing A means of masquerading on a network by making a transmission appear to come from an authorized computer.

SSL Stands for Secure Sockets Layer, a protocol developed by Netscape Communications Corporation for ensuring security and privacy in Internet communications. SSL supports authentication of client, server, or both, as well as encryption during a communications session. See also *PCT.*

star bus A network topology in which nodes connect to hubs in a star pattern, but the hubs are connected by a bus trunk. Star bus is a combination of star and bus topologies.

star topology A network configuration based on a central hub, from which nodes radiate in a star-shaped pattern.

start bit A bit (actually a timing signal) that represents the beginning of a character in asynchronous communications. Compare *parity bit, stop bit.*

star-wired ring A network topology in which hubs and nodes connect to a central hub in typical star fashion, but the connections within the central hub form a ring. Star-wired ring is a combination of star and ring topologies.

station In the IEEE 802.11 wireless LAN specification, a single, often mobile, node.

stop bit A bit (actually a timing signal) that represents the end of a character in asynchronous communications. Compare *parity bit, start bit.*

store and forward A method of delivering transmissions in which messages are held temporarily by an intermediary before being sent on to their destination. Store and forward is used by some switches in delivering packets to their destinations. Compare *cut-through switch.*

storm On a network, a sudden, excessive burst of traffic. Storms are often responsible for network outages.

STP See *twisted-pair wiring.*

striping A means of protecting data on a network by spreading it across multiple disks. In the most commonly used approach, striping is combined with parity (error-correcting information) to ensure that if some portion of the data is lost, it can be reconstructed. Striping is implemented in RAID security. See also *RAID.*

subdomain A domain, often representing an administrative or other organizational subgroup within a second-level domain.

subnet In general, a network that forms part of a larger network. In terms of the ISO/OSI Reference Model, the subnet comprises the layers below the transport layer—that is, the network, data link, and physical layers.

subnetwork A network that is part of another, larger network.

SVC See *switched virtual circuit.*

switch A network device capable of forwarding packets directly to the ports associated with particular network addresses.

Switched Multimegabit Data Service See *SMDS.*

Switched T1 A circuit-switched form of T1 communications.

switched virtual circuit A connection established by a connection-oriented service in which a temporary link is created between the communicating parties.

symmetric multiprocessing A method of processing in which multiple processors work together on the same tasks; a means of improving speed and increasing a computer's ability to handle large workloads.

synchronous communications Computer-to-computer communications in which transmissions are synchronized by timing between the sending and receiving machines.

Synchronous Digital Hierarchy An ITU recommendation implemented in Europe and similar in most respects to the SONET standard used in North America and Japan. See also *SONET.*

Synchronous Optical NETwork See *SONET.*

Systems Management Server A Microsoft BackOffice component that provides services for centralized network management.

Systems Network Architecture See *SNA.*

T1 A high-speed communications line, sometimes called T-1 carrier, originally developed to carry multiple conversations over standard twisted-pair telephone wiring. Currently, T1 provides digital communications and Internet access at the rate of 1.54 Mbps. T1 speed is attained through multiplexing 24 separate 64 kbps channels into a single data stream.

T-1 carrier See *T1.*

TA See *terminal adapter.*

tag In general, a marker of some sort. In the HTML markup language of the World Wide Web, tags are embedded codes used to identify and define the properties of the element within a document—images, formatted text, hyperlinks, and so on. These tags are used by browser software in determining how documents are displayed on screen.

TCP Stands for Transmission Control Protocol, the TCP/IP protocol responsible for creating and reassembling packets and ensuring that information is delivered correctly. TCP runs at the transport layer and relies on IP (Internet Protocol) for delivery. It is a connection-oriented, reliable protocol (reliable in the sense of ensuring error-free delivery). Compare *UDP.*

TCP/IP Stands for Transmission Control Protocol/Internet Protocol, a protocol suite (set of protocols) designed for enabling communications over interconnected, sometimes dissimilar, networks. TCP/IP is supported by almost all networks. It lies at the heart of Internet communications.

TCP/IP Reference Model A networking model designed around the concept of internetworking—the exchange of information among different networks, often built on different architectures. The TCP/IP Reference Model, often called the Internet

Reference Model, consists of four layers, the most distinctive of which is the internetwork that deals with routing messages and that has no equivalent in the ISO/OSI Reference Model or the SNA model. Compare *ISO/OSI Reference Model, SNA.*

telnet A protocol in the TCP/IP suite that enables individuals to log on to and use a remote computer as if they were sitting at a terminal directly connected to the machine.

terminal In terms of networking, a device with a keyboard and a monitor that is connected to a computer, such as a mainframe, through a communications link or cable and that relies on the larger machine for processing and data.

terminal adapter The correct name for an ISDN "modem," which connects a PC to an ISDN line but does not modulate or demodulate signals as a typical modem does.

terminal emulation The use of software to help a computer behave as if it were a particular kind of terminal attached to a larger computer, such as a mainframe.

terminator A hardware device used to "cap" the end of a cable in a bus network in order to keep signals from bouncing back along the line.

Thick Ethernet See *10Base5.*

thin client A network device that has the ability to process information independently but relies on servers for applications, data storage, and administration. See also *network computer, Windows terminal.*

Thin Ethernet See *10Base2.*

thread On the Internet and in e-mail discussions, a series of comments related to a particular topic.

throughput The data transfer rate of a network, measured as the number of bits per second transmitted.

timesharing A method, used primarily in the 60s and 70s, for sharing the capabilities (and cost) of a computer, such as a mainframe. Timesharing allowed different clients to "rent" time on a large computer and pay for only the portion of time they used.

token The special packet circulated by nodes in a token-passing network. Possession of the token gives a node the right to transmit.

token bus The IEEE 802.4 specification for token-passing networks based on a bus or tree topology. Token bus networks were designed primarily for manufacturing, but the specification also corresponds to the ARCnet architecture used for LANs.

token passing A means of controlling network access through the use of a small packet, the token, which is circulated through the network from node to node. A node can transmit only when it holds the token.

token ring Spelled with lowercase *t* and *r*, the IEEE specification 802.5 for token ring networks. See also *Token Ring.*

Token Ring Spelled with uppercase *T* and *R*, the token ring architecture developed by IBM and widely implemented in token-passing networks. Token Ring networks are usually star-wired rings in which nodes connect to hubs known as Multistation Access Units, or MAUs. These networks typically operate at 4 Mbps or 16 Mbps, although both 100 Mbps and 1 Gbps forms are under development.

top-level domain The highest-level domain in the Internet's DNS hierarchy.

topology The layout of a network; its configuration.

transceiver From transmitter/receiver, a device that both transmits and receives signals. On a network, a transceiver is the device that connects a computer to the network and that converts signals to and from parallel and serial form.

transceiver cable See *drop cable.*

Transmission Control Protocol See *TCP.*

transparent A term used to describe computer hardware or software that works so well and is so easy to use that its underlying complexity, or the means by which it performs its work, is invisible to the user.

trellis-coded modulation A variation of quadrature amplitude modulation that allows encoding of both data and error-checking information.

trunk The cable forming the main communications path on a network; on a bus network, the single cable to which all nodes connect. See also *backbone.*

tunneling A method of transmission over internetworks based on differing protocols. In tunneling, a packet based on one protocol is wrapped, or encapsulated, in a second packet based on whatever differing protocol is needed in order for it to travel over an intermediary network. In effect, the second wrapper "insulates" the original packet and creates the illusion of a tunnel through which the wrapped packet travels across the intermediary network. In real-life terms, tunneling is comparable to "encapsulating" a present (the original packet) in a box (the secondary wrapper) for delivery through the postal system.

twisted-pair wiring Wiring consisting of two insulated strands of copper twisted around one another to form a cable. Twisted-pair wiring comes in two forms, unshielded twisted pair (UTP) and shielded twisted pair (STP), the latter named for an extra protective sheath wrapped around each insulated pair of wires. Twisted-pair wiring can consist of a single pair of wires or, in thicker cables, two, four, or more pairs of wires. Twisted-pair wiring is typical of telephone cabling. Compare *coaxial cable, fiberoptic cable.*

UDP Stands for User Datagram Protocol, a transport-level TCP/IP protocol that breaks messages into packets for delivery by the IP protocol. Unlike TCP, UDP is a connectionless, unreliable protocol, meaning that it does not establish a path between sender and receiver before transmitting and does not verify that packets arrive correctly.

Universal Resource Locator See *URL.*

UNIX A powerful multitasking operating system developed in 1969 for use in a minicomputer environment; still a widely used network operating system.

unreliable protocol A communications protocol that makes a "best effort" attempt to deliver a transmission but does not provide for verifying that the transmission arrives without error.

unshielded twisted-pair wiring See *twisted-pair wiring.*

upstream Delivery of information from a client to a (Web) server. Compare *downstream.*

URL Stands for Uniform Resource Locator or, sometimes, Universal Resource Locator, the address for a resource (document) on the Internet.

User Datagram Protocol See *UDP.*

username The "friendly" name by which a user is known and addressed on a network.

UTP See *twisted-pair wiring.*

V series The series of recommendations devised by the CCITT (now part of the ITU) relating to modems and modem communications over the public phone system.

vampire tap A type of transceiver used on Ethernet networks that is equipped with sharp metal prongs that pierce the insulation on thicknet cable to make contact with the copper core over which signals travel.

VDSL Stands for Very high rate Digital Subscriber Line, a developing form of DSL that can transmit up to 52 Mbps downstream and up to 2.3 Mbps upstream, though only over short distances (up to 4500 feet).

Veronica See *Gopher.*

Very high rate Digital Subscriber Line See *VDSL.*

VINES A UNIX-based networking operating system from Banyan Systems.

virtual circuit A connection between communicating computers that provides the computers with what appears to be a direct link but can actually involve routing data over a defined, but longer path.

virtual private network A network that uses encryption and other technologies, including tunneling, to provide secure communications over the Internet. A virtual private network essentially provides users with an inexpensive, Internet-based equivalent of a network connected by private communications lines.

VPN See *virtual private network.*

W3C Abbreviation for the World Wide Web Consortium, a standards body based in the United States, Europe, and Japan. The W3C ("double-yew-three-see") is dedicated (in part) to encouraging the development of open Web standards, such as the HTML and XML document markup languages.

WAIS Stands for Wide Area Information Service, a UNIX-based document-search system that searches collections known as WAIS libraries for files matching keywords entered by the user.

WAN See *wide area network.*

Wide Area Information Service See *WAIS.*

wide area network A geographically widespread network, one that relies on communications capabilities to link the various network segments. A WAN can be one large network, or it can consist of a number of linked LANs.

Windows The name for any of the graphical, mouse-oriented operating systems from Microsoft, available in different forms and versions for desktop computers (Windows 95 and 98), workstations (Windows NT Workstation), and network servers (Windows NT/2000 Server).

Windows terminal A thin-client solution from Microsoft, designed to enable terminals and minimally configured computers to display Windows applications even if they are not, in themselves, capable of running Windows software. Windows terminals work in conjunction with Windows NT Server, Terminal Server edition. See also *thin client.*

Wireless LAN A local area network based either fully or in part on wireless transmission technologies, such as infrared light and radio signals.

WLAN See *wireless LAN.*

World Wide Web Consortium See *W3C.*

XDSL See *DSL.*

Xerox Network System See *XNS.*

XML Stands for Extensible Markup Language, an evolving Web markup language designed to extend the capabilities of HTML by giving page designers a means of describing not only the appearance of a document, but also its content.

XNS Stands for Xerox Network System, a set of protocols assigned to five numbered layers (0 through 4) that form a suite designed to (as usual) handle packaging and delivery of network transmissions.

Symbols and Numbers

A

About the Author

JoAnne Woodcock is the author of several popular computer books, including *Understanding Groupware in the Enterprise*, *The Ultimate Microsoft Windows 95 Book*, *The Ultimate MS-DOS Book*, and *PCs for Beginners*, all published by Microsoft Press. She is also a contributor to the *Microsoft Press Computer Dictionary*.

The manuscript for this book was prepared and submitted to Microsoft Press in electronic form. Text files were prepared using Microsoft Word 97 for Windows 98. Pages were composed by Helios Productions using Adobe PageMaker 6.51 for Windows, with text in Melior and display type in Frutiger Condensed. Composed pages were delivered to the printer as electronic prepress files.

Cover Designer
Tim Girvin Design, Inc.

Cover Illustrator
Tom Draper Design

Interior Graphic Artist
Ken Yaecker

Principal Compositor
Sybil Ihrig, Helios Productions

Principal Proofreader/Copy Editor
Rebecca Taff / Gail Taylor

Indexer
Rebecca Plunkett

END-USER LICENSE AGREEMENT FOR MICROSOFT SOFTWARE

Microsoft Skills 2000 IT Tour CD

IMPORTANT—READ CAREFULLY: This Microsoft End-User License Agreement ("EULA") is a legal agreement between you (either an individual or a single entity) and Microsoft Corporation, its suppliers, and third party content providers for the software product identified above, which includes computer software and may include "online" or electronic documentation ("SOFTWARE PRODUCT"). By installing, copying, or otherwise using the SOFTWARE PRODUCT, you agree to be bound by the terms of this EULA. If you do not agree to the terms of this EULA, do not install or use the SOFTWARE PRODUCT.

SOFTWARE PRODUCT LICENSE

The SOFTWARE PRODUCT is protected by copyright laws and international copyright treaties, as well as other intellectual property laws and treaties. The SOFTWARE PRODUCT is licensed, not sold.

1. **GRANT OF LICENSE.** This EULA grants you the following non-exclusive, worldwide, nontransferable, nonassignable license.

   - **License Grant.** You may install and use one copy of the SOFTWARE PRODUCT on a single computer. The primary user of the computer on which the SOFTWARE PRODUCT is installed may make a second copy for his or her exclusive use on a portable computer.

2. **DESCRIPTION OF OTHER RIGHTS AND LIMITATIONS.**

   - **Limitation on Reverse Engineering, Compilation, and Disassembly.** You may not reverse engineer, decompile, or disassemble the SOFTWARE PRODUCT, except and only to the extent that such activity is expressly permitted by applicable law notwithstanding this limitation.

   - **No Other Uses.** You may not use the SOFTWARE PRODUCT in any way other than expressly permitted under this EULA.

   - **Rental.** You may not rent, lease, or lend the SOFTWARE PRODUCT.

   - **Trademarks.** This EULA does not grant you any rights in connection with any trademarks or service marks of Microsoft, its suppliers, or third party content providers.

   - **Support Services.** No technical support shall be provided for the SOFTWARE PRODUCT.

   - **Termination**. Without prejudice to any other rights, Microsoft may terminate this EULA if you fail to comply with the terms and conditions of this EULA. In such event, you must destroy all copies of the SOFTWARE PRODUCT.

3. **COPYRIGHT.** All title and copyrights in and to the SOFTWARE PRODUCT (including but not limited to any images, photographs, animations, video, audio, music, text, and "applets" incorporated into the SOFTWARE PRODUCT), the accompanying printed materials, and any copies of the SOFTWARE PRODUCT are owned by Microsoft, its suppliers, or third party content providers. All title and intellectual property rights in and to the content which may be accessed through use of the SOFTWARE PRODUCT are the property of the respective content owner and may be protected by applicable copyright or other intellectual property laws and treaties. This EULA grants you no rights to use such content. All rights not expressly granted are reserved by Microsoft, its suppliers, or third party content providers.

4. **U.S. GOVERNMENT RESTRICTED RIGHTS.** The SOFTWARE PRODUCT is provided with RESTRICTED RIGHTS. Use, duplication, or disclosure by the Government is subject to restrictions as set forth in subparagraph (c)(1)(ii) of the Rights in Technical Data and Computer Software clause at DFARS 252.227-7013 or subparagraphs (c)(1) and (2) of the Commercial Computer Software—Restricted Rights at 48 CFR 52.227-19, as applicable. Manufacturer is Microsoft Corporation/One Microsoft Way/Redmond, WA 98052-6399.

5. **EXPORT RESTRICTIONS.** You agree that you will not export or re-export the SOFTWARE PRODUCT, any part thereof, or any process or service that is the direct product of the SOFTWARE PRODUCT (the foregoing collectively referred to as the "Restricted Components") to any country, person, entity, or end user subject to U.S. export restrictions. You specifically agree not to export or re-export any of the Restricted Components (i) to any country to which the U.S. has embargoed or restricted the export of goods or services, which currently include, but are not necessarily limited to, Cuba, Iran, Iraq, Libya, North Korea, Sudan, and Syria, or to any national of any such country, wherever located, who intends to transmit or transport the Restricted Components back to such country; (ii) to any end-user who you know or have reason to know will utilize the Restricted Components in the design, development, or production of nuclear, chemical, or biological weapons; or (iii) to any end-user who has been prohibited from participating in U.S. export transactions by any federal agency of the U.S. government. You warrant and represent that neither the BXA nor any other U.S. federal agency has suspended, revoked, or denied your export privileges.

6. **MISCELLANEOUS**

If you acquired this product in the United States, this EULA is governed by the laws of the State of Washington.

If you acquired this product in Canada, this EULA is governed by the laws of the Province of Ontario, Canada. Each of the parties hereto irrevocably attorns to the jurisdiction of the courts of the Province of Ontario and further agrees to commence any litigation which may arise hereunder in the courts located in the Judicial District of York, Province of Ontario.

If this product was acquired outside the United States, then local law may apply.

Should you have any questions concerning this EULA, or if you desire to contact Microsoft for any reason, please contact Microsoft, or write: Microsoft Sales Information Center/One Microsoft Way/Redmond, WA 98052-6399.

DISCLAIMER OF WARRANTY

NO WARRANTIES. THE SOFTWARE PRODUCT IS PROVIDED "AS IS" WITHOUT WARRANTY OF ANY KIND. TO THE MAXIMUM EXTENT PERMITTED BY APPLICABLE LAW, MICROSOFT AND ITS SUPPLIERS DISCLAIM ALL WARRANTIES, EITHER EXPRESS OR IMPLIED, INCLUDING, BUT NOT LIMITED TO, IMPLIED WARRANTIES OF MERCHANTABILITY AND FITNESS FOR A PARTICULAR PURPOSE AND ANY WARRANTY AGAINST INFRINGEMENT, WITH REGARD TO THE SOFTWARE PRODUCT. THIS LIMITED WARRANTY GIVES YOU SPECIFIC LEGAL RIGHTS. YOU MAY HAVE OTHERS, WHICH VARY FROM STATE/JURISDICTION TO STATE/JURISDICTION.

CUSTOMER REMEDIES. MICROSOFT'S ENTIRE LIABILITY AND YOUR EXCLUSIVE REMEDY SHALL NOT EXCEED THE PRICE PAID FOR THE SOFTWARE PRODUCT.

LIMITATION OF LIABILITY. TO THE MAXIMUM EXTENT PERMITTED BY APPLICABLE LAW, IN NO EVENT SHALL MICROSOFT OR ITS SUPPLIERS BE LIABLE FOR ANY SPECIAL, INCIDENTAL, INDIRECT, OR CONSEQUENTIAL DAMAGES WHATSOEVER (INCLUDING, WITHOUT LIMITATION, DAMAGES FOR LOSS OF BUSINESS PROFITS, BUSINESS INTERRUPTION, LOSS OF BUSINESS INFORMATION, OR ANY OTHER PECUNIARY LOSS) ARISING OUT OF THE USE OF OR INABILITY TO USE THE SOFTWARE PRODUCT OR THE FAILURE TO PROVIDE SUPPORT SERVICES, EVEN IF MICROSOFT HAS BEEN ADVISED OF THE POSSIBILITY OF SUCH DAMAGES. IN ANY CASE, MICROSOFT'S ENTIRE LIABILITY UNDER ANY PROVISION OF THIS EULA SHALL BE LIMITED TO THE GREATER OF THE AMOUNT ACTUALLY PAID BY YOU FOR THE SOFTWARE PRODUCT OR U.S.$5.00; PROVIDED, HOWEVER, IF YOU HAVE ENTERED INTO A MICROSOFT SUPPORT SERVICES AGREEMENT, MICROSOFT'S ENTIRE LIABILITY REGARDING SUPPORT SERVICES SHALL BE GOVERNED BY THE TERMS OF THAT AGREEMENT. BECAUSE SOME STATES/JURISDICTIONS DO NOT ALLOW THE EXCLUSION OR LIMITATION OF LIABILITY, THE ABOVE LIMITATION MAY NOT APPLY TO YOU.

RESTRICTIONS À L'EXPORTATION

VOUS CONSENTEZ À NE PAS EXPORTER OU RÉEXPORTER LE PRODUIT LOGICIEL, TOUTE PORTION DE CELUI-CI, OU TOUT PROCÉDÉ OU SERVICE QUI EST UN PRODUIT DIRECT DU PRODUIT LOGICIEL (TOUS LES PRODUITS CI-DESSUS SONT CI-APRÈS COLLECTIVEMENT APPELÉS LES "COMPOSANTS SOUS RESTRICTIONS"), VERS TOUT PAYS, PERSONNE OU ENTITÉ SOUMIS AUX RESTRICTIONS AMÉRICAINES EN MATIÈRE D'EXPORTATION. VOUS CONSENTEZ SPÉCIFIQUEMENT À NE PAS EXPORTER OU RÉEXPORTER TOUT COMPOSANT SOUS RESTRICTIONS (I) VERS TOUT PAYS À L'ENCONTRE DUQUEL LES ÉTATS-UNIS ONT DÉCRÉTÉ UN EMBARGO OU DES RESTRICTIONS À L'EXPORTATION DE BIENS OU DE SERVICES, LESQUELS INCLUENT NOTAMMENT, SANS ÊTRE NÉCESSAIREMENT LIMITÉS À, CUBA, L'IRAN, L'IRAQ, LA LIBYE, LA CORÉE DU NORD, LE SOUDAN ET LA SYRIE, OU VERS TOUT RESSORTISSANT DE TOUT TEL PAYS, QUELQUE SOIT SON LIEU DE SITUATION, QUI A L'INTENTION DE TRANSMETTRE OU DE TRANSPORTER LES COMPOSANTS SOUS RESTRICTIONS VERS CE PAYS; (II) VERS TOUTE PERSONNE OU ENTITÉ DONT VOUS SAVEZ, OU AVEZ DES RAISONS DE CROIRE, QU'ELLE UTILISERA LES COMPOSANTS SOUS RESTRICTIONS POUR LA CONCEPTION, LE DÉVELOPPEMENT OU LA PRODUCTION D'ARMES NUCLÉAIRES CHIMIQUES OU BIOLOGIQUES; OU (III) VERS TOUTE PERSONNE OU ENTITÉ QUI FAIT L'OBJET D'UNE INTERDICTION DE PARTICIPER À DES TRANSACTIONS À L'EXPORTATION IMPOSÉES PAR UNE QUELCONQUE ADMINISTRATION FÉDÉRALE DES ÉTATS-UNIS. VOUS GARANTISSEZ ET REPRÉSENTEZ QUE NI LE DXA NI TOUTE AUTRE AGENCE FÉDÉRALE AMÉRICAINE N'A SUSPENDU OU RÉVOQUÉ VOS PRIVILÈGES D'EXPORTATION NI NE VOUS LES A REFUSÉS.

Si vous avez acquis votre produit Microsoft au CANADA, la garantie limitée suivante vous concerne :

RENONCIATION AUX GARANTIES. Dans toute la mesure permise par la législation en vigueur, Microsoft et ses fournisseurs fournissent le Produit Logiciel et tous (selon le cas) les services d'assistance liés au Produit Logiciel ("Services d'assistance") TELS QUELS ET AVEC TOUS LEURS DÉFAUTS, et par les présentes excluent toute garantie ou condition, expresse ou implicite, légale ou conventionnelle, écrite ou verbale, y compris, mais sans limitation, toute (selon le cas) garantie ou condition implicite ou légale de qualité marchande, de conformité à un usage particulier, d'absence de virus, d'exactitude et d'intégralité des réponses, de résultats, d'efforts techniques et professionnels et d'absence de négligence, le tout relativement au Produit Logiciel et à la prestation ou à la non-prestation des Services d'assistance. DE PLUS, IL N'Y A AUCUNE GARANTIE ET CONDITION DE TITRE, DE JOUISSANCE PAISIBLE, DE POSSESSION PAISIBLE, DE SIMILARITÉ À LA DESCRIPTION ET D'ABSENCE DE CONTREFAÇON RELATIVEMENT AU PRODUIT LOGICIEL. Vous supportez tous les risques découlant de l'utilisation et de la performance du Produit Logiciel et ceux découlant des Services d'assistance (s'il y a lieu).

EXCLUSION DES DOMMAGES INDIRECTS, ACCESSOIRES ET AUTRES. Dans toute la mesure permise par la législation en vigueur, Microsoft et ses fournisseurs ne sont en aucun cas responsables de tout dommage spécial, indirect, accessoire, moral ou exemplaire quel qu'il soit (y compris, mais sans limitation, les dommages entraînés par la perte de bénéfices ou la perte d'information confidentielle ou autre, l'interruption des affaires, les préjudices corporels, la perte de confidentialité, le défaut de remplir toute obligation y compris les obligations de bonne foi et de diligence raisonnable, la négligence et toute autre perte pécuniaire ou autre perte de quelque nature que ce soit) découlant de, ou de toute autre manière lié à, l'utilisation ou l'impossibilité d'utiliser le Produit Logiciel, la prestation ou la non-prestation des Services d'assistance ou autrement en vertu de ou relativement à toute disposition de cette convention, que ce soit en cas de faute, de délit (y compris la négligence), de responsabilité stricte, de manquement à un contrat ou de manquement à une garantie de Microsoft ou de l'un de ses fournisseurs, et ce, même si Microsoft ou l'un de ses fournisseurs a été avisé de la possibilité de tels dommages.

LIMITATION DE RESPONSABILITÉ ET RECOURS. Malgré tout dommage que vous pourriez encourir pour quelque raison que ce soit (y compris, mais sans limitation, tous les dommages mentionnés ci-dessus et tous les dommages directs et généraux), la seule responsabilité de Microsoft et de ses fournisseurs en vertu de toute disposition de cette convention et votre unique recours en regard de tout ce qui précède sont limités au plus élevé des montants suivants: soit (a) le montant que vous avez payé pour le Produit Logiciel, soit (b) un montant équivalant à cinq dollars U.S. (5,00 $ U.S.). Les limitations, exclusions et renonciations ci-dessus s'appliquent dans toute la mesure permise par la législation en vigueur, et ce même si leur application a pour effet de priver un recours de son essence.

DROITS LIMITÉS DU GOUVERNEMENT AMÉRICAIN

Tout Produit Logiciel fourni au gouvernement américain conformément à des demandes émises le ou après le 1er décembre 1995 est offert avec les restrictions et droits commerciaux décrits ailleurs dans la présente convention. Tout Produit Logiciel fourni au gouvernement américain conformément à des demandes émises avant le 1er décembre 1995 est offert avec des DROITS LIMITÉS tels que prévus dans le FAR, 48CFR 52.227-14 (juin 1987) ou dans le FAR, 48CFR 252.227-7013 (octobre 1988), tels qu'applicables.

Sauf lorsqu'expressément prohibé par la législation locale, la présente convention est régie par les lois en vigueur dans la province d'Ontario, Canada. Pour tout différend qui pourrait découler des présentes, vous acceptez la compétence des tribunaux fédéraux et provinciaux siégeant à Toronto, Ontario.

Si vous avez des questions concernant cette convention ou si vous désirez communiquer avec Microsoft pour quelque raison que ce soit, veuillez contacter la succursale Microsoft desservant votre pays, ou écrire à: Microsoft Sales Information Center, One Microsoft Way, Redmond, Washington 98052-6399.